*The Prelude,* 1798–1799

# The Cornell Wordsworth

*General Editor*: Stephen Parrish
*Associate Editor*: Mark L. Reed

*Advisory Editors*: M. H. Abrams, Geoffrey Hartman, Jonathan Wordsworth

---

The Salisbury Plain Poems, edited by Stephen Gill
*The Prelude*, 1798–1799, edited by Stephen Parrish

# The Prelude, 1798–1799
by William Wordsworth

*Edited by* STEPHEN PARRISH

CORNELL UNIVERSITY PRESS
ITHACA, NEW YORK

THIS BOOK HAS BEEN PUBLISHED WITH THE AID OF A GRANT FROM THE
HULL MEMORIAL PUBLICATION FUND OF CORNELL UNIVERSITY.

Copyright © 1977 by Cornell University

First published 1977 by Cornell University Press.

Printed in the United States of America by Vail-Ballou Press, Inc.

Library of Congress Cataloging in Publication Data

Wordsworth, William, 1770–1850.
  The prelude, 1798–1799.

  (The Cornell Wordsworth)
  Includes the reading text of the earliest version of the two-part Prelude of 1798–1799, and
transcriptions of the manuscripts, usually with facing photographic reproductions of the manu-
scripts, JJ, RV, U, V, and Dove Cottage manuscripts 15, 16, and 33.
  I. Parrish, Stephen Maxfield. II. Title. III. Title: The prelude, 1798–1799.
PR5864.A2P3      821'.7      76-8550
ISBN 0-8014-0854-7

# Contents

Preface                                                                                          vii
Abbreviations                                                                                      xi
Introduction: The Growth of the Two-Part *Prelude*                           3
Editorial Procedure                                                                            37

The Two-Part *Prelude*, 1798–1799: Reading Text                            39
Texts Contributing to the First Part                                                    69
  MS. JJ                                                                                           71
    Photographic Reproductions and Transcriptions                           71
    Reading Text                                                                                121
  Letter to Coleridge, December 1798: Photographic Reproductions
  and Transcriptions                                                                        131
    Skating Scene                                                                             135
    Boat-Stealing Scene                                                                   136
  Dove Cottage MS. 15. Opening of the First Part: Photographic
  Reproduction and Transcription                                                     139
  Dove Cottage MS. 16                                                                   143
    Close of the First Part: Photographic Reproduction and Tran-
    scription                                                                                   145
    Aborted Opening of the Second Part: Photographic Reproduc-
    tion and Transcription                                                               145
    Skating Scene with Trailing Passages: Transcriptions                   147
Texts Contributing to the Second Part                                               149
  The Alfoxden Notebook (two leaves): Photographic Reproductions
  and Transcriptions                                                                       151
  *The Pedlar*, in Dove Cottage MS. 16: Transcriptions of Lines 1–20
  and Lines 204–222                                                                      157
  Dove Cottage MS. 33 (four passages): Photographic Reproductions
  and Transcriptions                                                                       161
  MS. RV: Photographic Reproductions and Transcriptions                167
MSS. U and V: Photographic Reproductions and Transcriptions of
MS. V, with Readings of MS. U in an *Apparatus Criticus*                   219

# Preface

Wordsworth began writing *The Prelude* when he was twenty-eight, finished it nearly seven years later, worked back over it at intervals that spanned another thirty-four years, and left it at his death untitled and unpublished. Within a few weeks his final text, given a title and touched up a little by his executors, was sent to the printer. When it was published in 1850 its reception was polite but not enthusiastic, and Matthew Arnold's opinion, uttered some thirty years afterward, that Wordsworth's longest poems "are by no means Wordsworth's best work," prevailed through the nineteenth century.

By 1926, however, when Ernest de Selincourt published his great variorum edition of *The Prelude*, presenting for the first time the version that Wordsworth had completed in 1805, opinions had altered: critical perception of the poem's intermittent magnificence and power had become widespread. Owing further to the intelligent use of the poem made by Wordsworth's first modern biographer, Emile Legouis, de Selincourt was able to declare, without seeming controversial: "*The Prelude* is the essential living document for the interpretation of Wordsworth's life and poetry; any details, therefore, that can be gathered of the manner and circumstances of its composition must be of interest alike to biographer and critic. But of more vital importance than these is a knowledge of its original text."

De Selincourt presented a plentiful gathering of these details, and his edition has lain behind modern appraisals of the poem which recognize both its radical originality and its place in important traditions as, for example, a spiritual journey of self-discovery. Yet, ironically, de Selincourt failed even to notice the two manuscripts which have the best right to be regarded as the "original text" of *The Prelude*. These two manuscripts, now known as JJ and RV, are here reproduced photographically and transcribed in full.

De Selincourt's omission was rectified in two stages: in 1932 he presented readings from JJ in "Supplementary Notes" to a new printing of his text, and in 1959 Helen Darbishire gave a transcription of it together with an account of RV in her revision of de Selincourt's *Prelude* edition. But even yet the nature of *The Prelude*'s "original text" was not made wholly clear. It was left to J. P. MacGillivray and John Finch to explain in 1964 that the manuscripts which followed JJ and RV constituted an early version of *The Prelude* in two Parts (not Books).¹ In this "proto-*Prelude*," MacGillivray observed, one finds "a much more unified theme and a much stronger sense of formal structure than in the poem completed first in 1805 and published in 1850. The time covered is restricted to childhood and school days only. The single theme is the awakening of the imagination. Each of the two parts has its own limit in time: the first being of childhood and to the age of about ten, the second until the end of school days when the narrator was seventeen." The version is found in two manuscripts, duplicate fair copies designated by de Selincourt as U and V, and it is here presented as the earliest state of *The Prelude*, representing the poem as it stood at the end of 1799.

How steady or terminal a state this was intended to be is uncertain. The text opens in mid-line and apparently in mid-thought with a hanging question, "Was it for this . . . ?" And in RV and V the text closes with an inscription, "End of the second Part," which according to Wordsworth's practice elsewhere implies another part to follow. Yet other signs suggest that Wordsworth may for a time have thought of this version as finished. Upon its completion he had duplicate fair copies made of it, just as he did of the thirteen-book version he completed in 1805. One of these, U, is entered in a hard-cover album which contains nothing else but fair copies of finished pieces, and here the text does not have the closing inscription which implies a part to follow. Internally, the two-part poem is coherent and thematically rounded, and it closes with a ceremonial "Fare thee well!" to the person who is addressed.

While this matter cannot be settled, it may in the end be enough to recognize that when he completed these two parts in 978 lines, Wordsworth reached a significant stopping place, and that this state of *The Prelude* can be looked upon as separate from later versions. Wordsworth did not resume steady work on *The Prelude* until more than four years had passed (though he wrote desultorily at the poem in 1801 and perhaps in 1803). When he started again in earnest, he did not simply extend the poem from where he had stopped: he broke up Part One of the 1798–1799 text and distributed portions of it among different sections of a new poem to be made up of five Books (not Parts); into the second book he put most of Part Two. In about eight weeks of work (by early March, 1804), he shaped and virtually finished this five-book *Prelude*. Anticipating its prompt completion, he once again had duplicate fair copies started, hurriedly this time because one of them was for Coleridge to take to Malta. But before he had brought the fifth and final

¹ MacGillivray's paper, "The Three Forms of *The Prelude* 1798–1805," was published in *Essays in English Literature from the Renaissance to the Victorian Age Presented to A. S. P. Woodhouse 1964* (Toronto, 1964); an earlier form was read at a meeting of the Royal Society of Canada in June, 1962. In February, 1964, John Finch presented his doctoral dissertation, "Wordsworth, Coleridge, and *The Recluse*, 1798–1814," to Cornell.

book to a close Wordsworth abruptly resolved to enlarge the scope of his poem. The fair copies, more than half finished, had to be tapered off into the new design, and what Wordsworth was obliged to give Coleridge was not the five-book *Prelude* he had projected, but simply the first five books of the new version. He then worked steadily on for over a year until he had completed the 1805 poem in thirteen books.

A full account of this later work will be given in other volumes of this series: the thirteen-book *Prelude*, edited by Mark Reed, and the fourteen-book *Prelude*, edited by W. J. B. Owen. This volume brings the account up to the end of 1799, tracing the stages through which the two-part *Prelude* grew to reach its final state. The beginnings were unpretentious. Wordsworth seems to have set out to compose some autobiographical verse much like *Tintern Abbey*, but he kept adding and inserting passages so that the poem grew in stages to more than four hundred lines, whereupon what he had written was suddenly thought of as the first part (Part One) and a second part was begun. The ending was swift. In a space of two or three weeks the second part was brought to a close and rapidly transcribed by Wordsworth's sister and Mary Hutchinson.

My account of this process of growth draws heavily upon, and elaborates, the fine account developed in "The Two-Part *Prelude* of 1798–9," *Journal of English and Germanic Philology*, LXXII (October, 1973), 503–525, by Jonathan Wordsworth and Stephen Gill, whose text of the two-part poem was published the following year in Volume II of the *Norton Anthology of English Literature*, 3d edition. I have also profited from reading three doctoral dissertations which deal with the two-part *Prelude*: John Finch's "Wordsworth, Coleridge, and *The Recluse*, 1798–1814" (Cornell, 1964), Michael Jaye's "The Growth of a Poem: The Early Manuscripts of William Wordsworth's *The Prelude*" (New York University, 1969), and Charles Stone's "Authorial Awareness in Wordsworth's Early Spots of Time" (Cornell, 1973).

Preparation of this volume, as of all volumes in this series, was made possible by the Trustees of Dove Cottage, who generously gave access to manuscripts in the Wordsworth Library at Grasmere and authorized their publication. My work at Grasmere has been supported by the American Philosophical Society and by Cornell Faculty Research grants. Throughout, my editorial partners have loyally shared their knowledge and helped me with advice.

STEPHEN PARRISH

*Ithaca, New York*

# Abbreviations

| | |
|---|---|
| *Chronology: EY* | Mark L. Reed, *Wordsworth: The Chronology of the Early Years, 1770–1799* (Cambridge, Mass., 1967). |
| *Chronology: MY* | Mark L. Reed, *Wordsworth: The Chronology of the Middle Years, 1800–1815* (Cambridge, Mass., 1975). |
| DC MS. | Dove Cottage manuscript. |
| DW | Dorothy Wordsworth. |
| *EY* | *Letters of William and Dorothy Wordsworth: The Early Years, 1787–1805*, ed. Ernest de Selincourt (2d ed.; rev. Chester L. Shaver; Oxford, 1967). |
| JJ | Manuscript JJ of *The Prelude*, DC MS. 19. |
| M | Manuscript M of *The Prelude*, DC MS. 44. |
| *Memoirs* | Christopher Wordsworth, *Memoirs of William Wordsworth* (2 vols.; London, 1851). |
| MH | Mary Hutchinson, later Mary Wordsworth. |
| *Prel.* | *The Prelude*, ed. Ernest de Selincourt; rev. Helen Darbishire (Oxford, 1959). |
| *Prose* | *The Prose Works of William Wordsworth*, ed. W. J. B. Owen and Jane Worthington Smyser (3 vols; Oxford, 1974). |
| *PW* | *The Poetical Works of William Wordsworth*, ed. Ernest de Selincourt and Helen Darbishire (5 vols.; Oxford, 1940–1949; Vols. I and II rev. 1952, Vol. IV rev. 1958). |
| RV | Manuscript RV of *The Prelude*, DC MS. 21. |
| SH | Sara Hutchinson. |
| *STCL* | *Collected Letters of Samuel Taylor Coleridge*, ed. Earl Leslie Griggs (6 vols.; Oxford, 1956–1971). |
| *TLS* | *The Times Literary Supplement.* |
| U | Manuscript U of *The Prelude*, DC MS. 23. |
| V | Manuscript V of *The Prelude*, DC MS. 22. |
| WW | William Wordsworth. |

*The Prelude*, 1798–1799

# Introduction: The Growth
# of the Two-Part *Prelude*

I

The origins of *The Prelude* lie in Wordsworth's boyhood experience of nature in the north of England, but the making of the poem began in Germany in Wordsworth's twenty-ninth year. When he settled at Goslar, in October, 1798, where he was to spend the winter, he entered an isolation—shared with his sister Dorothy—as intense as any he had ever known. Following close upon the year of creative intimacy he had just shared with Coleridge, this isolation drove Wordsworth back to the sources of memory and led him to trace in wondering and thankful tones the beginnings of the growth of a poet's mind.

The *Prelude* verse that Wordsworth began to compose at Goslar survives in what has been known as MS. JJ of *The Prelude* (DC MS. 19), described and published by Helen Darbishire (*Prel.*, pp. xxvi–xxvii and 633–642). JJ is a small notebook bound in boards, originally made up of 96 leaves; 7 leaves have been torn out. The notebook was used by Dorothy in Germany to write out an account of the journey from Hamburg to Goslar (11 pages) and to set down some notes on German grammar (10 pages near the front of the book, 4 pages toward the back). Nearly four years later Dorothy took up the book again and used it for a portion of her Grasmere journal (14 February to 2 May, 1802). But before then William had also used the book in Hamburg and Goslar to write out a 19-page account of his conversations with Klopstock and a 7-page fragment of a moral essay (these were published in *Prose*, I, 91–95 and 103–104), and to draft the beginnings of the poem that became *The Prelude*.

The *Prelude* composition, in ink with some scattered drafts in pencil, starts at the back of the book and runs forward, mostly by pairs of pages in a zigzag fashion, for 11 leaves, stopping where Wordsworth came up against his sister's German notes and exercises. He also scribbled drafts on the inside back cover and, at the other end of the book, on leaves 1$^v$ and 2$^r$. A reading text of JJ, showing the earliest readings, is given here, and photographic reproductions with facing transcriptions are provided. As these show, the composition falls into three separate elements:

1. A page of drafts, amounting to 21 lines, opening with a passage later taken into the "glad preamble" of the 1805 *Prelude*:

> a mild creative breeze
> a vital breeze that passes gently on
> Oer things which it has made and soon becomes
> A tempest a redundant energy. . . .

2. A coherent passage of about 150 lines in fair copy, occasionally interrupted by drafts, beginning with the hanging question that opened the 1798–1799 *Prelude*:

> was it for this
> That one, the fairest of all rivers, loved
> To blend his murmurs with my nurse's song. . . .

The passage goes on to present two boyhood experiences—bathing in the river and clinging to the rock above the raven's nest (in the thirteen-book *Prelude* completed in 1805 these stand in Book I at lines 291–304 and 333–350)—followed by two apostrophes to nature—"Ah not in vain ye beings of the hills" and "Ah! not in vain ye spirits of the springs"—another boyhood scene, the trap-robbing (1805 *Prelude*, I, 311–332), evidently meant to be inserted earlier, and a closing tribute to the landscapes of childhood and the response they generated:

> Nor unsubservient even to noblest ends
> Are these primordial feelings how serene
> How calm those seem amid the swell
> Of human passion even yet I feel
> Their tranquillizing power.

Most of this 150-line passage was taken into Part One of the 1798–1799 *Prelude*.

3. Several detached pieces, mainly fair copy but with some draft, evidently intended for later inclusion (three of them were taken into the 1798–1799 *Prelude*, these three and a fourth into the 1805):

> a. There was a boy ye knew him well, ye rocks
> And islands of Winander. . . .

(24 lines, omitted from 1798–1799, but published in the 1800 *Lyrical Ballads*, and used in the 1805 *Prelude*, Book V, lines 389–413).

b. The boat-stealing episode (about 49 lines, found in 1805 in Book I, lines 373–375 and 383–427).

> c. The soul of man is fashioned & built up
> Just like a strain of music. . . .

(11 lines in Dorothy's hand, evidently here intended to follow the boat-stealing episode and lead into the trap-robbing; roughly equivalent to I, 351–371, in 1805).

d. "I would not strike a flower . . ." (about 17 lines later incorporated into a version of *Nutting*; 6 lines were taken into the 1805 *Prelude* at XII, 47–52).

e. "Those beauteous colours of my early years . . ." (a fragment of about 11 lines, including revisions, containing phrases which seem to recollect the deepest origins of the poem and may have been intended to bring it to a close, as they later close Part One of 1798–1799):

> Those hours that cannot die those lovely forms
> And sweet sensations which throw back our life
> And make our infancy a visible scene
> On which the sun is shining.

f. Then dearest maiden on whose lap I rest
  My head    do not deem that these
  Are idle sympathies—.

(a three-line fragment addressed tenderly to Dorothy, resembling lines that later showed up in *Nutting*).

The order of the detached passages is somewhat uncertain, owing to Wordsworth's peculiar manner of procedure: starting at the back of the notebook, when he filled a page he would move forward to a fresh page, sometimes turning to the next unused recto, sometimes skipping across to the facing verso. However, the reading text of JJ presents a plausible order, and one that may for a number of reasons seem the likeliest. "There was a boy . . ." was started on an early leaf of the notebook, one that contains drafts for the central 150-line passage, then broken off; where it is later copied out in full, drafts of the boat-stealing episode are found both back of it and ahead of it, as though it already stood on the page when the boat-stealing lines were composed—and it is worth remembering that "There was a boy . . ." was sent to Coleridge in Ratzeburg several weeks before the boat-stealing lines were sent him.[1] With the pieces in this order, the "steady lake" at the end of "There was a boy . . ." could lead to the lake on which the stolen boat was moored. The "soul of man" lines, which pretty clearly follow these pieces, are like them inscribed horizontally, not vertically like the remaining passages in the notebook. In these final passages, "Those beauteous colours of my early years" appears to have been developed as a continuation of "I would not strike a flower," supplanting an aborted continuation that stopped after three lines; the address to Dorothy, which is entered in a different ink, has the look of a disconnected afterthought.

---

[1] Coleridge acknowledged it on 10 December 1798; later in December Dorothy copied the skating scene for him (see *STCL*, I, 452, and *EY*, p. 239).

This important manuscript, unrecognized until 1931,[2] unpublished as a whole until 1959, allows us to judge something of Wordsworth's intentions and his state of mind when he began to write *The Prelude*. The preamble drafts stand first in the book (that is, on the back page) and could well have been entered first (though Miss Darbishire misleadingly printed them last in her transcription of JJ (*Prel.*, pp. 633–642). They must have been on the page by the time the central section of some 150 lines was written down, for drafts toward some of these lines are scrawled on the inside of the book's back cover, and it is unlikely that Wordsworth would have used that space had the last page been empty. The preamble drafts express in images of wind and storm the turbulence of feeling that marked a surge of creative energy:

> trances of thought
> And mountings of the mind compared to which
> The wind that drives along th[']autumnal [?leaf]
> Is meekness.

Whether they were entered first or last, there is no reason to doubt that these drafts were meant to precede the coherent central passage which follows overleaf in the notebook—as in fact some of them do by 1804. Thus they provide the only clue we have to the original antecedent of "was it for this" which opens that passage. "This" seems here to have been the powerful disturbance of mind occasioned by a superabundant flow of inspiration—not incapacity, or guilt, or self-reproach of the type that later entered the "post-preamble." The tone of "was it for this" may not, in fact, be ironic, or regretful, but wondering, perhaps confused, even perhaps quietly exultant.

Certain revisions help to reveal the tone by showing us phrases that Wordsworth must have held to be equivalent. In the course of writing out the central passage of JJ, Wordsworth altered the opening of one apostrophe to nature from "Ah! not in vain ye spirits of the springs" (line 80 of the reading version) to "Ah! not for this . . . ," evidently to throw it back into parallel with an earlier passage. If the second phrase is solely regretful, Wordsworth would have to have turned 180 degrees in what looks like a casual revision. And "was [it] for this," pluralized at the opening of the river-bathing lines, seems almost to become a grateful allusion to nature's tempering consolations:

> Was it for these perhaps I speak of things
> Complacent fashioned fondly to adorn
> The years of unrememberable being
> Was it for this that I a four years child
> A naked boy among thy silent pools
> Made one long bathing of a summers day. . . .

---

[2] See de Selincourt's account of it in *TLS*, 12 November 1931, p. 886.

Whatever the original force of the hanging "this," JJ, and especially its central passage, represented for Wordsworth an extension of a mode of verse he had already adopted, a mode based upon Coleridge's conversation poems (line 29 of JJ quotes a phrase from *Frost at Midnight*). The last poem Wordsworth wrote before leaving England was *Tintern Abbey*, completed in mid-July, and the affinities between *Tintern Abbey* and the autobiographical verse he began to write in Germany three months later help to point up *The Prelude*'s earliest design. *Tintern Abbey*, addressed in part to a murmuring river ("O sylvan Wye"), can be described as an autobiographical blank-verse meditation in which Wordsworth sums up in tones of quiet exultation what he owes to memories of a landscape and traces the growth of a poet's response to nature. However much he learned to hear over nature's voices the "still, sad music of humanity," he recognized

> In nature and the language of the sense
> The anchor of my purest thoughts, the nurse,
> The guide, the guardian of my heart, and soul
> Of all my moral being.

At the close of the poem, he turned to his sister, who shared this scene with him, talked of her "wild eyes," and invoked for her—"my dearest Friend, / My dear, dear Friend"—the future healing solace of nature and of memory, using tones rather different from those of the preceding autobiographical reminiscences.

In like manner JJ, addressed to a river ("O Derwent"), expresses a wondering and grateful memory of the "ceaseless music"

> Which with its steady cadence tempering
> Our human waywardness compose[d] my thought
> To more than infant softness giving me
> Amid the fretful tenements of man
> A knowledge, a dim earnest of the calm
> That Nature breathes among her woodland h[aunts].

The poet's intention is plainly specified after a pause in composition marked by a line number (94, inscribed by Wordsworth in the margin) and a self-conscious, rather fumbling effort to find a way through "the mazes of this argument." It is quite simply to "paint"

> How Nature by collateral interest
> And by extrinsic passion peopled first
> My mind with beauteous objects,

even if this requires that he set aside "what might demand a loftier song"— perhaps *The Recluse*. This intention is carried out through evocation of remembered landscapes, interspersed with meditative tributes cast in eloquent verse, tributes to the agencies that interwove the passions

> with eternal things
> With life & nature, purifying thus
> The elements of feeling & of thought
> And sanctifying by such disipline
> Both pain & fear untill we recognize
> A grandeur in the beatings of the heart—

and to the spirits of nature which, for the growing boy,

> Impressd upon all form[s] the character
> Of danger & desire & thus did make
> The surface of the universal earth
> With meanings of delight of hope & fear
> Work like a sea.

At the close of composition in JJ, Wordsworth turned again to his sister to point up the meaning of their shared experience.

The earliest state of *The Prelude* may now be summed up as follows: fragments of a preamble appear to precede a coherent 150-line passage which, expanded and rearranged, became the basis for Part One of the 1798–1799 *Prelude*; this passage is followed by detached pieces written to be inserted into it. The speaker of the poem and its tones are not significantly different from the speaker and the tones of *Tintern Abbey*, and where a listener is identified at the close, it seems, as in *Tintern Abbey*, to be the poet's sister.

The circumstances and the state of mind in which Wordsworth composed JJ are probably revealed in a letter he and Dorothy wrote to Coleridge toward the end of December, 1798, shortly after they had broken a six-week silence—an "ominous silence," Coleridge had called it, caused by Wordsworth's "violent hatred of letter-writing."[3] Having been without books in Goslar, Wordsworth said, he had been "obliged to write in self-defense." Yet the act of writing provoked unpleasant sensations of a sort that had long afflicted him: "uneasiness at my stomach and side, with a dull pain about my heart." As a consequence, reading—when there were books to read—"is now become a kind of luxury to me. When I do not read I am absolutely consumed by thinking and feeling and bodily exertions of voice or of limbs, the consequence of those feelings." Here, one supposes, is something like the turbulence described in JJ's preamble drafts, the "tempest," the "redundant energy,"

> Creating not but as it may
> disturbing things created.

---

[3] Coleridge was writing to Thomas Poole; *STCL*, I, 445.

Wordsworth, or rather Dorothy, went on in the letter to copy out for Coleridge some "little Rhyme poems" about Lucy and three passages of blank verse probably connected with *The Prelude*—William laconically called them "a few descriptions." Transcribing first a version of "a nutting scene . . . like the rest, laid in the North of England," Dorothy called it "the conclusion of a poem of which the beginning is not written,"[4] and the lines she transcribed correspond roughly to the lines that Wordsworth years later said were at first "intended as part of a poem on my own life, but struck out as not being wanted there" (Fenwick note; *PW*, II, 504). They close with a tender address to Dorothy:

> —Then, dearest Maiden! move along these shades
> In gentleness of heart; with gentle hand
> Touch, for there is a spirit in the woods.

The other passages that Dorothy copied were later put into the 1798–1799 *Prelude*. One was the skating scene (in 36 lines), taken, Dorothy said, "from a description of Williams boyish pleasures." The other was the boat-stealing scene (in 49 lines), drafted in JJ then revised; her version corresponds to the version of 1798–1799. "I select it from the mass of what William has written," Dorothy said, "because it may be easily detached from the rest." What the rest of the mass was Dorothy did not tell Coleridge. She had earlier, as we have noticed, sent him the "boy of Winander," but no lines from the central section of William's growing poem were offered to Coleridge at this stage.

II

That *The Prelude* was growing there can be no doubt. The passages that Dorothy copied in the December letter came not from JJ but from another text, and much of this text probably paralleled the entries in a notebook in which the second state of *The Prelude* had been entered, without any preamble this time, but trailed again by disconnected passages meant for later inclusion. This notebook is DC MS. 15, which has come to be known as the "*Christabel* Notebook" from the presence in it of the earliest surviving version of Coleridge's poem. MS. 15 is a pocket notebook bound in red leather, with a clasp. Most of its leaves have been cut or torn out in bunches, so that groups of stubs appear at intervals in the book. Only 41 leaves are now intact, including some of the leaves on which *Christabel* is entered, which were not part of the original notebook, but were sewn in. An account of the contents of this book is given by Mark Reed in Appendix IX to his *Chronology: EY*, and Appendix II to *Chronology: MY*.

---

[4] *EY*, 235–243; for the correct order of the parts of this complicated letter see de Selincourt's publication of it in *The Early Letters of William and Dorothy Wordsworth* (1785–1805), (Oxford, 1935), pp. 203–211.

The *Prelude* composition in MS. 15 was entered, largely in fair copy, on seven consecutive leaves toward the middle of the book, but only the first of the seven remains intact. On the back of this first leaf stands a fair copy of the beginning of the poem in its second state (full transcription and a photograph may be found on pages 140–141):

> was it for this
> That one the fairest of all rivers loved
> To blend his murmurs with my nurse's song . . . ,

and so on for 26 lines, through the introduction and the river-bathing scene. There follow not the raven's-nest lines, as in JJ, but the opening five lines of the trap-robbing episode, introduced by an asterisk, as though freshly inserted here. The episode reaches the bottom of the page with line 5, making a total of 31 lines that survive. That this version is later than JJ's can be easily shown. Where JJ has in line 27 "To intertwine my dreams," MS. 15 has "That flowed along my dreams" written above that reading as an alternate, and this alternate reading is adopted in later texts. Similarly, at line 37, MS. 15 departs from JJ by substituting one line ("Beloved Derwent fairest of all streams") for three:

> Was it for these perhaps I speak of things
> Complacent fashioned fondly to adorn
> The years of unrememberable being.

The one-line variant is later adopted.

Beyond the first 31 lines, the second state of *The Prelude* has to be reconstructed from the writing visible on the six stubs which follow the intact leaf in MS. 15. Nothing can be seen on the versos of the stubs, but scraps of letters on the rectos show with fair certainty what the poem contained. Following the introduction, the river-bathing scene, and the opening lines of the trap-robbing episode (on page 1), the first missing leaf held on its recto (page 2) the rest of the trap-robbing passage and the opening 13 lines of the raven's-nest scene, as the stub shows (lines are supplied below from Part One of MS. U, a fair copy of the final text, though the readings of JJ are virtually identical, and line numbers refer to the reading texts):

*Stub 1ʳ (page 2)*
]

| | JJ | U |
|---|---|---|
| A[long the moonlight turf. In thought and wish | 102 | 33 |
| T[hat time, my shoulder all with springes hung, | 103 | 34 |
| I[ was a fell destroyer. Gentle Powers | 104 | 35 |
| W[ho give us happiness and call it peace | 105 | 36 |
| W[hen scudding on from snare to snare I plied | 106 | 37 |
| M[y anxious visitation, hurrying on | 107 | 38 |
| S[till hurrying hurrying onward how my heart | 108 | 39 |
| | [109] | [40] |

| | | |
|---|---|---|
| T[hat looked upon me how my bosom beat | 110 | 41 |
| - | [111] | [42] |
| - | [112] | [43] |
| - | [113] | [44] |
| B[ecame my prey, and when the deed was done | 114 | 45 |
| I[ heard among the solitary hills | | 46 |
| Lo[w breathings coming after me and sounds | 115 | 47 |
| Of[ undistinguishable motion, steps | 116 | 48 |
| Al[most as silent as the turf they trod | 117 | 49 |
| ] | | |
| ] | [51] | [50] |
| Th[e shining sun had from his knot of leaves | 52 | 51 |
| De[coyed the primrose flower, and when the vales | 53 | 52 |
| And[ woods were warm was I a rover then | 54 | 53 |
| In[ the high places, on the lonesome peaks | 55 | 54 |
| Am[ong the mountains and the winds. Though mean | 56 | 55 |
| An[d though inglorious were my views the end | 57 | 56 |
| Wa[s not ignoble. Oh when I have hung | 58 | 57 |
| Ab[ove the raven's nest by knots of grass | 59 | 58 |
| A[nd half-inch fissures in the slipp'ry rock | 60 | 59 |
| B[ut ill sustained and almost, as it seemed, | 61 | 60 |
| Su[spended by the blast which blew amain | 62 | 61 |
| Sh[ouldering the naked crag, oh at that time | 63 | 62 |

On the back of this leaf (page 3) would have had to be the remaining four lines of the raven's-nest scene followed by a passage of about 24 lines before the text can be picked up again on the front of the second stub (page 4). There we find the concluding five lines of the two apostrophes to nature which stood in JJ in an equivalent position, following the raven's-nest scene; the missing 24 lines on the facing verso must therefore have been the beginning of these apostrophes. The first apostrophe amounted to 12 lines in both JJ and U; the second had 17 in JJ but only 12 in U, and the version here would therefore have been that of JJ (5 lines of the 17 are on the next stub, leaving 12 for the missing verso, which added to 12 for the first apostrophe give the needed 24). The second stub shows, moreover, that after the apostrophes came the long conclusion to the poem, intermittently running parallel in JJ and U but here mainly following U (from which again readings are supplied):

*Stub 2ʳ (page 4)*

| | | |
|---|---|---|
| - | [JJ 92] | [U 194] |
| Of[ danger or desire, and thus did make | JJ 93 | U 195 |
| T[he surface of the universal earth | 94 | 196 |
| W[ith meanings of delight, of hope and fear | 95 | 197 |
| W[ork like a sea | 96 | 198 |
| ] | | |
| - | | [376] |
| - | | [377] |
| - | | [378] |

A[nd made me love them may I well forget                                379
-                                                                      [380]
Of[ subtler origin how I have felt                                      381
-                                                                      [382]
T[hose hallowed and pure motions of the sense            136           383
W[hich seem in their simplicity to own                   137           384
An[ intellectual charm, that calm delight                138           385
W[hich, if I err not, surely must belong                 139           386
To[ those first born affinities that fit                 140           387
Ou[r new existence to existing things                    141           388
An[d in our dawn of being constitute                     142           389
Th[e bond of union betwixt life and joy                  143           390
]                                                       [144]         [391]
A[nd twice five seasons on my mind had stamped           145           392
Th[e faces of the moving year, even then,                146           393
A[ Child, I held unconscious intercourse                 147           394
W[ith the eternal Beauty drinking in                     148           395
A[ pure organic pleasure from the lines                  149           396
Of[ curling mist or from the level plain                 150           397

Another gap of about 30 lines on the missing verso (page 5) is easily filled by continuing straight on in U (lines 398–427), for the third stub shows the poem concluding (on page 6) with the final lines of Part One as it stands in U. Some of the lines that lead up to this conclusion can be found in U, but some cannot, hence are unrecoverable. The full stub reads as follows (with lines again supplied from U):

*Stub 3ʳ (page 6)*

]                                                                  [U 428]
]                                                                  [429]
-                                                                  [430]
D[epicted on the brain and to the eye                              U 431
W[ere visible, a daily sight; and thus                             432
B                                                              [433 or 434]
-                                                                  [435]
O[f obscure feelings representative                                436
Of[ joys that were forgotten, these same scenes                    437
So[ beauteous and majestic in themselves                           438
-
-
A
W
M
M
W
B
An
**To[ understand myself, nor thou to know**                        456
**Wi[th better knowledge how the heart was framed**                457

**Of[ him thou lovest, need I dread from thee**          458
**Ha[rsh judgements if I am so loth to quit**            459
Th[ose recollected hours that have the charm            460
Of[ visionary things, and lovely forms                  461
An[d sweet sensations that throw back our life          462
An[d make our infancy a visible scene                   463
On[ which the sun is shining—                           464

The last five lines are taken over from JJ, where they stood at the close of the last or next-to-last passage in the manuscript ("Those beauteous colours of our early time . . ."). The lines that lead up to them (in boldface here) are evidently fresh composition, and they introduce a new element into the main body of the poem. Here for the first time is a loving person addressed, and here for the first time are signs on the speaker's part of a concern to justify the self-indulgence of composing these boyhood memories—a concern growing out of anxiety about expectations of him held by the friend, who might still be Dorothy, though by now is more probably Coleridge.

It is easy to summarize what Wordsworth did to the main body of his poem when he converted the first state, as in JJ, into the second state, as in MS. 15. He simply rearranged the pieces by pulling out the trap-robbing episode and moving it ahead of the raven's-nest scene, and then rewrote the conclusion, extending it some 30 lines to make a poem of about 180 lines, as compared with JJ's 150 or so. A simple tabulation of the pieces will make this procedure clear:

| MS. JJ | Number of lines | MS. 15 | | Number of lines |
|---|---|---|---|---|
| Intro., river-bathing | 29 | Intro., river-bathing | | 26 |
| Raven's-nest | 17 | Trap-robbing | | 25 |
| Apostrophe 1 | 12 | Raven's-nest | | 17 |
| Apostrophe 2 | 17 | Apostrophe 1 | | 12 |
| Trap-robbing | 21 | Apostrophe 2 | | 17 |
| Conclusion | 53 | Conclusion | about | 83 |
| Total | 149 | Total | about | 180 |

But Wordsworth did not stop here, as the next stubs in MS. 15 show. When he had finished copying out his poem he once again rewrote the ending. The fourth stub (page 8) contained the new ending, running down the page about three-fourths of the way. The revision probably started on the back of the previous leaf (page 7), but there is no way of telling. Subsequent revision again makes some of the new lines unrecoverable, but what can be seen (again in boldface) introduces a distinctly darker tone, in lines 451 to 455 of U, which speak of "Reproaches from my former years" and raise the possibility of "impotent desire." In these lines, moreover, the mention of "honourable toil" suggests *The Recluse* and promises made to Coleridge before leaving England.

*Stub 4ʳ (page 8)*

| | |
|---|---|
| ] | [U 442?] |
| - [My story early, feeling, as I fear,] | [443?] |
| - [The weakness of a human love, for days] | [444?] |
| D[isowned by memory, 'ere the birth of spring] | [445?] |
| - [Planting my snow-drops among winter snows.] | [446?] |
| - | |
| A | |
| - | |
| - | |

| | |
|---|---|
| **R[eproaches from my former years, whose power** | U 451 |
| **M[ay spur me on, in manhood now mature,** | 452 |
| **To[ honorable toil. Yet, should it be** | 453 |
| **Th[at this is but an impotent desire** | 454 |
| **T[hat I by such enquiry am not taught** | 455 |
| To[ understand myself, nor thou to know | 456 |
| W[ith better knowledge how the heart was framed | 457 |
| Of[ him thou lovest, need I dread from thee | 458 |
| H[arsh judgements if I am so loth to quit | 459 |
| Tho[se recollected hours that have the charm | 460 |
| Of[ visionary things, and lovely forms | 461 |
| An[d sweet sensations that throw back our life | 462 |
| An[d make our infancy a visible scene | 463 |
| On[ which the sun is shining— | 464 |

After a space, the page concludes with some crowded lines of draft; readings of the first four are conjectural.

D
B
Afo
Wi
The
sky
-

The last two leaves of the original seven were only partially filled. Writing on the fifth stub (page 10) stops about three-fourths of the way down the page, and the letters show clearly that the last 22 lines of the boat-stealing episode were present; the beginning of the episode, 27 lines, would just fit on the preceding verso (page 9). Again the lines are supplied from MS. U:

*Stub 5ʳ (page 10)*

| | |
|---|---|
| - | [U 108] |
| As[ if with voluntary power instinct | U 109 |
| Up[reared its head: I struck and struck again | 110 |
| An[d growing still in stature the huge cliff | 111 |

R[ose up between me and the stars, and still                                         112
W[ith measured motion, like a living thing                                           113
St[rode after me. With trembling hands I turned                                      114
An[d through the silent water stole my way                                           115
B[ack to the cavern of the willow-tree                                               116
T[here, in her mooring-place I left my bark                                          117
A[nd through the meadows homeward went with grave                                    118
A[nd serious thoughts: and after I had seen                                          119
T[hat spectacle, for many days my brain                                              120
W[orked with a dim and undetermined sense                                            121
Of[ unknown modes of being: in my thoughts                                           122
Th[ere was a darkness, call it solitude                                              123
O[r blank desertion; no familiar shapes                                              124
Of[ hourly objects, images of trees                                                  125
Of[ sea or sky, no colours of green fields                                           126
B[ut huge and mighty forms that do not live                                          127
Li[ke living men moved slowly through my mind                                        128
By[ day, and were the trouble of my dreams                                           129

Letters on the final stub, which again stop well short of the bottom of the page, show that three separate pieces were entered (two of them were taken into the 1798–1799 *Prelude*): (1) the last seven lines of the skating scene (there would be just room for the first 28 lines on the facing verso, page 11); (2) a version of the passage called "Redundance," copied in another notebook, MS. 16, from which the lines are supplied below (the passage is printed in *PW*, V, 346); and (3) the image of splitting ice, which follows "Redundance" in MS. 16 and became lines 230–233 of MS. U:

*Stub 6ʳ (page 12)*
H[ave I reclining back upon my heels,                                         U 179
S[topped short, yet still the solitary cliffs                                   180
W[heeled by me, even as if the earth had rolled                                181
W[ith visible motion her diurnal round.                                        182
B[ehind me did they stretch in solemn train                                    183
F[eebler and feebler, and I stood and watched                                  184
Til[l all was tranquil as a summer's sea.                                      185


]
F[ailed I to lengthen out my watch. I stood
W[ithin the area of the frozen vale,
-

Of[ one that listens, for even yet the scene,
I[ts fluctuating hues and surfaces,
A[nd the decaying vestiges of forms,
D[id to the dispossessing power of night
I[mpart a feeble visionary sense
Of[ movement and creation doubly felt

Wh[ile it sank down towards the water sent                                    U 230
Am[ong the meadows and the hills its long                                       231
An[d frequent yellings imitative some                                           232
Of[ wolves that howl along the Bothnic main.                                    233

The reverse side of this leaf must have held the first 28 lines of the passage copied out in MS. 14 (the Alfoxden Notebook) beginning "There is an active principle . . ." (reproduced in part in *PW*, V, 286–291 and 472–473), because lines 29–45 in fair copy appear on the intact leaf which follows the last stub. It is hard to say whether this passage, most of which was later used in *The Excursion* (IX, 1–26 and 125–152), belongs here among the pieces being kept available for inclusion in the developing poem on the growth of Wordsworth's boyhood sensibilities. It is followed by a 24-line passage, "For let the impediment be what it may . . . ," reflecting on the inhibiting weight, the bondage, of domestic obligation (the passage is printed in *PW*, V, 344–345), then by a version of *Nutting* which seems to have become a separate poem (it ends with the passage Dorothy copied for Coleridge in December, 1798, and into its lengthy beginning, which Dorothy said had not then been written, is incorporated "I would not strike a flower . . ." from JJ). The line that divides pieces of verse associated with *The Prelude* from pieces that break off or are detached is not always clear in the manuscripts, and may not always have been clear to Wordsworth.

To sum up the second state of the *Prelude*: the fragmentary preamble drafts of JJ are missing; in the central section the trap-robbing scene has been moved up ahead of the raven's-nest scene with no significant revision, and the conclusion has been rewritten and extended, then again rewritten, to introduce a person addressed in a tone of self-doubt and self-reproach; of the separate passages trailing along behind, only the boat-stealing episode remains closely attached; to it have been added the skating scene and some other fragments— the boy of Winander is gone; "I would not strike a flower" is worked into *Nutting* (stubs show that it was separately entered later in the notebook as well—see *Chronology: EY*, p. 325); and the lines comparing the soul of man to a strain of music are nowhere visible.

III

Growing still, *The Prelude* reached its third state in another German notebook, DC MS. 16 (earlier known as 18A). Once again a labor of reconstruction has to be undertaken on the scanty evidence of stubs, but once again it is possible to form a precise idea of the poem's shape and contents.

MS. 16 is another red leather pocket notebook with a clasp, like MS. 15. A number of the leaves have been torn out, but 59 remain intact. The contents of the notebook are again detailed by Mark Reed in *Chronology: EY*, Appendix

IX; among them is the second full version of *Salisbury Plain*. The main *Prelude* composition was entered on five consecutive leaves, of which only the last survives. These leaves are preceded by a long passage, part draft, part fair copy, of lines later contributive to the 1805 *Prelude*, V, 370–388; these lines run right into a version of "There was a boy . . ." (1805: V, 389–413).

The surviving leaf of *The Prelude*, following four stubs, contains the closing twelve lines of the poem (Part One), a line count, and a fragmentary continuation. Overleaf is a fresh start headed "2nd Part"; it consists of six lines of fair copy which have been heavily crossed out (photographs of both leaves are presented below, pages 144–145). Setting aside for the moment these aborted continuations, we can see that the closing here is identical to that of Part One in MS. U. In the transcription below, the text and the line numbers are in Wordsworth's hand:

```
To honourable toil. Yet, should it be
That this is but an impotent desire
That I by such enquiry am not taught
To understand myself, nor thou to know
With better knowledge, how the heart was framed
Of him thou lovest need I dread from thee                    240
Harsh judgements if I am so loth to quit
Those recollected hours that have the charm
Of visionary things and lovely forms
And sweet sensations that throw back our life
And make our infancy a visible scene
On which the sun is shining?—                                246
                                                            145
                                                            ———
                                                            391
                                                            400
```

Working back from the end of Part One, we can tell, first, that the missing four leaves (8 pages) must have been filled, averaging close to 30 lines on a page, to contain the needed 234 lines (which added to 12 give 246). On the front of the first stub, eleven lines down, can be detected a portion of the beginning of the poem, as in MS. 15 and MS. U:

```
T[o more than infant softness giving me                     U 12
A[mong the fretful dwellings of mankind,                      13
A[ knowledge a dim earnest of the calm                        14
W[hich Nature breathes among the fields and groves            15
]                                                            [16]
```

Nothing further can be read before the bottom of the recto of the second stub, which would represent page 3 of the poem. Here we can pick up the ending of the "soul of man" lines and the opening of the boat-stealing episode, lines 79–83 of MS. U:

| | |
|---|---|
| S[everer interventions, ministry | U 79 |
| M[ore palpable, and of their school was I. | 80 |
| ] | [81] |
| I[ went alone into a Shepherd's boat | 82 |
| A[ skiff which to a willow-tree was tied | 83 |

On the verso of the third stub (page 6 of the text) is visible a single word, "plains," about seven lines down. This is clearly the end of line 84 of JJ, for alongside it, written vertically into the margin as an insert, are traces of two more lines from the second apostrophe to nature (the lines are in JJ and were probably in MS. 15; they must have been struck out or omitted by the copyist here, then restored in the margin):

| | |
|---|---|
| Of moonlight frost and in the stormy day | JJ 85 |
| [Did ye with such] assiduous love pursue | 86 |

Finally, most initial letters on the recto of the fourth stub (page 7) are visible, and they show that we have reached line 388 of U:

| | |
|---|---|
| T[he bond of union betwixt life and joy | U 390 |
| ] | [391] |
| An[d twice five seasons on my mind had stamped | 392 |
| Th[e faces of the moving year, even then, | 393 |
| A C[hild, I held unconscious intercourse | 394 |
| - | [395] |
| A[ pure organic pleasure from the lines | 396 |
| Of[ curling mist or from the level plain | 397 |
| Of[ waters coloured by the steady clouds. | 398 |
| ] | [399] |
| Of[ Cumbria's rocky limits, they can tell | 400 |
| How[ when the sea threw off his evening shade | 401 |
| And[ to the Shepherd's hut beneath the crags | 402 |
| D[id send sweet notice of the rising moon | 403 |
| Ho[w I have stood to images like these | 404 |
| A[ stranger, linking with the spectacle | 405 |
| No b[ody of associated forms | 406 |
| An[d bringing with me no peculiar sense | 407 |
| Of[ quietness or peace, yet I have stood | 408 |
| Ev[en while my eye has moved o'er three long leagues | 409 |
| Of[ shining water, gathering, as it seemed | 410 |
| T[hrough the wide surface of that field of light | 411 |
| - | [412] |
| - | [413] |
| - | [414] |

| | [415] |
|---|---|
| - | [416] |
| - | [417] |
| - | [418] |

A[nd common face of nature spake to me                              419
R[emembrable things: sometimes 'tis true                            420
B[y quaint associations yet not vain                                421

The make-up of this state of the poem can now be laid out page by page. It corresponds to the version in MS. 15, but there is one addition: here the "soul of man" lines and the boat-stealing episode (both drafted as early as JJ) are inserted following the raven's-nest scene. They total some 63 lines, which, subtracted from 246, make the previous version (in MS. 15) 183 lines. In the reconstruction below, the line numbers in italics refer to lines that can be detected on the stubs or on the surviving leaf.

*Third state of* The Prelude *(MS. 16)*

| Leaf | Page | Lines | Total | Contents |
|---|---|---|---|---|
| 1ʳ | 1 | U 1–11, *12–16,* 17–27 | 27 | Introduction; trap-robbing begins |
| 1ᵛ | 2 | U 28–55 | 28 | Trap-robbing ends; raven's-nest begins |
| 2ʳ | 3 | U 56–78; *79–83* | 28 | Raven's-nest ends; soul of man put in; boat-stealing begins |
| 2ᵛ | 4 | U 84–112 | 29 | Boat-stealing continues |
| 3ʳ | 5 | U 113–129; 130–141 | 29 | Boat-stealing concludes; first apostrophe |
| 3ᵛ | 6 | JJ 58–83, *84–86,* 87–96; U 376–389 | 30½ | Second apostrophe; conclusion begins |
| 4ʳ | 7 | *U 390–421* | 32 | Conclusion continues |
| 4ᵛ | 8 | U 422–452 | 31 | Conclusion continues |
| 5ʳ | 9 | *U 453–464* | 11½ | Conclusion ends |
| | Total lines | | 246 | |

At this stage the trailing passages, even two that later came into the 1798–1799 *Prelude*, are cleanly detached. Toward the other end of the notebook, following transcriptions of *The Ruined Cottage*, *Salisbury Plain*, *The Pedlar*, and the *Discharged Soldier*, are entered a series of blank-verse pieces, some of them possibly associated with the growing *Prelude*. Each of the first three carries the title "Fragment": "There is an active principle . . . ," "There is a law severe of penury . . ." (both taken into *The Excursion*), and the skating scene. The skating scene is followed, exactly as in MS. 15, by "Redundance" and the image of splitting ice. Then come "For let the impediment be what it may" and a long version of *Nutting* later than that in MS. 15. Finally, after *Nutting* breaks off onto stubs, come some stanzas from *Andrew Jones* and a version of "I would not strike a flower."

IV

The fourth state of *The Prelude* is even more ghostly than the two earlier states. No evidence survives to show that it was ever copied out, and reconstruction of it rests not on stubs but on the single line count that Wordsworth entered at the close of the poem in MS. 16. Nonetheless, this state of the poem clearly existed as a conception in the poet's mind, and it deserves to be recognized because it was meant to contain for the first time the passages that lay at the center of the 1798–1799 *Prelude*, the celebrated "spots of time." These consisted of three childhood scenes that came to haunt the imagination of the poet, grouped around the summarizing tribute:

> There are in our existence spots of time
> Which with distinct preeminence retain
> A fructifying virtue, whence, depressed
> By trivial occupations, and the round
> Of ordinary intercourse, our minds,
> (Especially the imaginative power)
> Are nourished and invisibly repaired.

The scenes are introduced by a paragraph in which Wordsworth seeks rather fumblingly to hold "the unity of this my argument" and lays out his subject pretty much as he had in JJ: "the growth of mental power / And love of Nature's works." The three scenes that follow are, first, the episode of the drowned man in Esthwaite Lake, then the discovery of the mouldered gibbet, and finally the scene of waiting for the horses at the Christmas holidays. As he looked back upon this last scene Wordsworth summed up the elements that gave the experience its terrible power to chasten and to nourish him. His lines communicate their own distinctively Wordsworthian power:

> . . . the wind and sleety rain
> And all the business of the elements
> The single sheep, and the one blasted tree
> And the bleak music of that old stone wall
> The noise of wood and water and the mist
> That on the line of each of those two roads
> Advanced in such indisputable shape
> All these were spectacles and sounds to which
> I often would repair, and thence would drink
> As at a fountain.

The manuscript in which these lines were drafted does not survive, and their inclusion in the fourth state of *The Prelude* has to be inferred from the number 145, which Wordsworth added to the 246 in MS. 16 to get his new total of 391 lines (or roughly 400). We can suppose that he was thinking of the "spots of time" because there are no other pieces of composition that give the right total. The skating scene was only 35 lines; the "home amusements" scene, describing the card-playing, was only 36. The "spots of time" totaled 139 lines, revised in transcription to 141, and the few extra lines would have had to form some sort of link passage to introduce them. Where the "spots" were fitted in can be seen from MSS. U and V, which contain the fifth and final state of Part One: they just precede the long conclusion, beginning at U 376, by now made up of some 35 lines taken over in blocks from JJ and some 50 composed along the way but complete by the stage of MS. 16.

The final insertions which brought the finished Part One to 464 lines, from 391, can now be identified and placed. They were two passages clearly set in parallel, one representing outdoor amusements of boyhood, the other indoor. The skating scene (36 lines taken over virtually unaltered from the manuscript that furnished lines for the letter to Coleridge of December 1798) went in between the two apostrophes to nature, and the card-playing scene (some 28 lines of later composition, finished off by the image of splitting ice) went in after the second apostrophe and just before the "spots of time."

The poem's growth, from the composition in JJ to the final form of Part One as in MSS. U and V can at last be summarized. For Wordsworth, it was mainly a matter of fitting pieces of verse together, like parts of a puzzle; only one rearrangement of parts took place, and only the conclusion was extensively rewritten and expanded. About half the inserted passages had been drafted in JJ; about half were later composition. Here a rough columnar array, showing what was added at each stage, may be helpful.

*The Growth of Part One of the Two-Part Prelude*

| *State 1*<br>MS. JJ<br>149 lines | *State 2*<br>MS. 15<br>183 lines | *State 3*<br>MS. 16(a)<br>246 lines | *State 4*<br>MS. 16(b)<br>391 lines | *State 5*<br>MSS. U & V<br>464 lines |
|---|---|---|---|---|

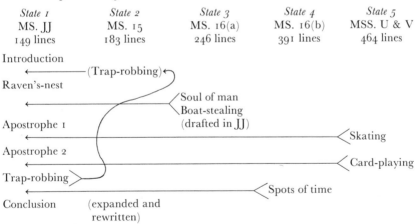

It will of course be recognized that this process of re-sorting, inserting, and expanding resumed when *The Prelude* of 1798–1799 grew toward its later forms.

V

To complete the account of the growth of Part One of the poem, we must turn now to the final manuscripts of 1799, MSS. U and V (DC MSS. 23 and 22).

U and V are fair copies of Parts One and Two made respectively by Mary Hutchinson and Dorothy Wordsworth. U is a vellum-bound notebook of 92 leaves. *The Borderers* with its preface is copied into the first 72 leaves, followed directly by the *Prelude* fair copy, followed in turn by a fair copy of *The Beggar* (in a hand that is probably Sara Hutchinson's) which runs right to the end of the book. V is a smaller notebook, now taken apart, with only 19 leaves surviving (an extra loose leaf has been inserted at the front). A fair copy of the 1798–1799 *Prelude* begins at the top of the first surviving original leaf and runs through three leaves before breaking off, and resumes on the verso of the next leaf (Wordsworth later used the recto of that leaf for drafts of revisions that were incorporated in the 1805 *Prelude*). Throughout most of the *Prelude* fair copy line numbers, running by twenties, are entered in pencil, apparently in Wordsworth's hand.

It seems clear that U and V were transcribed from a copy of Part One that had not yet been fully assembled. There is a gap in U just after the first apostrophe to nature, evidently left for a link passage to introduce the skating scene which follows. In V this gap was filled by eight linking lines, but only on the second try: Dorothy at first went right on to the second apostrophe, leaving out the skating scene, then had to go back in her text, break in again on a fresh page, and this time insert the link lines and the skating scene. Similarly, both U and V have a gap at the end of the "spots of time" left for a link line which was needed to open the long conclusion to the poem. This evidence suggests that U and V were copied from MS. 16, which did not incorporate the "spots of time" or the skating scene. The copyists, at Wordsworth's direction, could pick up the skating scene from among the detached passages in MS. 16, but for the link lines and the "spots of time" they would have had to turn to another manuscript now lost.

Before Dorothy broke off her transcription of V, in order to go back and insert the skating scene, she seems to have been following the text of MS. 16 for the second apostrophe to nature. This included the passage based on JJ:

> familiars of the lakes
> And standing pools. ah! not for trivial ends
> Through snow and sunshine, through the sparkling plains
> Of moonlight frost and in the stormy day
> Did ye with such assiduous love pursue
> Your favourite and your joy. I may not think . . .

In V this passage bears pencil revisions apparently in Coleridge's hand; four lines are struck out and revised readings written in above them. But when Dorothy turned back and recopied this apostrophe she did not follow the pencil revisions, nor did she follow the underlying text. She left out the line ending "plains" together with the next following line, and recopied only the other lines of the passage. After she had done that, however, she overscored three of them and inserted a couple of words so that the passage read at last the way it reads in U:

Familiars of the lakes and

   of the
And˄standing pools, ~~ah not for trivial ends~~
~~Did ye with such assiduous love pursue~~
~~Pursue your favorite and your joy~~. I may not think

The incorporation of V's revisions here into the base text of U points to V as the earlier of these two fair copies, but the evidence is contradictory: U has two gaps which are filled in V—one the eight-line gap left at the beginning of the skating scene, the other a partial line at I, 9—and these, of course, point to U as the earlier. The matter is complicated by the fact that V bears at least two levels of revision. One level, clearly visible on the photographs, belongs to the years 1801–1803, when Wordsworth worked rather desultorily at extending the poem. Another level of revision seems to be contemporary with preparation of the duplicate fair copies: Wordsworth himself erased a number of words or phrases in Dorothy's text of V, sometimes first jotting a revision down in pencil, then neatly entered revisions in the line, in ink. Most of these revisions show up in MS. U, but some do not, and it is apparent that the process of revision went forward while U was being copied, occasionally involving U as well. One rather ambiguous instance occurs at lines 247–248:

                          demand
V:   All these and ~~many~~ more with rival claims
     {Grateful
     {Demand acknowledgement. It were a song

U:   All these and more with rival claims demand
     {Grateful acknowledgement
     {Acknowledgement. It were a song.

(Entries in reduced type are additions; a brace signifies an overwriting.) It is impossible to say where the revision began—with Wordsworth's (or the copyist's) perception that the second line in U was short, or with Wordsworth's desire to insert "grateful" in V. But clearer instances can be found, and four of them—taken from the early lines of the poem, before transcription of V was broken off—may suffice to show the pattern. In each case the alteration seems to be in Wordsworth's hand:

| Line | MS. 15 or JJ | MS. V | MS. U |
|------|------|------|------|
| 24 | all the distant mountain tops | distant Skiddaw's lofty height *over erasure* | distant Skiddaw's lofty height |
| 29 | nipp'd | nipp'd *altered to* snapped | snapped |
| 59 | | Or *over erasure* | And *the reading of later MSS.* |
| 83 | which | that *over erasure* | which *the reading of later MSS.* |

Evidently V was altered at lines 24 and 29 before U was copied, and at lines 59 and 83 afterward.

The most sustained revision of this sort in V can be seen at lines 295–298, where Wordsworth erased two full lines and crowded them back with two new lines between them. Where U reads:

> Such moments chiefly seem to have their date
> In our first childhood. I remember well
> While yet an urchin, one who scarce
> Could hold a bridle, . . .

V reads:

> Such moments chiefly seem to have their date
> **In our first childhood. I remember well**
> **(Tis of an early season that I speak**
> **The twilight of rememberable life,)**
> **While I was yet an urchin, one who scarce**
> Could hold a bridle, . . .

The lines printed in boldface are in Wordsworth's hand, written over erasure.

This matter of priority will be taken up again when we reach Part Two of the poem, for the evidence there comes into clearer focus owing to the survival of the underlying manuscript, RV. But whatever the priority, it is plain that V has to be regarded as the primary manuscript. It bears marks of Wordsworth's close attention, not only in the revisions he neatly entered but in the dozens of added punctuation marks (visible on the transcriptions), and it was V to which he turned in later years in the course of extending his poem to three, to five, to thirteen books. Hence the final text of the poem of 1798–1799 follows V rather than U where discrepancies arise that cannot be accounted simple errors of copying.

In this final version of Part One, the various pieces of Wordsworth's growing poem come together in a powerful and moving sequence, beginning with happy recollections of a "four years child," touching on other boyhood memories, rising to a climax in the "spots of time," then dropping into the long, nostalgic summary of the pleasure and inspiration which the mature poet now owes to

> Those recollected hours that have the charm
> Of visionary things and lovely forms
> And sweet sensations that throw back our life
> And make our infancy a visible scene
> On which the sun is shining.—

The sequence was rearranged one last time when Wordsworth broke up Part One of 1798–1799 in the course of extending his poem. The way in which parts were redistributed, sometimes revised or expanded, can be shown by a simple listing of their positions, first in JJ (when they originated there), then in 1798–1799, then in 1805:

| JJ | 1798–1799 Part One | | 1805 |
|---|---|---|---|
| 22–50 | Intro.; river-bathing | 1–26 | I, 271–304 |
| 97–117 | Trap-robbing | 27–49 | 310–332 |
| 51–67 | Raven's-nest | 50–66 | 332–350 |
| 242–252 | Soul of man | 67–80 | 351–371 |
| 195–241 | Boat-stealing | 81–129 | 372–427 |
| 68–79 | Apostrophe 1 | 130–141 | 428–441 |
| | Transition | 142–149 | 442–451 |
| | Skating | 150–185 | 452–489 |
| 80–96 | Apostrophe 2 | 186–198 | 490–501 |
| | Transition | 198–205 | 501–503 |
| | Card-playing | 206–233 | 504; 535–570 |
| | Transition to spots of time (1) | 234–246 | 509–524 |
| | (2) | 247–258 | |
| | Drowned man | 258–279 | V, 450–472 |
| | Transition | 279–287 | |
| | Spots of time | 288–296 | XI, 258–265; 274–276 |
| | Gibbet scene | 296–330 | 279–316 |
| | Waiting for horses | 330–374 | 346–389 |
| 119–122; 136–165 | Conclusion, paras. 1–3 | 375–412 | I, 571–608 |
| | para. 4 | 413–442 | 609–640 |
| 273–276 | para. 5 | 442–464 | 640–663 |

While the first half of Part One and its long conclusion remained in order in 1805, the breaking up of the "spots of time" and their distribution to other books pulled the center out of the poem of 1798–1799. Moreover, these moves radically altered the function and the meaning of the "spots." As Jonathan Wordsworth has observed, in 1798–1799 "the Drowned Man exerts his influence on the whole sequence, setting up an expectation of the sort of memories that are to be talked about, and preparing for the mood of 'visionary dreariness' that is to be invoked."[5] When "exiled" to Book V the passage serves more prosaically as a specimen of the sort of incident to which a child

---

[5] "The Growth of a Poet's Mind," *Cornell Library Journal*, No. 11 (Spring, 1970), 3–24.

can become hardened by reading fairy tales and romances. But at the same time, the other "spots" were cast into a darkened perspective in 1805 by the moving passage which connected them (Book XI), and served there to summarize some of the somber tones of the longer poem:

> Oh! mystery of Man, from what a depth
> Proceed thy honours! I am lost, but see
> In simple childhood something of the base
> On which thy greatness stands; . . .
>                     The days gone by
> Come back upon me from the dawn almost
> Of life: the hiding places of my power
> Seem open; I approach, and then they close;
> I see by glimpses now; when age comes on,
> May scarcely see at all. . . .

VI

Part Two of the 1798–1799 *Prelude* suffered no such dispersal as Part One, being taken over almost intact into Book II of 1805. Nor did it go through the same slow process of assembly; hence the story of its growth is rather less complicated.

After Wordsworth reached the end of his transcription in MS. 16 and summed up his line counts, including the "spots of time" passages to be inserted, he seems to have decided to extend the poem. His first self-conscious effort is drafted on the same page, following the line counts, and it resembles the rather faltering resumption that followed the line count in JJ (". . . thou[gh] doubting yet not lost I tread / The mazes of this argument . . ."):

> Here we pause
> Doubtful; or lingering with a truant heart
>    Slow & of stationary character
> Rarely adventurous studious more of peace
> And soothing quiet which we here have found.—

(The indented line was crowded in between the other two; see the photograph, page 144). There is nothing here to show that this extension was to be any different from the others that had brought the poem to its fourth state, in some 400 lines, but it cannot have been long before Wordsworth made a major decision about the shape of the growing *Prelude*, for just overleaf in MS. 16 is a firm new start (later heavily crossed out; see the photograph):

> 2nd Part
> Friend of my heart & genius we had reach'd
> A small green island which I was well pleased
> To pass not lightly by for though I felt
> Strength unabated yet I seem'd to need
> Thy cheering voice or ere I could pursue
> My voyage, resting else for ever there.

The shift of tense from the earlier draft, and the direct address here, show Wordsworth looking back with fresh understanding and forward with fresh resolve, both evidently reached as a consequence of talks with Coleridge, whose "cheering voice" helped to bring *The Prelude* into focus and (ironically) encouraged Wordsworth to go on with it. The talks must have taken place at Göttingen in March or April, 1799, as the Wordsworths were making their way from Goslar back to England. The subject of the talks cannot be guessed, but it certainly was not *The Prelude*. Perhaps unwilling to let Coleridge know that he had made no progress with *The Recluse*, perhaps reticent about sharing an unfinished piece of personal writing, Wordsworth seems not to have told Coleridge about his poem, nor shown any of it to him. For not until October, 1799, close to a year after the *Prelude* drafts had been begun, did Coleridge learn that Wordsworth was working at something which was going to be addressed to him, and he was understandably both delighted and curious. "I long to see what you have been doing," he wrote on October 12, but the reason for his longing cannot have sounded encouraging to Wordsworth: "O let it be the tail-piece of the 'Recluse'! for of nothing but the 'Recluse' can I hear patiently. That it is to be addressed to me makes me more desirous that it should not be a poem of itself."[6]

Coleridge may thus have helped to keep *The Prelude* hanging uncompleted, an appendage to be attached somewhere, sometime, but it was too late for him to alter the shape of the swelling poem, for by this time Wordsworth was well along in Part Two. He had come back to England with Dorothy at the beginning of May, and they had settled with the Hutchinsons at Sockburn, on the river Tees in County Durham. Here, after more than two months of wandering, Wordsworth began writing again, and here Part Two of the 1798–1799 *Prelude* was composed.

The manuscript in which his Sockburn work on *The Prelude* survives is known as RV (DC MS. 21), described by Miss Darbishire, *Prel.*, p. xxix.[7] RV is a reasonably fair copy of Part Two, bearing some drafts and some marginal insertions, alternately in Wordsworth's hand and in Dorothy's, with one passage in the hand of Mary Hutchinson. It seems to have been put together from working drafts, most of which are now lost. The manuscript was made up by folding 18 sheets of heavy accountant's paper so as to form a booklet of 36 leaves; the leaves were then stitched together at the fold. Wordsworth began writing on the inside front cover of the booklet—that is, on the verso of the first leaf. Having turned the booklet sideways, he wrote across the leaf and his lines descended from the outer edge down to the center

---

[6] *STCL*, I, 538. The letter survives only as quoted by Christopher Wordsworth in *Memoirs*, I, 159.

[7] Michael Jaye has published an account of RV: "Wordsworth at Work: MS. RV Book II of *The Prelude*," *Papers of the Bibliographical Society of America*, LXVIII (1974), 251–265.

fold, then filled the next leaf from the center fold outward to the edge. Each successive pair of facing pages was filled in the same manner. Only the first 13 leaves of the booklet were used; the rest were left blank save for some scraps of pencil draft (of another poem) on the margin of the next-to-last leaf. A full transcription of RV with facing photographs is provided on pages 168–217.

The RV copy of Part Two can be thought of as an extension of the fourth state of *The Prelude*, Part One, as it stood in MS. 16; RV and 16 together underlie the final state, represented by U and V. Although RV is a fair copy which only occasionally degenerated into a working draft, several stages of composition can be discerned in it. To open Part Two, Wordsworth set aside both the link passage he had drafted in MS. 16 and the formal opening over-leaf and started with five lines that roughly summarized what he had written to that point:

> Thus far my Friend have we retraced the way
> Through which I travelled when I first began
> To love the woods and fields: the passion yet
> Was in its birth sustained as might befall
> By nourishment that came unsought for still.

From here Wordsworth went directly on to further accounts of "boyish sport," this time, as he grew more mature, pursued more thoughtfully, in deeper consciousness of nature's presence—rowing in the summer on Windermere, picnicking in school holidays, horseback riding through the ruins of Furness Abbey, bowling on the green at a country inn on Windermere's shore. He summed up these experiences by touching once again on what had become his central theme:

> Thus day by day my sympathies encreased
> And thus the common range of visible things
> Grew dear to me.

But while Part Two of the 1798–1799 *Prelude* started out like an extension of Part One, it shortly took on a different character. After adding a brief tribute to the beauty of the sun, Wordsworth made a major alteration of course, and began to trace the changes in his relationship to nature very much the way he had done in *Tintern Abbey*, and later was to do in the "Intimations" *Ode*: dismissing his central theme in language that made it sound trivial, he turned to a fresh stage of his growth:

> Those incidental charms which first attached
> My heart to rural objects day by day
> Grew weaker and I hasten on to tell
> How nature intervenient till this time
> And secondary, now at length was sought
> For her own sake.

Impelled by this new subject to undertake an analysis of the growing soul,
Wordsworth contemptuously pronounced the task impossible. Apart from
mock-heroic touches in the card-playing scene, these are the first tones of
satiric irony to enter *The Prelude*:

> But who shall parcel out
> His intellect by geometric rules
> Split like a province into round & square
> Who knows the individual hour in which
> His habits were first sown even as a seed
> Who that shall point as with a wand & say
> This portion of the river of my mind
> Came from yon fountain.

Rejecting any such mechanical analysis, Wordsworth resolved his difficulty
by tracing the organic growth of sensibility in the infant who, still in his
mother's arms, develops a reciprocal intimacy with nature, receiving and
giving, his mind,

> Even as an agent of the one great mind
> Creating creator & receiver both.

Another significant break of tone follows, as the poet looks forward with
anxiety along the path that stretches ahead, fearful

> That in its broken windings we shall need
> The Chamois sinews & the eagle's wing
> For now a trouble came into my mind
> From obscure causes: I was left alone
> Seeking this visible world nor knowing why
> The props of my affection were removed
> And yet the building stood as if sustained
> By its own spirit.

As he developed his account of this new stage of his growth, Wordsworth
drew upon some autobiographical lines he had drafted in the third person for
*The Pedlar*,[8] casting them back into the first person. The lines speak of drinking
in a "visionary power" in "moods / Of shadowy exaltation," a power that
emanates from the sounds of nature,

> sounds that are
> The ghostly language of the antient earth
> Or make their dim abode in distant winds.

Just following these lines, transcription of RV seems to have been broken off,
stopping where Wordsworth recalled hours of solitude at sunrise when he

---

[8] Lines 1–20 of the MS. D text presented by Jonathan Wordsworth in *The Music of Humanity*
(London, 1969), p. 172; earlier drafts are found in the Alfoxden Notebook, DC MS. 14.

would sit and gaze over the vale until the world appeared to melt into his own sensations:

> Oft in those moments such a holy calm
> Did overspread my soul that I forgot
> The agency of sight & what I saw
> Appeared like something in myself—a dream
> A prospect in my mind.

As at earlier stopping places, Wordsworth here summed up his line count. Numbering every twentieth line up to 280, he wrote the figure 292 where Dorothy had stopped.

The date of this interruption cannot be fixed, but it is clear that before Wordsworth resumed transcription the presence of Coleridge once more fell across *The Prelude*. After hearing about Wordsworth's poem, and alarmed by reports of Wordsworth's failing health (the symptoms of distress that writing generally produced had reappeared), Coleridge came over to Sockburn in late October, and for three weeks Wordsworth and Coleridge were together on a walking tour through the Lake Country, occasionally accompanied, occasionally alone. It was Coleridge's first visit to the scenes of Wordsworth's boyhood. The two poets went to Hawkshead, where Wordsworth was shocked by changes in the village, and to Grasmere, where they stayed five days before moving on north. During the trip Wordsworth resolved his long uncertainty about where to make his home by fixing upon Grasmere. He and Coleridge parted on November 18. Coleridge went back to Sockburn, where he stopped long enough to pick up a letter offering him employment on the *Morning Post* in London—and to suffer the first sting of the wounding, hopeless passion for Sara Hutchinson that was to torment him for years; Wordsworth lingered alone in the Lakes, probably to make arrangements for leasing Dove Cottage, and returned at last to Sockburn on November 26, a day after Coleridge had gone off to London.

Wordsworth must have set at once to finishing Part Two of his poem to Coleridge. Before he resumed the copying himself, however, he turned back to the opening of Part Two in RV, erased the first 5 lines, and began again with them on the cover of the booklet (the recto of the first leaf), this time adding 39 new lines before going on with line 6 of the original version. The new lines speak of the distance that now separated him from his childhood, so that he seemed at times "two consciousnesses, conscious of myself / And of some other being." They go on to describe the distressing changes that he and Coleridge had found at Hawkshead. The gray stone which he remembered as the center of his boyhood games was now

> split, & gone to build
> A smart assembly room that perk'd and flared
> With wash & rough-cast elbowing the ground
> Which had been ours.

Once he had developed the new opening, Wordsworth wrote the figure 43 under the line number 292 and did the sum to get 335 as the amended line number. It is not clear where the 43 came from, but the most plausible explanation is that Wordsworth simply totaled the 44 freshly copied lines at the beginning (the original 5 plus 39 new ones) and miscounted by one. This would help to explain the way in which the line-numbering resumes after Wordsworth did his sum: 30 lines following 335 is the number 360. The discrepancy of 5 can be resolved if one supposes that before calculating the second line number Wordsworth realized that he had counted the first 5 lines twice, and made the appropriate correction.

The final paragraphs of Part Two in RV (118 lines), which bring the history of the growth of a poet's mind up to Wordsworth's seventeenth year, show signs of having been assembled as much as composed: substantial pieces of them are grafted in from other manuscripts. The 118 lines fall into two sections, again marked by a number entered at a stopping place in the transcription, at line 398. In the first of these sections, which is mainly in his own hand, Wordsworth rises to some of the boldest and most eloquent assertions of nature's power to be found in *The Prelude*. Here are his grateful tributes to the poet's "first creative sensibility" and to the "plastic power" that shaped his way of seeing. In the original version these lines are leaner and more direct than in their later form:

> my vision often times
> Was from within and an auxiliar light
> Came from my mind which on the setting sun
> Bestowed new splendor & the midnight storm
> Grew darker in the presence of my eye
> Hence my obeisance my devotion hence
> And hence my joy.

The passage culminates in a straightforward pantheistic statement of "the one life" that runs through all "forms," all "things" (the words are left as alternatives) in nature.

The passage may have been brought to mind by Wordsworth's talks with Coleridge, but the lines are taken over from an earlier piece of autobiographical blank verse, *The Pedlar*, in MS. 16 (full transcription may be found on page 159). In RV this passage is followed by 16 lines drawn largely from the last of a series of drafts in another manuscript (DC MS. 33), the one in which the second full version of *Peter Bell* is copied (the manuscript is described and the drafts are presented in full with photographs, pages ooo–ooo). The first three drafts deal with the trials and the labor of composition, the exhaustion of mind and the discontent that accompany creation, almost as though intended to form part of a preamble leading up to "was it for this." The fourth draft, drawn upon for RV, both here and in a marginal insertion, seems to speak of distractions created out of sensory images by "that false secondary power by which / In weakness we create distinctions," and re-emphasizes "the one interior life"

> In which all beings live with god themselves
> Are god existing in one mighty whole. . . .

In RV the lines read:

> In which all beings live with god, are lost
> In god & nature in one mighty whole,

then follow on like the manuscript draft:

> As undistinguishable as the cloudless east
> At noon is from the cloudless west, when all
> The hemisphere is one cerulean blue.

Following the interruption here, Dorothy copied the final section of the poem, up to the last paragraph, which Wordsworth first drafted for her. This paragraph turns again to Coleridge, with another quotation from *Frost at Midnight* and a parting blessing much like the one that closes *Tintern Abbey*:

> Fare thee well!
> Health & the quiet of a healthy mind
> Attend thee! seeking oft the haunts of men
> But yet more often living with thyself,
> And for thyself, so haply shall thy days
> Be many & a blessing to mankind. . . .

According to Wordsworth's line count, which jumps from 420 to 430 then stops before Dorothy took over, Part Two in this stage reached a total of 447 lines. But it did not remain long at that figure, for Wordsworth turned back and wrote into the margins of RV six passages to be inserted, totaling some 40 lines. One of them expands the satiric account of the mind's growth and, picking up some more lines from MS. 33, praises Coleridge for being "no slave"

> Of that false secondary power by which
> In weakness we create distinctions then
> Believe our puny boundaries are things
> Which we perceive & not which we have made.

Incorporation of these marginal passages, together with other scattered revisions of RV, into the base texts of Part Two in U and V shows, of course, the priority of RV. But further analysis of priority again has to start with Wordsworth's in-line revisions of V, over erasure, which are just as numerous in Part Two as in Part One. As before, most, but not all, of them show up in the base text of U. A cluster of examples will reveal the pattern; as before, all alterations appear to be in Wordsworth's hand:

| Line | MS. RV | MS. V | MS. U | MS. M (1804) |
|------|--------|-------|-------|--------------|
| 62 | fractur'd | moulder'd *over erasure* | fractured | mouldered |
| 75 | A modesty and diffidence ensued | Ensued a modesty and diffidence *over erasure* | *like corrected V* | *like U* |
| 84 | poverty, but | poverty. But *capital and period added* | *like corrected V* | *like U* |
| 104 | More than once we | sometimes we have *over erasure* | more than once we | sometimes we have |
| 119 | through the gateway | by the Chantry *over erasure* | through the gateway | by the Chantry |

At lines 75 and 84, V was revised before U was copied; at lines 62, 104, and 119 it was revised afterward, and one again has to suppose that revision took place as the copying went forward.

What U was being copied from has yet to be considered. Some evidence suggests that the source was V, not the underlying RV. At three places U appears to pick up errors in V (the extra phrase "of night" at the end of line 204, erased at once; "of" for "off" in line 209, corrected at once; and the extra word "and" in line 252, later deleted from V). Where V departs from RV either in wording or in paragraphing, U nearly always follows it, although where gaps were left in V, evidently because revision was planned, the copyist of U had to turn back to RV to get a reading (at line 322 for "obscure," actually crossed out in RV, but visible, and at line 236 for "native vale," which became "darling vale" in later manuscripts). There are two other places where U departs from V to pick up the RV reading, but in both of them V has the pertinent reading penciled above the line, and it is plausible to suppose that the penciling, like most other penciling in V, may have been entered before or along with the copying of U: at line 377 V has an incomplete word, "pow," with "soul" (the reading of RV) penciled above; at line 479 V has "world," with "waste," an alternate reading in the margin of RV, penciled above.

While this evidence is less than conclusive, there can be no doubt that V has, once again, to be regarded as the primary manuscript of 1798–1799, the one Wordsworth was closest to, and the one he used for drafting revisions toward later forms of *The Prelude*.

Before he reached the stage of later revision, however, one last change in the poem of 1798–1799 had been made. When the fifth and final state of 1798–1799 was put together—Part One presumably from MS. 16 and one or more lost manuscripts, Part Two from RV and other sources—the lines from MS. 33 were dropped, and a long passage was inserted between the scenes of horseback riding and bowling. This passage, the last to go into *The Prelude* of 1798–1799 and very likely the last to be written for it (it was taken out again by 1804 but by 1850 part of it had been picked up for lines 463–475 of Book VIII), touches once more with perfect simplicity upon the theme which Wordsworth had made the center of his poem. It describes a boating picnic on Coniston Lake in Wordsworth's fourteenth summer, a season when he first began to notice

> That sense of dim similitude which links
> Our moral feelings with external forms,

and records the poet's resolve to turn back in memory to these "fair scenes" with his mind's dying eye.[9]

It may in summary be helpful to lay out in columnar array the stages by which Part Two of the 1798–1799 *Prelude* was put together. The line numbers, facing, are those of the final (1799) text, except of course for the 16-line portion of RV put in at stage 3 and taken out again at stage 6. In stage 5 a few marginal insertions that amounted to only two or three lines are omitted from the array.

The final insertion, with RV's marginal additions, brought Part Two up to 514 lines, which with the 464 of Part One made a total of 978. Even as these last insertions were made, the poem was doubtless being copied in MSS. U and V, and this work was probably completed in about three weeks, for on December 17, Wordsworth and Dorothy departed from the Hutchinsons and made their way to Grasmere, where they arrived and settled into Dove Cottage on the evening of December 20. Minor revision of MS. V could have dragged over into 1800, but Wordsworth was by then looking in other directions, and the two-part *Prelude* was almost certainly behind him.

VII

The state of mind in which Wordsworth brought his poem to a stop in 1799 is revealed in the "glad preamble" to the 1805 *Prelude*, which incorporated some of the earliest lines that Wordsworth had drafted in JJ—drafts which in their turn revealed the state of mind in which the poem was begun. For the "glad preamble," as John Finch has demonstrated,[10] records the feelings that swept over Wordsworth after he had parted from Coleridge in the Lakes on November 18, 1799. In these 54 lines Wordsworth celebrates his freedom to settle where he chooses and to take up the poet's life, using a series of metaphors which do not bear literal interpretation: he is "a captive" liberated from a "house of bondage," from "prison," from a "city's walls"— able to "breathe again," free at last to "quit the tiresome sea and dwell on

---

[9] The resolve is echoed in several other poems, one of late December 1799, *To M. H. (PW,* II, 118): should a man plant his cottage near Rydal, a spot "made by Nature for herself,"

> He would so love it, that in his death-hour
> Its image would survive among his thoughts.

[10] "Wordsworth's Two-Handed Engine," *Bicentenary Wordsworth Studies in Memory of John Alban Finch,* ed. Jonathan Wordsworth (Ithaca, 1970), pp. 1–13.

*The Growth of Part Two of the Two-Part Prelude*

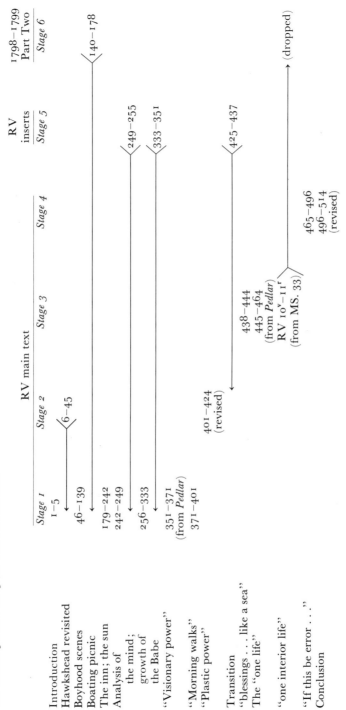

| | RV main text | | | RV inserts | 1798–1799 Part Two |
|---|---|---|---|---|---|
| | *Stage 1* | *Stage 2* | *Stage 3* | *Stage 4* | *Stage 5* | *Stage 6* |

Introduction — 1–5
Hawkshead revisited — 6–45 (Stage 2)
Boyhood scenes — 46–139
Boating picnic — 140–178 (Stage 6)
The inn; the sun — 179–242
Analysis of — 242–249
   the mind; — 249–255 (Stage 5)
   growth of — 256–333
   the Babe — 333–351 (Stage 5)
"Visionary power" — 351–371 (from *Pedlar*)
   371–401
"Morning walks" — 401–424 (revised)
"Plastic power"
Transition — 425–437 (Stage 5)
"blessings . . . like a sea" — 438–444
The "one life" — 445–464 (from *Pedlar*)
   RV 10ᵛ–11ʳ (from MS. 33)
"one interior life" — (dropped)
"If this be error . . ." — 465–496
Conclusion — 496–514 (revised)

shore." The "mild creative breeze" that fans his cheek, though mounting to a "tempest, a redundant energy," becomes

> a storm
> Which, breaking up a long-continued frost,
> Brings with it vernal promises, the hope
> Of active days, of dignity and thought,
> Of prowess in an honourable field,
> Pure passions, virtue, knowledge, and delight,
> The holy life of music and of verse.

Finch's dating of this passage has looked persuasive, but it must be added that the passage in its present form reflects more than the parting with Coleridge. As Mark Reed has observed, it seems also "to draw upon the experience of W's journey of removal to his home at Grasmere" in late December (*Chronology: MY*, p. 629). Thus we cannot confidently date it until after completion of the duplicate fair copies of the two-part *Prelude*. But as it stands it would hardly have fitted that poem. Despite the phrases carried over from the scraps of preamble draft in JJ, the tone of this effusion would have seemed too buoyant, too flatly joyous, to lead directly into the ambiguous hanging question, "was it for this?" The bridging passage—the remainder of the preamble and the "post-preamble" (1805, ll. 55–271)—had still to be composed, and by the time he turned to them Wordsworth's mood had altered. His hopes of carrying out some high poetic ambition had become stalled, and his bewildered mind had fallen into "listlessness" and "vain perplexity." But at the end of 1799 Wordsworth was apparently content to leave his poem as it stood, a record of the growth of his poetic sensibility under the ministering powers of nature.

# Editorial Procedure

Like other volumes in this series, this edition provides two kinds of texts: (1) "reading texts," from which all complexities and variant readings are stripped away, and (2) transcriptions of manuscripts, usually with facing photographic reproductions of the manuscripts. Editorial procedures have been adapted to the different aims of these two styles of presentation.

In this volume, the reading texts in turn are of two sorts. The reading text of the earliest *Prelude* manuscript, JJ, is designed to help bring into view the earliest version of the two-part *Prelude* of 1798–1799. Only the earliest readings, therefore, are given; overwritings, revisions, and rearrangements of the text are not shown except where the original drafts are fragmentary or are rendered incoherent by later readings, or where the original reading is an obvious error or false start. On the other hand, the reading text based on the two fair copies of the 1798–1799 *Prelude* has the aim of showing the final state of the poem. This text, therefore, omits not only later revision, probably entered in 1801 or later, but also the earliest readings where those were supplanted or over-written as the copies were being made. These separate aims have required different ways of treating accidentals. Spelling, capitals, and punctuation are given exactly as they stand in JJ, whereas in the reading text of 1798–1799, which is based on a collation of manuscripts, these features are corrected or modernized where appropriate. In both sorts of reading texts brackets en-closing blank spaces indicate gaps or blanks left in the manuscripts. Particulars of these tactics are given in headnotes to the separate texts.

The other main sort of text, transcription of a manuscript, is more com-plicated. Here the aim is to show with reasonable typographic accuracy everything in the manuscript which could be helpful to a study of the poem's growth and development. Even false starts and corrected letters can sometimes reveal the writer's intention, and they are here recorded, though reinforced letters and random marks are normally not. Passages in Wordsworth's hand are discriminated from those in the hands of his amanuenses by printing his in roman type, theirs in italic with footnotes identifying the copyist, though identification of hands must sometimes be conjectural, especially in the case of scattered words or parts of words. Revisions are shown in type of reduced size just above or below the line to which they pertain, and an effort has been made to show deletion marks, spacing, and other such physical features so that they resemble those of the manuscript itself, though some minor adjustments have been made in the interest of clarity; where transcripts face photographs, doubled-back lines are shown approximately as they appear in the manuscript. In the numbering of leaves, stubs are counted, but not pasted-down end papers. Line numbers correspond to those of the final text of 1798–1799: in transcriptions of fair copy these numbers are carried in the left-hand margin, while in transcriptions of drafts the pertinent range of roughly corresponding line numbers is shown within brackets in the upper right-hand corner of each page.

The following symbols are used in both reading texts and transcriptions:

| | |
|---|---|
| [ ] | Gap or blank in the manuscript. |
| [?peace] | Conjectural reading. |
| [ ? ] | Illegible word. |

The following symbols are used in transcriptions; the first two also appear in the *apparatus criticus*:

d<br>
have }   An overwriting: original reading, "have," converted to "had" by writing "d" on top of the "ve".

{ ;   A short addition, sometimes only a mark of punctuation.

[——?——]   Illegible word deleted.

That more   Words written over an erasure; the original reading is now illegible.

# The Two-Part *Prelude*, 1798–1799

Reading Text

This text, which represents the final form of the two-part *Prelude* of 1798–1799, is based upon the two fair copies in MSS. U and V. Discrepancies between them have been resolved, for the most part, in favor of V, which Wordsworth appears to have been closer to, but not where idiosyncratic habits of the copyists are involved (Dorothy Wordsworth, the copyist of V, sometimes wrote "&" for "and"; both copyists occasionally used "'d" in place of "ed" as a verbal ending). Punctuation, always a problem for Wordsworth, hence for his editors, generally follows V, which Wordsworth went over after transcription with an eye to adding and improving punctuation, though his zeal and attentiveness clearly flagged as the work went on. Even the improved punctuation, like the original, tended to be largely rhetorical, marking pauses, and some modernizing has been done. In these instances, later texts of the poem have been consulted: MS. M, where possible, otherwise MSS. A and B (see *Prel.*, pp. xx–xxii and xxx–xxxi).

Since virtually all of this text is to be included in separate editions of the thirteen-book and fourteen-book *Prelude*s, annotations here have been limited to identifying poems quoted and to commenting on an occasional textual problem.

## First Part

Was it for this
That one, the fairest of all rivers, loved
To blend his murmurs with my Nurse's song,
And from his alder shades, and rocky falls,
And from his fords and shallows, sent a voice          5
That flowed along my dreams? For this didst thou
O Derwent, travelling over the green plains
Near my "sweet birth-place," didst thou beauteous Stream
Make ceaseless music through the night and day,
Which with its steady cadence tempering               10
Our human waywardness, composed my thoughts
To more than infant softness, giving me,
Among the fretful dwellings of mankind,
A knowledge, a dim earnest of the calm
Which Nature breathes among the fields and groves?    15
 Beloved Derwent! fairest of all Streams!
Was it for this that I, a four year's child,
A naked Boy, among thy silent pools
Made one long bathing of a summer's day?
Basked in the sun, or plunged into thy streams,       20
Alternate, all a summer's day, or coursed
Over the sandy fields, and dashed the flowers
Of yellow grunsel, or when crag and hill,
The woods and distant Skiddaw's lofty height
Were bronzed with a deep radiance, stood alone,       25
A naked Savage in the thunder shower?
 And afterwards, 'twas in a later day
Though early, when upon the mountain-slope
The frost and breath of frosty wind had snapped
The last autumnal crocus, 'twas my joy                30

---

8 Here and at the close of the two-part *Prelude* Wordsworth quotes *Frost at Midnight*, Coleridge's autobiographical reflection which served as a model for *Tintern Abbey*.

To wander half the night among the cliffs
And the smooth hollows, where the woodcocks ran
Along the moonlight turf. In thought and wish,
That time, my shoulder all with springes hung,
I was a fell destroyer. Gentle Powers!                                35
Who give us happiness and call it peace!
When scudding on from snare to snare I plied
My anxious visitation, hurrying on,
Still hurrying hurrying onward, how my heart
Panted; among the scattered yew-trees, and the crags              40
That looked upon me, how my bosom beat
With expectation. Sometimes strong desire,
Resistless, overpowered me, and the bird
Which was the captive of another's toils
Became my prey; and when the deed was done                        45
I heard among the solitary hills
Low breathings coming after me, and sounds
Of undistinguishable motion, steps
Almost as silent as the turf they trod.
      Nor less, in spring-time, when on southern banks           50
The shining sun had from his knot of leaves
Decoyed the primrose-flower, and when the vales
And woods were warm, was I a rover then
In the high places, on the lonesome peaks,
Among the mountains and the winds. Though mean                    55
And though inglorious were my views, the end
Was not ignoble. Oh, when I have hung
Above the raven's nest, by knots of grass,
Or half-inch fissures in the slipp'ry rock,
But ill sustained, and almost, as it seemed,                      60
Suspended by the blast which blew amain,
Shouldering the naked crag, oh at that time,
While on the perilous ridge I hung alone,
With what strange utterance did the loud dry wind
Blow through my ears! the sky seemed not a sky                    65
Of earth, and with what motion moved the clouds!
      The mind of man is fashioned and built up
Even as a strain of music: I believe
That there are spirits, which, when they would form
A favored being, from his very dawn                               70
Of infancy do open out the clouds
As at the touch of lightning, seeking him

With gentle visitation; quiet Powers!
Retired and seldom recognized, yet kind,
And to the very meanest not unknown;    75
With me, though rarely, [in my early days]
They communed: others too there are who use,
Yet haply aiming at the self-same end,
Severer interventions, ministry
More palpable, and of their school was I.    80
    They guided me: one evening, led by them,
I went alone into a Shepherd's boat,
A skiff that to a willow-tree was tied
Within a rocky cave, its usual home;
The moon was up, the lake was shining clear    85
Among the hoary mountains: from the shore
I pushed, and struck the oars, and struck again
In cadence, and my little Boat moved on
Just like a man who walks with stately step
Though bent on speed. It was an act of stealth    90
And troubled pleasure; not without the voice
Of mountain-echoes did my boat move on,
Leaving behind her still on either side
Small circles glittering idly in the moon
Until they melted all into one track    95
Of sparkling light. A rocky steep uprose
Above the cavern of the willow tree,
And now, as suited one who proudly rowed
With his best skill, I fixed a steady view
Upon the top of that same craggy ridge,    100
The bound of the horizon, for behind
Was nothing—but the stars and the grey sky.
—She was an elfin pinnace; twenty times
I dipped my oars into the silent lake,
And, as I rose upon the stroke, my Boat    105
Went heaving through the water, like a swan—
When from behind that rocky steep, till then
The bound of the horizon, a huge Cliff,
As if with voluntary power instinct,
Upreared its head: I struck, and struck again,    110
And, growing still in stature, the huge cliff
Rose up between me and the stars, and still

---

76   The line is incomplete in both U and V, but "in my early" is penciled lightly into V.

With measured motion, like a living thing,
Strode after me. With trembling hands I turned,
And through the silent water stole my way                    115
Back to the cavern of the willow-tree.
There, in her mooring-place I left my bark,
And through the meadows homeward went with grave
And serious thoughts: and after I had seen
That spectacle, for many days my brain                       120
Worked with a dim and undetermined sense
Of unknown modes of being: in my thoughts
There was a darkness, call it solitude
Or blank desertion; no familiar shapes
Of hourly objects, images of trees,                          125
Of sea or sky, no colours of green fields:
But huge and mighty forms, that do not live
Like living men, moved slowly through my mind
By day, and were the trouble of my dreams.
     Ah! not in vain ye Beings of the hills!                 130
And ye that walk the woods and open heaths
By moon or star-light, thus from my first dawn
Of childhood did ye love to intertwine
The passions that build up our human soul,
Not with the mean and vulgar works of man,                  135
But with high objects, with eternal things,
With life and nature, purifying thus
The elements of feeling and of thought,
And sanctifying by such discipline
Both pain and fear, until we recognise                       140
A grandeur in the beatings of the heart.
     Nor was this fellowship vouchsafed to me
With stinted kindness. In November days,
When vapours, rolling down the valleys, made
A lonely scene more lonesome, among woods                    145
At noon, and 'mid the calm of summer nights
When by the margin of the trembling lake
Beneath the gloomy hills I homeward went
In solitude, such intercourse was mine.
     And in the frosty season when the sun                   150
Was set, and, visible for many a mile,
The cottage windows through the twilight blazed,
I heeded not the summons: clear and loud
The village clock tolled six; I wheeled about

Proud and exulting like an untired horse                           155
That cares not for its home.— All shod with steel
We hissed along the polished ice, in games
Confederate, imitative of the chace
And woodland pleasures, the resounding horn,
The pack loud bellowing, and the hunted hare.                      160
So through the darkness and the cold we flew,
And not a voice was idle: with the din,
Meanwhile, the precipices rang aloud,
The leafless trees and every icy crag
Tinkled like iron, while the distant hills                         165
Into the tumult sent an alien sound
Of melancholy not unnoticed while the stars,
Eastward, were sparkling clear, and in the west
The orange sky of evening died away.
   Not seldom from the uproar I retired            170
Into a silent bay, or sportively
Glanced sideway leaving the tumultuous throng
To cut across the shadow of a star
That gleamed upon the ice: and oftentimes
When we had given our bodies to the wind                           175
And all the shadowy banks on either side
Came sweeping through the darkness, spinning still
The rapid line of motion, then at once
Have I, reclining back upon my heels,
Stopped short; yet still the solitary cliffs                       180
Wheeled by me, even as if the earth had rolled
With visible motion her diurnal round;
Behind me did they stretch in solemn train
Feebler and feebler, and I stood and watched
Till all was tranquil as a summer sea.                             185
   Ye Powers of earth! ye Genii of the springs!
And ye that have your voices in the clouds
And ye that are Familiars of the lakes
And of the standing pools, I may not think
A vulgar hope was yours when ye employed                           190
Such ministry, when ye through many a year
Thus by the agency of boyish sports
On caves and trees, upon the woods and hills,
Impressed upon all forms the characters
Of danger or desire, and thus did make                             195
The surface of the universal earth

With meanings of delight, of hope and fear,
Work like a sea.
                                    Not uselessly employed
I might pursue this theme through every change
Of exercise and sport to which the year                                    200
Did summon us in its delightful round.
We were a noisy crew: the sun in heaven
Beheld not vales more beautiful than ours
Nor saw a race in happiness and joy
More worthy of the fields where they were sown.                           205
I would record with no reluctant voice
Our home amusements by the warm peat fire
At evening, when with pencil, and with slate
In square divisions parcelled out, and all
With crosses and with cyphers scribbled o'er,                             210
We schemed and puzzled, head opposed to head
In strife too humble to be named in verse,
Or round the naked table, snow-white deal,
Cherry or maple, sate in close array
And to the combat—Lu or Whist—led on                                      215
A thick-ribbed army, not as in the world
Discarded and ungratefully thrown by
Even for the very service they had wrought,
But husbanded through many a long campaign.
Oh with what echoes on the board they fell—                               220
Ironic diamonds, hearts of sable hue,
Queens gleaming through their splendour's last decay,
Knaves wrapt in one assimilating gloom,
And Kings indignant at the shame incurr'd
By royal visages. Meanwhile abroad                                        225
The heavy rain was falling, or the frost
Raged bitterly with keen and silent tooth,
And interrupting the impassioned game
Oft from the neighbouring lake the splitting ice
While it sank down towards the water sent                                 230
Among the meadows and the hills its long
And frequent yellings, imitative some
Of wolves that howl along the Bothnic main.
    Nor with less willing heart would I rehearse
The woods of autumn and their hidden bowers                               235
With milk-white clusters hung; the rod and line,
True symbol of the foolishness of hope,

Which with its strong enchantment led me on
By rocks and pools where never summer-star
Impressed its shadow, to forlorn cascades                          240
Among the windings of the mountain-brooks;
The kite, in sultry calms from some high hill
Sent up, ascending thence till it was lost
Among the fleecy clouds, in gusty days
Launched from the lower grounds, and suddenly                       245
Dash'd headlong—and rejected by the storm.
All these and more with rival claims demand
Grateful acknowledgement. It were a song
Venial, and such as if I rightly judge
I might protract unblamed; but I perceive                           250
That much is overlooked, and we should ill
Attain our object if from delicate fears
Of breaking in upon the unity
Of this my argument I should omit
To speak of such effects as cannot here                             255
Be regularly classed, yet tend no less
To the same point, the growth of mental power
And love of Nature's works.
       Ere I had seen
Eight summers (and 'twas in the very week
When I was first transplanted to thy vale,                          260
Beloved Hawkshead! when thy paths, thy shores
And brooks were like a dream of novelty
To my half-infant mind) I chanced to cross
One of those open fields which, shaped like ears,
Make green peninsulas on Esthwaite's lake.                          265
Twilight was coming on, yet through the gloom
I saw distinctly on the opposite shore
Beneath a tree and close by the lake side
A heap of garments, as if left by one
Who there was bathing: half an hour I watched                       270
And no one owned them: meanwhile the calm lake
Grew dark with all the shadows on its breast,
And now and then a leaping fish disturbed
The breathless stillness. The succeeding day
There came a company, and in their boat                             275
Sounded with iron hooks and with long poles.
At length the dead man 'mid that beauteous scene
Of trees, and hills, and water, bolt upright

Rose with his ghastly face. I might advert
To numerous accidents in flood or field,                    280
Quarry or moor, or 'mid the winter snows,
Distresses and disasters, tragic facts
Of rural history that impressed my mind
With images, to which in following years
Far other feelings were attached, with forms              285
That yet exist with independent life
And, like their archetypes, know no decay.
    There are in our existence spots of time
Which with distinct pre-eminence retain
A fructifying virtue, whence, depressed                    290
By trivial occupations and the round
Of ordinary intercourse, our minds
(Especially the imaginative power)
Are nourished, and invisibly repaired.
Such moments chiefly seem to have their date              295
In our first childhood. I remember well
('Tis of an early season that I speak,
The twilight of rememberable life)
While I was yet an urchin, one who scarce
Could hold a bridle, with ambitious hopes                 300
I mounted, and we rode towards the hills;
We were a pair of horsemen: honest James
Was with me, my encourager and guide.
We had not travelled long ere some mischance
Disjoined me from my comrade, and through fear            305
Dismounting, down the rough and stony moor
I led my horse and, stumbling on, at length
Came to a bottom where in former times
A man, the murderer of his wife, was hung
In irons; mouldered was the gibbet mast,                  310
The bones were gone, the iron and the wood,
Only a long green ridge of turf remained
Whose shape was like a grave. I left the spot,
And, reascending the bare slope, I saw
A naked pool that lay beneath the hills,                  315
The beacon on the summit, and more near
A girl who bore a pitcher on her head
And seemed with difficult steps to force her way

---

297–298   These lines were inserted by WW in MS. V, over erasure.

Against the blowing wind. It was in truth
An ordinary sight but I should need                    320
Colours and words that are unknown to man
To paint the visionary dreariness
Which, while I looked all round for my lost guide,
Did, at that time, invest the naked pool,
The beacon on the lonely eminence,                     325
The woman and her garments vexed and tossed
By the strong wind. Nor less I recollect
(Long after, though my childhood had not ceased)
Another scene which left a kindred power
Implanted in my mind.                                  330
            One Christmas time,
The day before the holidays began,
Feverish, and tired and restless, I went forth
Into the fields, impatient for the sight
Of those three horses which should bear us home,
My Brothers and myself. There was a crag,              335
An eminence which from the meeting point
Of two highways ascending overlooked
At least a long half-mile of those two roads,
By each of which the expected steeds might come,
The choice uncertain. Thither I repaired               340
Up to the highest summit; 'twas a day
Stormy, and rough, and wild, and on the grass
I sate, half-sheltered by a naked wall;
Upon my right hand was a single sheep,
A whistling hawthorn on my left, and there,            345
Those two companions at my side, I watched
With eyes intensely straining as the mist
Gave intermitting prospects of the wood
And plain beneath. Ere I to school returned
That dreary time, ere I had been ten days              350
A dweller in my Father's house, he died,
And I and my two Brothers, orphans then,
Followed his body to the grave. The event
With all the sorrow which it brought appeared
A chastisement, and when I called to mind              355
That day so lately passed when from the crag
I looked in such anxiety of hope,
With trite reflections of morality
Yet with the deepest passion I bowed low

To God, who thus corrected my desires;                        360
And afterwards the wind, and sleety rain,
And all the business of the elements,
The single sheep, and the one blasted tree,
And the bleak music of that old stone wall,
The noise of wood and water, and the mist                     365
Which on the line of each of those two roads
Advanced in such indisputable shapes,
All these were spectacles and sounds to which
I often would repair, and thence would drink
As at a fountain, and I do not doubt                          370
That in this later time when storm and rain
Beat on my roof at midnight, or by day
When I am in the woods, unknown to me
The workings of my spirit thence are brought.
       [Nor sedulous to trace]                    375
How Nature by collateral interest
And by extrinsic passion peopled first
My mind with forms, or beautiful or grand,
And made me love them, may I well forget
How other pleasures have been mine, and joys                  380
Of subtler origin, how I have felt
Not seldom, even in that tempestuous time,
Those hallowed and pure motions of the sense
Which seem in their simplicity to own
An intellectual charm, that calm delight                      385
Which, if I err not, surely must belong
To those first-born affinities that fit
Our new existence to existing things
And in our dawn of being constitute
The bond of union betwixt life and joy.                       390
   Yes, I remember when the changeful earth
And twice five seasons on my mind had stamped
The faces of the moving year, even then,
A Child, I held unconscious intercourse
With the eternal Beauty, drinking in                          395
A pure organic pleasure from the lines
Of curling mist or from the level plain
Of waters coloured by the steady clouds.

---

375 The line is incomplete in both U and V but "Nor sedulous to trace" is penciled into V.

The sands of Westmoreland, the creeks and bays
Of Cumbria's rocky limits, they can tell                          400
How when the sea threw off his evening shade
And to the Shepherd's hut beneath the crags
Did send sweet notice of the rising moon,
How I have stood to images like these
A stranger, linking with the spectacle                           405
No body of associated forms
And bringing with me no peculiar sense
Of quietness or peace, yet I have stood
Even while my eye has moved o'er three long leagues
Of shining water, gathering, as it seemed,                       410
Through the wide surface of that field of light
New pleasure, like a bee among the flowers.
    Thus often in those fits of vulgar joy
Which through all seasons on a child's pursuits
Are prompt attendants, 'mid that giddy bliss                     415
Which like a tempest works along the blood
And is forgotten, even then I felt
Gleams like the flashing of a shield; the earth
And common face of Nature spake to me
Rememberable things: sometimes, 'tis true,                       420
By quaint associations, yet not vain
Nor profitless if haply they impressed
Collateral objects and appearances,
Albeit lifeless then, and doomed to sleep
Until maturer seasons called them forth                          425
To impregnate and to elevate the mind.
——And if the vulgar joy by its own weight
Wearied itself out of the memory,
The scenes which were a witness of that joy
Remained, in their substantial lineaments                        430
Depicted on the brain, and to the eye
Were visible, a daily sight: and thus
By the impressive agency of fear,
By pleasure and repeated happiness,
So frequently repeated, and by force                             435
Of obscure feelings representative
Of joys that were forgotten, these same scenes
So beauteous and majestic in themselves,
Though yet the day was distant, did at length
Become habitually dear, and all                                  440

Their hues and forms were by invisible links
Allied to the affections.
                    I began
My story early, feeling, as I fear,
The weakness of a human love for days
Disowned by memory, ere the birth of spring                    445
Planting my snow-drops among winter snows.
Nor will it seem to thee, my Friend, so prompt
In sympathy, that I have lengthened out
With fond and feeble tongue a tedious tale.
Meanwhile my hope has been that I might fetch                    450
Reproaches from my former years, whose power
May spur me on, in manhood now mature,
To honourable toil. Yet, should it be
That this is but an impotent desire,
That I by such inquiry am not taught                    455
To understand myself, nor thou to know
With better knowledge how the heart was framed
Of him thou lovest, need I dread from thee
Harsh judgements if I am so loth to quit
Those recollected hours that have the charm                    460
Of visionary things, and lovely forms
And sweet sensations that throw back our life
And make our infancy a visible scene
On which the sun is shining?—


Second Part


Thus far my Friend, have we retraced the way
Through which I travelled when I first began
To love the woods and fields: the passion yet
Was in its birth, sustained as might befall
By nourishment that came unsought, for still                    5
From week to week, from month to month, we lived
A round of tumult: duly were our games
Prolonged in summer till the day-light failed;
No chair remained before the doors, the bench

---

7   Two extra lines once present here were canceled (see MS. U transcript, p. 275):
    A round of tumult. 'Twas a rustic spot
    The town in which we dwelt a small domain
    And there each evening duly were our games

And threshold steps were empty, fast asleep          10
The labourer and the old man who had sate
A later lingerer, yet the revelry
Continued and the loud uproar: at last
When all the ground was dark, and the huge clouds
Were edged with twinkling stars, to bed we went     15
With weary joints and with a beating mind.
Ah! is there one who ever has been young
And needs a monitory voice to tame
The pride of virtue and of intellect,
And is there one, the wisest and the best           20
Of all mankind, who does not sometimes wish
For things which cannot be, who would not give,
If so he might, to duty and to truth
The eagerness of infantine desire?
A tranquillizing spirit presses now                 25
On my corporeal frame, so wide appears
The vacancy between me and those days
Which yet have such self-presence in my heart
That sometimes when I think of them I seem
Two consciousnesses, conscious of myself            30
And of some other being. A grey stone
Of native rock, left midway in the square
Of our small market-village, was the home
And centre of these joys, and when, returned
After long absence, thither I repaired,             35
I found that it was split and gone to build
A smart assembly-room that perked and flared
With wash and rough-cast, elbowing the ground
Which had been ours. But let the fiddle scream
And be ye happy! yet I know, my Friends,            40
That more than one of you will think with me
Of those soft starry nights and that old dame
From whom the stone was named, who there had sate
And watched her table with its huckster's wares,
Assiduous, for the length of sixty years.          45
—We ran a boisterous race, the year span round
With giddy motion. But the time approached
That brought with it a regular desire
For calmer pleasures, when the beauteous scenes
Of nature were collaterally attached               50
To every scheme of holiday delight

And every boyish sport, less grateful else
And languidly pursued.
                    When summer came
It was the pastime of our afternoons
To beat along the plain of Windermere                    55
With rival oars; and the selected bourn
Was now an island musical with birds
That sang for ever, now a sister isle
Beneath the oak's umbrageous covert sown
With lilies of the valley like a field,                    60
And now a third small island where remained
An old stone table and one mouldered cave,
A hermit's history. In such a race,
So ended, disappointment could be none,
Uneasiness, or pain, or jealousy;                    65
We rested in the shade all pleased alike,
Conquered and conqueror. Thus our selfishness
Was mellowed down, and thus the pride of strength
And the vain-glory of superior skill
Were interfused with objects which subdued                    70
And tempered them, and gradually produced
A quiet independence of the heart.
And to my Friend who knows me I may add,
Unapprehensive of reproof, that hence
Ensued a diffidence and modesty,                    75
And I was taught to feel, perhaps too much,
The self-sufficing power of solitude.
    No delicate viands sapped our bodily strength;
More than we wished we knew the blessing then
Of vigorous hunger, for our daily meals                    80
Were frugal, Sabine fare! and then exclude
A little weekly stipend, and we lived
Through three divisions of the quartered year
In pennyless poverty. But now to school
Returned from the half-yearly holidays,                    85
We came with purses more profusely filled,
Allowance which abundantly sufficed
To gratify the palate with repasts
More costly than the Dame of whom I spake,
That ancient woman, and her board supplied,                    90
Hence inroads into distant vales, and long
Excursions far away among the hills;

Hence rustic dinners on the cool green ground
Or in the woods or by a river-side
Or fountain, festive banquets that provoked                    95
The languid action of a natural scene
By pleasure of corporeal appetite.
    Nor is my aim neglected if I tell
How twice in the long length of those half-years
We from our funds perhaps with bolder hand                   100
Drew largely, anxious for one day at least
To feel the motion of the galloping steed;
And with the good old Innkeeper in truth
I needs must say that sometimes we have used
Sly subterfuge, for the intended bound                        105
Of the day's journey was too distant far
For any cautious man, a Structure famed
Beyond its neighbourhood, the antique walls
Of a large Abbey with its fractured arch,
Belfry, and images, and living trees,                         110
A holy scene! Along the smooth green turf
Our horses grazed: in more than inland peace
Left by the winds that overpass the vale
In that sequestered ruin trees and towers
Both silent, and both motionless alike,                       115
Hear all day long the murmuring sea that beats
Incessantly upon a craggy shore.
    Our steeds remounted, and the summons given,
With whip and spur we by the Chantry flew
In uncouth race, and left the cross-legged Knight            120
And the stone Abbot, and that single wren
Which one day sang so sweetly in the nave
Of the old church that, though from recent showers
The earth was comfortless, and touched by faint
Internal breezes from the roofless walls                      125
The shuddering ivy dripped large drops, yet still
So sweetly 'mid the gloom the invisible bird
Sang to itself that there I could have made
My dwelling-place, and lived for ever there
To hear such music. Through the walls we flew                130
And down the valley, and, a circuit made
In wantonness of heart, through rough and smooth
We scampered homeward. O ye rocks and streams
And that still spirit of the evening air,

Even in this joyous time I sometimes felt                         135
Your presence, when with slackened step we breathed
Along the sides of the steep hills, or when,
Lightened by gleams of moonlight from the sea,
We beat with thundering hoofs the level sand.
  There was a row of ancient trees, since fallen,               140
That on the margin of a jutting land
Stood near the lake of Coniston and made
With its long boughs above the water stretched
A gloom through which a boat might sail along
As in a cloister. An old Hall was near,                          145
Grotesque and beautiful, its gavel end
And huge round chimneys to the top o'ergrown
With fields of ivy. Thither we repaired,
'Twas even a custom with us, to the shore
And to that cool piazza. They who dwelt                          150
In the neglected mansion-house supplied
Fresh butter, tea-kettle, and earthen-ware,
And chafing-dish with smoking coals, and so
Beneath the trees we sate in our small boat
And in the covert eat our delicate meal                          155
Upon the calm smooth lake. It was a joy
Worthy the heart of one who is full grown
To rest beneath those horizontal boughs
And mark the radiance of the setting sun,
Himself unseen, reposing on the top                             160
Of the high eastern hills. And there I said,
That beauteous sight before me, there I said
(Then first beginning in my thoughts to mark
That sense of dim similitude which links
Our moral feelings with external forms)                         165
That in whatever region I should close
My mortal life I would remember you,
Fair scenes! that dying I would think on you,
My soul would send a longing look to you:
Even as that setting sun while all the vale                     170
Could nowhere catch one faint memorial gleam
Yet with the last remains of his last light
Still lingered, and a farewell lustre threw
On the dear mountain-tops where first he rose.
  'Twas then my fourteenth summer, and these words               175
Were uttered in a casual access

Of sentiment, a momentary trance
That far outran the habit of my mind.
   Upon the eastern shore of Windermere,
Above the crescent of a pleasant bay,               180
There was an Inn, no homely-featured shed,
Brother of the surrounding cottages,
But 'twas a splendid place, the door beset
With chaises, grooms, and liveries, and within
Decanters, glasses, and the blood-red wine.        185
In ancient times, or ere the Hall was built
On the large island, had the dwelling been
More worthy of a poet's love, a hut
Proud of its one bright fire and sycamore shade.
But though the rhymes were gone which once inscribed    190
The threshold, and large golden characters
On the blue-frosted sign-board had usurped
The place of the old Lion in contempt
And mockery of the rustic painter's hand,
Yet to this hour the spot to me is dear         195
With all its foolish pomp. The garden lay
Upon a slope surmounted by the plain
Of a small bowling-green; beneath us stood
A grove, with gleams of water through the trees
And over the tree-tops; nor did we want         200
Refreshment, strawberries and mellow cream,
And there through half an afternoon we played
On the smooth platform, and the shouts we sent
Made all the mountains ring. But ere the fall
Of night, when in our pinnace we returned       205
Over the dusky lake, and to the beach
Of some small island steered our course with one,
The minstrel of our troop, and left him there
And rowed off gently while he blew his flute
Alone upon the rock—oh then the calm        210
And dead still water lay upon my mind
Even with a weight of pleasure, and the sky,
Never before so beautiful, sank down
Into my heart and held me like a dream.
   Thus day by day my sympathies increased    215
And thus the common range of visible things
Grew dear to me: already I began
To love the sun, a Boy I loved the sun

Not, as I since have loved him, as a pledge
And surety of my earthly life, a light                                220
Which while I view I feel I am alive,
But for this cause, that I had seen him lay
His beauty on the morning hills, had seen
The western mountain touch his setting orb
In many a thoughtless hour, when from excess                          225
Of happiness my blood appeared to flow
With its own pleasure and I breathed with joy.
And from like feelings, humble though intense,
To patriotic and domestic love
Analogous, the moon to me was dear,                                   230
For I would dream away my purposes
Standing to look upon her while she hung
Midway between the hills as if she knew
No other region but belonged to thee,
Yea, appertained by a peculiar right                                  235
To thee and thy grey huts, my native vale.
   Those incidental charms which first attached
My heart to rural objects day by day
Grew weaker, and I hasten on to tell
How nature, intervenient till this time                               240
And secondary, now at length was sought
For her own sake.— But who shall parcel out
His intellect by geometric rules,
Split like a province into round and square;
Who knows the individual hour in which                                245
His habits were first sown, even as a seed;
Who that shall point as with a wand and say,
This portion of the river of my mind
Came from yon fountain? Thou, my Friend, art one
More deeply read in thy own thoughts, no slave                        250
Of that false secondary power by which
In weakness we create distinctions, then
Believe our puny boundaries are things
Which we perceive and not which we have made.
To thee, unblinded by these outward shews,                            255
The unity of all has been revealed,
And thou wilt doubt with me, less aptly skilled
Than many are to class the cabinet
Of their sensations and in voluble phrase
Run through the history and birth of each                             260

As of a single independent thing.
Hard task to analyse a soul in which
Not only general habits and desires
But each most obvious and particular thought,
Not in a mystical and idle sense                                    265
But in the words of reason deeply weighed,
Hath no beginning.
               Bless'd the infant Babe
(For with my best conjectures I would trace
The progress of our being) blest the Babe
Nursed in his Mother's arms, the Babe who sleeps                    270
Upon his Mother's breast, who when his soul
Claims manifest kindred with an earthly soul
Doth gather passion from his Mother's eye!
Such feelings pass into his torpid life
Like an awakening breeze, and hence his mind                       275
Even in the first trial of its powers
Is prompt and watchful, eager to combine
In one appearance all the elements
And parts of the same object, else detached
And loth to coalesce. Thus day by day                              280
Subjected to the discipline of love
His organs and recipient faculties
Are quickened, are more vigorous, his mind spreads
Tenacious of the forms which it receives.
In one beloved presence, nay, and more,                            285
In that most apprehensive habitude
And those sensations which have been derived
From this beloved presence, there exists
A virtue which irradiates and exalts
All objects through all intercourse of sense.                      290
No outcast he, bewildered and depressed:
Along his infant veins are interfused
The gravitation and the filial bond
Of nature that connect him with the world.
Emphatically such a being lives                                     295
An inmate of this *active* universe;
From nature largely he receives, nor so
Is satisfied but largely gives again,
For feeling has to him imparted strength,
And powerful in all sentiments of grief,                           300
Of exultation, fear and joy, his mind,

Even as an agent of the one great mind,
Creates, creator and receiver both,
Working but in alliance with the works
Which it beholds.— Such verily is the first                    305
Poetic spirit of our human life,
By uniform control of after years
In most abated and suppressed, in some
Through every change of growth or of decay
Preeminent till death.
                              From early days,                 310
Beginning not long after that first time
In which, a Babe, by intercourse of touch
I held mute dialogues with my Mother's heart,
I have endeavoured to display the means
Whereby this infant sensibility,                               315
Great birth-right of our being, was in me
Augmented and sustained. Yet is a path
More difficult before me, and I fear
That in its broken windings we shall need
The Chamois' sinews and the Eagle's wing:                      320
For now a trouble came into my mind
From obscure causes. I was left alone
Seeking this visible world, nor knowing why:
The props of my affections were removed
And yet the building stood as if sustained                     325
By its own spirit. All that I beheld
Was dear to me, and from this cause it came
That now to Nature's finer influxes
My mind lay open, to that more exact
And intimate communion which our hearts                        330
Maintain with the minuter properties
Of objects which already are beloved,
And of those only. Many are the joys
Of youth, but oh! what happiness to live
When every hour brings palpable access                         335
Of knowledge, when all knowledge is delight,
And sorrow is not there. The seasons came
And every season brought a countless store
Of modes and temporary qualities
Which but for this most watchful power of love                 340
Had been neglected, left a register
Of permanent relations, else unknown:

Hence life, and change, and beauty, solitude
More active even than "best society,"
Society made sweet as solitude                              345
By silent inobtrusive sympathies
And gentle agitations of the mind
From manifold distinctions, difference
Perceived in things where to the common eye
No difference is: and hence from the same source          350
Sublimer joy; for I would walk alone
In storm and tempest or in starlight nights
Beneath the quiet heavens, and at that time
Would feel whate'er there is of power in sound
To breathe an elevated mood by form                        355
Or image unprofaned: and I would stand
Beneath some rock listening to sounds that are
The ghostly language of the ancient earth
Or make their dim abode in distant winds.
Thence did I drink the visionary power.                    360
I deem not profitless these fleeting moods
Of shadowy exaltation, not for this,
That they are kindred to our purer mind
And intellectual life, but that the soul
Remembering how she felt, but what she felt               365
Remembering not, retains an obscure sense
Of possible sublimity to which
With growing faculties she doth aspire,
With faculties still growing, feeling still
That whatsoever point they gain, they still               370
Have something to pursue.
                              And not alone
In grandeur and in tumult, but no less
In tranquil scenes, that universal power
And fitness in the latent qualities
And essences of things, by which the mind                 375
Is moved with feelings of delight, to me
Came strengthened with a superadded soul,
A virtue not its own. My morning walks
Were early; oft before the hours of school
I travelled round our little lake, five miles             380
Of pleasant wandering, happy time more dear

344   The quotation is from *Paradise Lost*, IX, 249: "For solitude sometimes is best society."

For this, that one was by my side, a Friend
Then passionately loved; with heart how full
Will he peruse these lines, this page, perhaps
A blank to other men, for many years                                385
Have since flowed in between us, and, our minds
Both silent to each other, at this time
We live as if those hours had never been.
Nor seldom did I lift our cottage latch
Far earlier, and before the vernal thrush                           390
Was audible, among the hills I sate
Alone upon some jutting eminence
At the first hour of morning when the vale
Lay quiet in an utter solitude.
How shall I trace the history, where seek                           395
The origin of what I then have felt?
Oft in those moments such a holy calm
Did overspread my soul that I forgot
The agency of sight, and what I saw
Appeared like something in myself—a dream,                          400
A prospect in my mind. 'Twere long to tell
What spring and autumn, what the winter-snows
And what the summer-shade, what day and night,
The evening and the morning, what my dreams
And what my waking thoughts supplied, to nurse                      405
That spirit of religious love in which
I walked with nature. But let this at least
Be not forgotten, that I still retained
My first creative sensibility,
That by the regular action of the world                             410
My soul was unsubdued. A plastic power
Abode with me, a forming hand, at times
Rebellious, acting in a devious mood,
A local spirit of its own, at war
With general tendency, but for the most                             415
Subservient strictly to the external things
With which it communed. An auxiliar light
Came from my mind which on the setting sun
Bestowed new splendour, the melodious birds,
The gentle breezes, fountains that ran on                           420
Murmuring so sweetly in themselves, obeyed
A like dominion, and the midnight storm
Grew darker in the presence of my eye.

Hence my obeisance, my devotion hence,
And *hence* my transport.
              Nor should this perchance       425
Pass unrecorded, that I still had loved
The exercise and produce of a toil
Than analytic industry to me
More pleasing, and whose character, I deem,
Is more poetic, as resembling more       430
Creative agency: I mean to speak
Of that interminable building reared
By observation of affinities
In objects where no brotherhood exists
To common minds. My seventeenth year was come,   435
And whether from this habit rooted now
So deeply in my mind, or from excess
Of the great social principle of life
Coercing all things into sympathy,
To unorganic natures I transferred       440
My own enjoyments, or, the power of truth
Coming in revelation, I conversed
With things that really are. I at this time
Saw blessings spread around me like a sea.
Thus did my days pass on, and now at length    445
From Nature and her overflowing soul
I had received so much that all my thoughts
Were steeped in feeling; I was only then
Contented when with bliss ineffable
I felt the sentiment of being spread     450
O'er all that moves, and all that seemeth still,
O'er all that, lost beyond the reach of thought
And human knowledge, to the human eye
Invisible, yet liveth to the heart,
O'er all that leaps, and runs, and shouts and sings   455
Or beats the gladsome air, o'er all that glides
Beneath the wave, yea, in the wave itself
And mighty depth of waters: wonder not
If such my transports were, for in all things
I saw one life and felt that it was joy.     460
One song they sang, and it was audible,
Most audible then when the fleshly ear,
O'ercome by grosser prelude of that strain,
Forgot its functions, and slept undisturbed.

If this be error, and another faith                                465
Find easier access to the pious mind,
Yet were I grossly destitute of all
Those human sentiments which make this earth
So dear, if I should fail with grateful voice
To speak of you, ye mountains! and ye lakes             470
And sounding cataracts! ye mists and winds
That dwell among the hills where I was born.
If, in my youth, I have been pure in heart,
If, mingling with the world, I am content
With my own modest pleasures, and have lived          475
With God and Nature communing, removed
From little enmities and low desires,
The gift is yours: if in these times of fear,
This melancholy waste of hopes o'erthrown,
If, 'mid indifference and apathy                                480
And wicked exultation, when good men
On every side fall off we know not how
To selfishness disguised in gentle names
Of peace, and quiet, and domestic love,
Yet mingled, not unwillingly, with sneers               485
On visionary minds, if in this time
Of dereliction and dismay I yet
Despair not of our nature, but retain
A more than Roman confidence, a faith
That fails not, in all sorrow my support,                   490
The blessing of my life, the gift is yours,
Ye Mountains! thine, O Nature! thou hast fed
My lofty speculations, and in thee
For this uneasy heart of ours I find
A never-failing principle of joy                                 495
And purest passion.
        Thou, my Friend, wast reared
In the great city 'mid far other scenes,
But we, by different roads, at length have gained
The self-same bourne. And from this cause to thee
I speak unapprehensive of contempt,                      500
The insinuated scoff of coward tongues,
And all that silent language which so oft
In conversation betwixt man and man

---

496–497    Another quotation from Coleridge's *Frost at Midnight*; see above, First Part, line 8.

Blots from the human countenance all trace
Of beauty and of love. For thou hast sought                505
The truth in solitude, and thou art one,
The most intense of Nature's worshippers,
In many things my brother, chiefly here
In this my deep devotion.
                              Fare thee well!
Health and the quiet of a healthful mind                   510
Attend thee! seeking oft the haunts of men
But yet more often living with thyself
And for thyself, so haply shall thy days
Be many and a blessing to mankind.—

        End of the Second Part

# Texts Contributing
to the First Part

## MS. JJ: Photographic Reproductions and Transcriptions

MS. JJ (DC MS. 19) is a small notebook bound in boards; it was originally made up of 96 leaves, but 7 leaves have been torn out. The leaves, in gatherings of 16, measure 9.5 by 14.8 centimeters, with chain lines at intervals of 2.7 centimeters; they are watermarked with a design showing two warriors and the legend PRO PATRIA. The contents of the notebook are described in the Introduction, Section I, above. In the transcription that follows, leaves of the manuscript which carry *Prelude* composition are presented in order, from front to back, and for convenience of reference to other texts the nomenclature adopted by de Selincourt and Darbishire is preserved: leaves A and B come first, then P through Z, followed by the inside back cover. Line numbers of the final text of 1798–1799 are shown bracketed in the running head of each leaf, roughly corresponding to the lines entered on the leaf. Extended passages of revision, often indistinguishable from fresh drafting, are set in larger type.

Who give us happiness & call it peace
[?While ?thus ?from] snare to snare I plied
My anxious visitation hurrying on [?ward]

                          & the crags
[?Reclined] among the lonely eughtrees that
That looked upon me how my bosom
                  beat

With expectation

---

Pencil drafts, expanding upon drafts on V<sup>v</sup> and leading toward version on X<sup>r</sup>.

When shape was [?not ?no] figure to be seen
Low [?breathing]    and steps
            and sounds
Of undistinguishable motion, steps

Pencil drafts, expanding upon drafts on V<sup>v</sup> and leading toward version on X<sup>r</sup>.

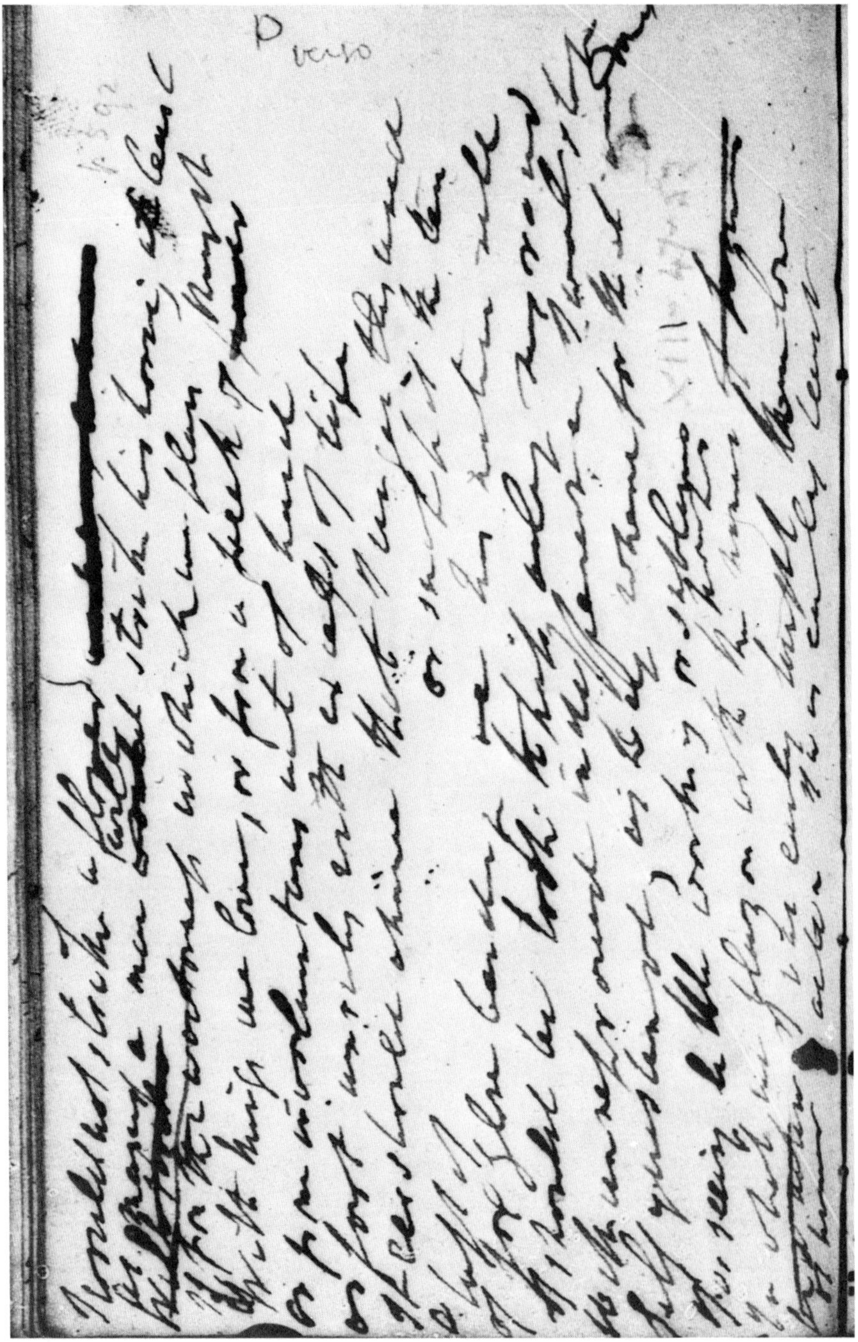

I would not strike a flower as ~~many a man~~
        will
    As many a man ~~would~~ strike his horse; at least
~~Will strike~~
If from the wantonness in which we play                    thought
With things we love, or from a freak of ~~power~~
Or from involuntary act of hand
        s)
Or foot unruly with excel⟩s of life
It eer should chance that I ungently used
A tuft of              or snappd the stem
Of foxglove bending oer his native rill
I should be loth to pass along my road
With unreproved indifference I would stop
Self questined, asking wherefor that was done
For seeing little worthy or sublime
                pompous
In what we blazon with the names ~~of power~~
                                   ⎰ to
~~And action~~ I was early taught ⎱ the love
        Of power & action I was early taugh

---

Probably the last passage in the notebook to be started, after the "soul of man" lines had been entered on R^r. The passage, never used in *The Prelude*, was later merged into *Nutting*, described by DW in December 1798 as "the conclusion of a poem of which the beginning is not written."

to love

hold

Those unassuming things, that occupy

A Silent station in this beauteous world

each thing have

let all things be

Its little lot of life but more than all

Their lot of life

The things that live in [?peace]

Then dearest maiden on whose lap I rest

[?]

My head    do not deem that these

Are idle sympathies—

Continuation of "I would not strike a flower," which begins on Pᵛ, facing. The last three lines, in a different ink, open in the same way ("Then, dearest Maiden") as the last three lines of the version of *Nutting* which DW sent to Coleridge in December 1798.

our                    time
Those beauteous colours of my early years
Which make the starting-place of being fair
And worthy of the goal to which the tends
                                and
Those hours that cannot die these lovely forms
And sweet sensations which throw back our life
And make our infancy a visible scene
x On which the sun is shining
x Those recollect hours that have the charm
                            things—
                   onary    things
Of visi bl    [?thoughts]
islands in the unnavigable depth
Of our departed time—

---

These lines, which cannot stand alone grammatically, seem to be a conclusion of the passage that runs over from P<sup>v</sup> to Q<sup>r</sup>, perhaps replacing a fragmentary and aborted conclusion on Q<sup>r</sup>: Part One of the 1799 *Prelude* ends: "On which the sun is shining." The X appears to mark a substitution to be made at the fourth line, above; the last two lines WW never used.

The soul of man is fashioned X
just like a strain of musee    built up
                              I believe
That there are spirits which when
                    they would form
a favor'd being open out the clouds
As at the touch of lightning
Seeking him with gentle visitation
                    and with
Though rarely to my wanderings
Communion others too there    held
                              are who
Yet haply aiming at the self-same    use
Severer intervention minister
Of grosser kind X of their school
and oft when on the withered    to as
                              mountain
The frost X breath  ↑ 311    slope

                    Theni held

Communion with heaven in his boyhood
Thought rarely

                    Prelude J. 351-37
                              (1806)

R

*The soul of man is fashioned &*
                              *built up*
*Just like a strain of music*
*I believe*              *I believe*
*That there are spirits which when*
                   *they would form*
*A favor'd being open out the clouds*
*As at the touch of lightning*
*Seeking him with gentle visitation*
                     *and with such*
*I Though rarely in my wanderings I have*
                              *held*
*Communion Others too there are who*
                              *use*
*Yet haply aiming at the self-same end*
*Severer interventions ministry*
*Of grosser kind & of their school*
                          *was I*
*And oft when on the withered mountain*
                              *slope*
*The frost & breath*
                    I have held
Communion with ~~them~~ in my boyish days
Though rarely

---

This passage was evidently written to follow the boat-stealing scene and lead into the trap-robbing scene, but WW never arranged the pieces in that order. All but the last three lines are in the hand of DW. Taking dictation, she mistakenly ended a line after "lightning," making it too short and the next line too long. Following "ministry" the word "and" appears to be erased.

When from behind that rocky steep, till then
The bound of the horizon a huge cliff
As if with voluntary power instinct
Upreard its head I struck & struck again
And growing still in stature the huge cliff
Rose up between me and the stars & still
With measured motion like a living thing
Strode after me. With trembling hand I turn'd
And to the willow tree, the mooring place
of my small boat, pursud a

                    it was & was not houses
                    Unusual was the hower
Heavd
that strange sight for many days my brain
Workd with a dim & undetermind sense
of unknown modes of being in my thoughts
                              vacancy
There was a darkness call it solitude
or blank desertion no familiar shapes
of hourly objects images of trees
of sea or sky no colours of green fields
but huge & mighty forms that do not
                                    live
like living men movd slowly through my
by day, and were —— the trouble of my
                                    mind
and I to —— the one through their house
Twas of familiar or the grave & —
                                    precious one

When from behind that rocky steep, till then

⌠o
The b⌡und of the horizon a huge cliff

As if with voluntary power instinct

Uprear'd its head I struck & struck again

And growing still in stature the huge cliff

Rose up between me and the stars & still

With measured motion like a living

              thing

Strode after me. With trembling hands I

    And through the silent water stole my way

                       turnd

Back to the willow tree, the mooring place

            pinnace

Of my small ~~bark~~


                       ⌠unusual
          A most ⌡usual power

  Had           Unusual was the power

Of that strange sight for many day my brain

Workd with a dim & undetermin'd sense

Of unknown modes of being in my thought

                vacancy

There was a darkness call it solitude

   ⌠blank

Or ⌡strange desertion no familiar shapes

Of hourly objects images of trees

Of sea or sky no colours of green fields

But huge & mighty forms that do not

              d ⌉       live

Like living men move[?]⌡ slowly through my

                        mind

By day, and were the trouble of my

                dreams—

    And straightway through [?home] I [?went]

    Though fearless with a grave & [?]

          serious [?]

---

Extension and development of the boat-stealing scene on S<sup>v</sup> and T<sup>r</sup>. The last two lines were probably meant for insertion after "Of my small bark," above.

There was a boy ye knew him well, ye cliffs
And islands of Winander & ye green
peninsulas of Esthwaite many a time
                              When the stars began

to move along the edges of the hills
rising or setting would he stand alone
Beneath the trees, or by the glimmering
And through his fingers woven in both
                                    dire nois
Blow mimic hootings to the       silent owls
And bid them answer him. And they
                                      would shout
Across the watery vale & shout again
Responsive to my call with tremulous
hollow hallows & screams & echoes loud
redoubled & redoubled & wild scream
of mirth & jocund din. And when it heard
that [...] of deep silence mock'd my
[...] oftimes in that silence while they
                                    hung
listening [...] thick of [...]
would enter [...] far into my heart the
of mountain torrents; or the visible
would enter unawares into my
with all its solemn imagery & rocks
[...] received into the [...]
into the bosom of the [...] lake

                              S         S

There was a boy ye knew him well, ye rocks
And islands of Winander & ye green
Peninsulas of Esthwaite many a time
                    When the stars began
To move along the edges of the hills
Rising or setting would he stand alone
Beneath the trees or by the glimmering
                              lakes
And through his fingers woven in one
                 ⎧ings        close knot
Blow mimic hoot⎨[ ? ] to the silent owls
And bid them answer him. And they
                         would shout
Across the watry vale & shout again
Responsive to my call with tremulous
                              sobs
                  ⎧screams
And long halloos & ⎨[?] & echoes loud
Redoubld & redoubld a wild scene
Of mirth & jocund din. And when it chanced
That pauses of deep silence mockd my
     sometimes              skill
Then, often, in that silence while I hung
           gentle
Listening a sudden shock of mild
                         surprize
Would carry far into my heart the
                    voice
Of mountain torrents: or the visible
                         scene
Would enter unawares into my mind
With all its solemn imagery its rocks
Its woods & that uncertain heaven
                    receved
Into the bosom of the steady lake

---

The boy of Winander passage, not used in 1799 but taken into the 1805 *Prelude* at V, 364ff., was probably entered here after the second full unit of composition had been brought to a close on V$^r$. "Sometimes," above the line beginning "Then often," is in pencil, as is "gentle" above the line that follows.

I went alone into a shepherds boat
A skiff which to a willow tree was tied
With                     it usual home
The moon was up the lake was shining clear
Among the hoary mountains: from the shore
I pushd and struck the oars and struck again
In a cadence and my little boat moved on
Just like a man who walks with stately step
Though bent on speed & a rocky steep uprose
Above the cavern of the willow tree
And as I [struck] a man who proudly rowed
With his best speed I fixd a steady view
Upon the top of that same shaggy ridge
The bound of the horizon for behind
Was nothing but the stars & the grey sky
She was an elfin pinnace, lustily
I dippd my oars into the silent lake
And as I rose upon the stroke my boat
Went heaving through the water like a swan
                    It was an act of stealth
And troubled pleasure after that the huge
Mountain columns that my boat moved
Leaving behind still on either side
In all a silver glittering idly in the
Untill they melted all into one
                    to act

One evening [?I ?ran ?alone] [   ?   ]
I went alone into a shepherd's boat
A skiff which to a willow tree was tied
With            it usual home
The moon was up the lake was shining clear
Among the hoary mountains: from the shore
I push'd and struck the oars and struck again
In cadence and my little boat moved on
Just like a man who walks with stately step
Though bent on speed: A rocky steep uprose
Above the cavern of the willow-tree
     so as fitted
And as beseemd a man who proudly rowed
With his best speed I fixd a steady view
Upon the top of that same shaggy ridge
The bound of the horizon for behind
Was nothing but the stars & the gray sky

She was an elfin pinnace, twenty {[ ?]imes
I dipp'd my oars into the silent lake
And I rose upon a the stroke my boat
Went heaving through the water like a
               swan

---

          It was an act of stealth
And troubled pleasure not without the
               voice
Of mountain echoes did my boat move
               on
Leaving behind still on either side
Small circles glittering idly in the
               moon
Untill they melted all into one
               track

---

Beginning of the boat-stealing scene, probably written after the boy of Winander passage on S<sup>r</sup> (see the Introduction, pp. 4–5). The opening lines of this scene echo scraps of verse WW had composed 10 years earlier, found in DC MS. 5: see Carol Landon, "Some Sidelights on *The Prelude*," *Bicentenary Wordsworth Studies in Memory of John Alban Finch* (Ithaca, N.Y., 1970). The revision above the first line is in pencil. The line drawn across the page apparently marks the passage that follows for insertion earlier, on T<sup>r</sup>, as in the final text of 1798–1799, I, 90–96.

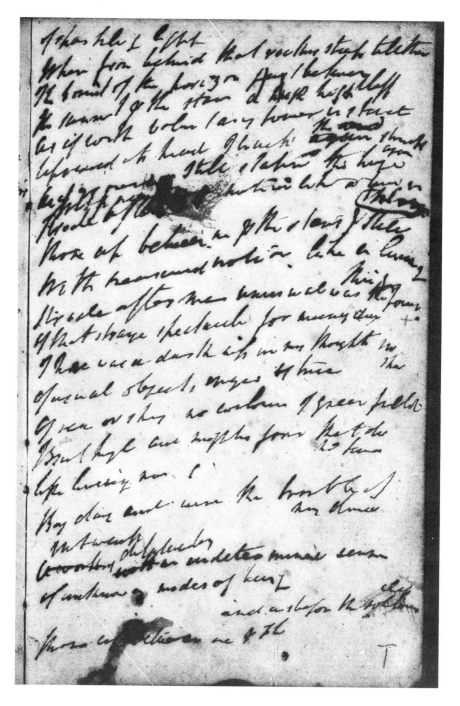

Of sparkling light
When from behind that rocky steep till then
The bound of the horizon just between

                                e}
The summit & the stars a hugh} high cliff
As if with voluntary power instinct
                              ⌠and
                        the ⌡oars
Upreared its head I truck ~~again~~    struck
                                       again
And growing still stature the huge
   With measured motion like a living
                            ⌠thing___
Stride after [?me]
Rose up between me & the stars & still
With measured motion like a living
                                thing
Strode after me unusual was the power
Of that strange spectaccle for many day
There was a darkness in my thoughts no
                                      show
Of usual objects images of trees
Of sea or sky no colours of green fields
But huge and mighty forms that do
                            not live
Like living men [?&]
By day and were the trouble of
                        my dream
      But work
         [?dilated]   by
~~A working with an~~ undetermined sense
Of unknown modes of being
                              cliff
                  and as before the solitary
   Rose up between me & the

The boat-stealing scene follows from Sᵛ; these drafts break down and are more fully developed
on Rᵛ.

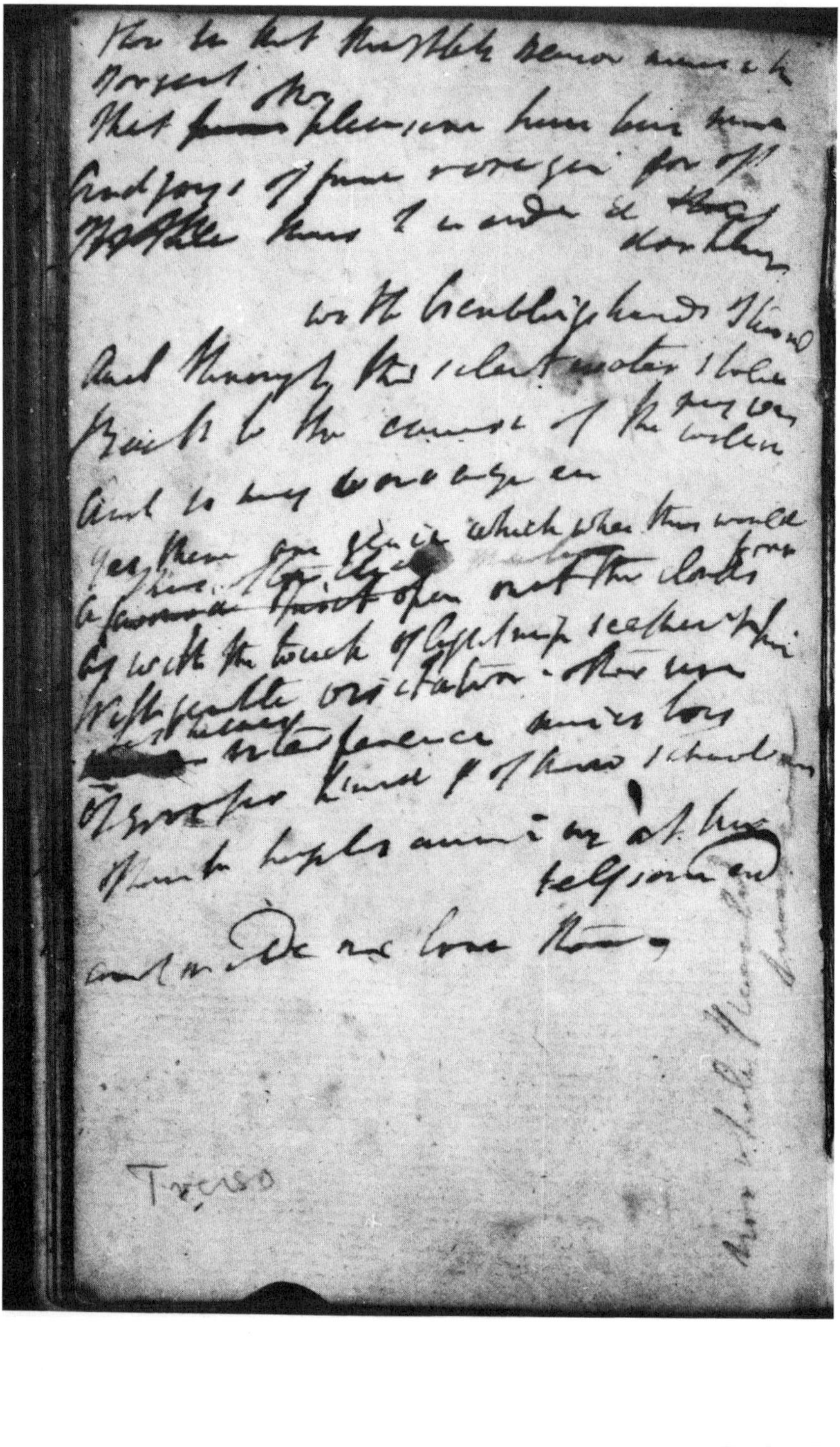

Nor in that thoughtless season [ ? ? ?]
   Forget    other
That ~~purer~~ pleasure have been mine
And joys of purer origin for oft
⎧ While
⎨ For while thus I wander'd ~~thus~~
⎩
                doubting


          with trembling hands I turnd
And through the silent water stole
               my way
Back to the cavern of the willow
And to my [?home] again


Yes there are genii which when they would
  Thus often did make          form
A ~~favour'd spirit~~ open out the clouds
As with the touch of lightning seeking him
With gentle visitation—other use
  Less [?hidden]
[—?—] interference ministry
Of grosser kind & of their school was
Though haply aiming at the
              selfsame end
And made me love them,

*(written vertically, right margin:)* Nor while I would   [?preserve]

---

Four separate pieces of draft. The four lines at the top of the page are connected with similar drafts on Uʳ and Uᵛ. They seem intended to help bridge the gap between the two sections of composition that end on Xʳ and begin on Uʳ, respectively; they appear finally as lines 379–381 of Part One, 1798–1799. The next two sections of draft, here, are connected with the boat-stealing scene and with the "soul of man" lines on Rʳ. The single line written vertically, in pencil, looks like a variant of the top vertical line on Uʳ, facing.

                    [?wandered]   [ ? ]        heat
How while I ran whereer the working heat
Of Passion drove me at that thoughtless time
        unknown
A͜power ~~unknown~~ would open out the clouds
As with the touch of lightning seeking me
With gentle visitation the n unknown

Nor while, thou doubting yet not lost, I tread
The mazes of this argument, and paint
How Nature by collateral interest
        extrinsic
        extrinsic
And by [ ? ] } passion peopled first
My mind with beauteous objects may I well
Forget what might demand a loftier song
{For
{How oft the eternal spirit, he that has
His life in unimaginable things
And he who painting what he is in all
The visible imagery of all the worlds
Is yet apparent chiefly as the soul
Of our first sympathies —— Oh bounteous power
In childhood, in rememberable days
How often did thy love renew for me
Those naked feelings which when thou wouldst
        (form
A living thing thou sendest like a breeze
Into its infant being. Soul of things

    The vertical lines appear to begin a fresh section of composition which runs through Vʳ, following the summary line count on Xʳ which ended the first main section. Draftings across the top of the page are connected with drafts on Tᵛ.

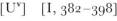

for often-times      [?]
In that tempestuous season I have fellt
Even in that                    & tempestuous time

I felt that age

How often did thy love renew 'd  for me
Those hallowed & pure motions of the sense
Which seem in their simplicity to own
An intellectual charm: that calm delight

Which if I eer ʳ not surely must belong
To those first born affinities which fit
Our new existence to existing things
And in our dawn of being constitute
The bond of union betwixt life & joy.
Yes, I remember when the changeful // earth
And twice five seasons on my mind had
                              (stampd
moving
The faces of the changeful year, even then,
A child I held unconscious intercourse
With the eternal beauty drinking in
A pure organic pleasure from the lines
Of curling mist or from the smooth expanse
Of waters coloured by the cloudless moon
                              clouds of heaven

Continued from Uʳ; the lines across the top of the page likewise appear to be extended from drafts at the top of Uʳ. The double slash below "joy," entered before the following line was written, may indicate a pause in composition or transcription.

The sands of Westm{o oorland the creeks &
                    {bays
Of Cumbria's rocky limits they can tell

How when the sea threw off his e[?]}ening shade
And to the shepherds hut beneath the craggs
Did send sweet notice of the rising moon
How I have stood to images like this
A stranger liking with the spectacle
No body of associated forms
And bearing with no peculiar sense
Of quietness or peace yet I have stood
Even while my eye has moved oer three long lea
                                        leagues
Of shining water, gathering as it seemd

New pleasure like a bee among the flowers—
Nor unsubservient even to noblest ends
Are these primordial feeling how serene
How calm those seem amid the swell
Of human passion even yet I feel
Their tranquillizing power

---

Continued from U$^v$. Dots after "No body of associated forms" may represent a dash or an omission. Deletion of part of "linking," miswritten "liking," in the line above, appears to be unintentional. The blank line, lower, is filled in MSS. U and V by "Through the wide surface of that field of light."

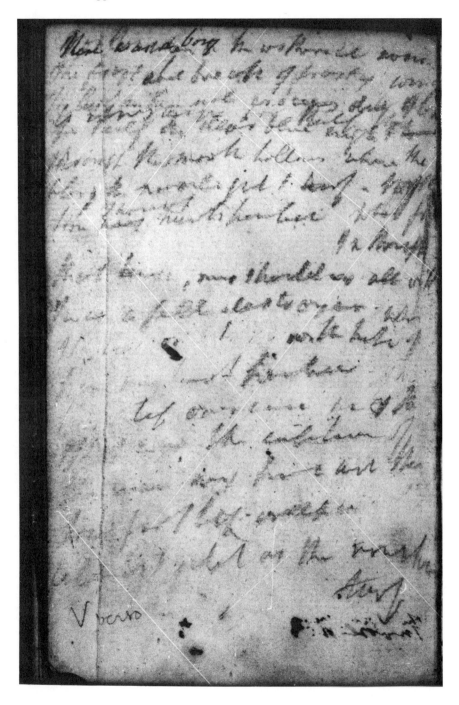

⎰There was a boy
⎱For this when on the withered moun          tain slope
The frost and breath of frosty wind          s had nipped
The last autumnal crocus did I lov           e
                                                      [ ? ]
    [?to ?range ?for]    half the      [?night] [? ? ] cliff
For half the clear blue night to      range alone
Through the smooth hollows where the  woodcocks ran
Along the moonlight turf. [?With]     hopes & fears
          [?Though]
[?How ?my ?heart ?panted] What [?        ?] I [?ran]
                        In though     t and wish
That time, my shoulder all with       springes hung
I was a fell destroyer When           from [ ? ]
I [ ?   ? ] with hope &               fear
[?How ?my ?heart ?panted ?]           strong desire
Resistless overcame me & the          bird
That was the captive of               anothers toil
[?Became ?my ?prey] and then                      ye [?that]
[?Low ?footsteps ?creepin]
Almost silent as the [?mountain]
                turf

---

"There was a boy," an aborted start on the passage copied onto S<sup>r</sup>, is in ink. The other lines, all in pencil, run over onto W<sup>r</sup> as shown; they are draftings toward the passage on W<sup>v</sup> and X<sup>r</sup>.

The mountains & the [...] hills

[...] of earth

Ah not in vain ye spirits of the [...]
And ye that have your voices in the
                                    clouds
And ye that are familiars of the
And standing pools, ah not for trivial [...]
[...]
[...]
[...]
                    [...]

The mountains & the fluctuating
                    hills

Ye powers of earth
Ah not in vain ye spirits of the springs
And ye that have your voices in the
                              clouds
And ye that are familiars of the
                        Lakes
And standing pools, ah not for trivi
                    al ends
Through snow & sunshine & through rain
       the sparkling plains      ~~and storm~~
   Of moonlight frost and through the
                          stormy [?day]
Did ye with such assiduous love
             pursue

---

Only the ink lines, most of them revision of drafts on Y$^r$, are transcribed here; for the pencil lines, which were apparently entered later, see V$^v$. The top line appears again inside the back cover. "The sparkling plains," toward the bottom of the page, seems intended to come in before "Of moonlight frost," but it is not clear how much WW meant to cancel.

Your favorite and your joy
            I may not think
A vulgar hope was your's when ye employd
Such ministry when ye through many
                              a year
Thus by the agency of boyish sports
    Upon the cave the trees
Impressd upon the stream the woods the
                                    hill
        On caves & trees upon on the [?caves]
Impressd upon all form the character
                ⌠or
Of danger ⌡& desire & thus did make
    The surface of the universal earth
With meanings of delight of hope & fear
Work like a sea. —

---

                              slope
For this when on the witherd mountain
The frost and breath of frosty wind had
        ⌠autumnal              nippd
The last ⌡[   ?   ] crocus did I love
    wander
To range through half the night among
                          the ⟨cliffs
And the smooth hollows where the
                      woodcocks ran
Along the moonlight turf. In thought
                      and wish
That time my shoulder all with
                    springes hung
I was a fell destroyer
                  Gentle power,
Who give us happiness & call
                    it peace

---

Continued from W$^r$ as development of drafts on Y$^r$ which had broken down. The horizontal rule seems to indicate that the episode which follows was to be inserted earlier, probably on Y$^v$.

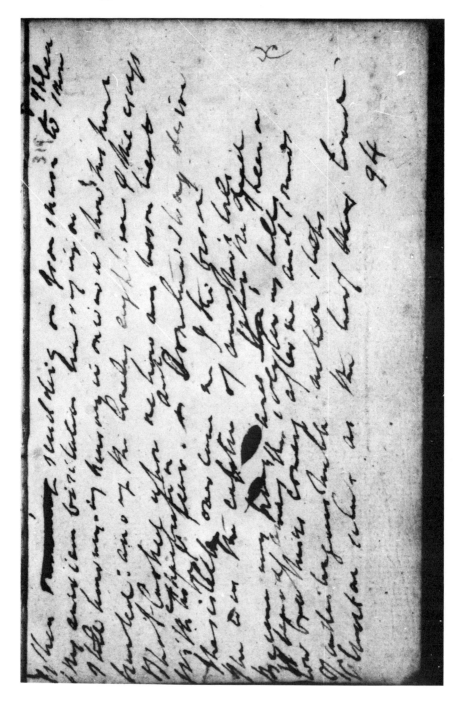

I plied
When ~~running~~ scudding on from snare to snare
My anxious visitation hurrying on
Still hurrying hurryin onward, how my heart
Panted: among the lonely eughtrees & the crags
That looked upon me how my bosom beat
    expectation    And {s
With hope & fear. + {Sometimes strong desire
  le} {s
Resistel{s} over came me & the bird
The was the captive of another's toils
          when the deed
Became my prey and ~~then~~ /     I heard
  I heard among the solitary hills
Low breathings coming after me and sounds
Of undistinguishable motion steps
Almost as silent as the turf they trod.
      94

---

Continued from W<sup>v</sup>. WW's summary line count, which began at "was it for this," Z<sup>r</sup>, is a rough one; there would appear to be 96 or 97 good lines up to this point. Diagonal marks in lines 6 and 9 seem to be intended as carets.

With what strange utterance did
Blow through my ears the

the colour of the sky

the sky was dark

the perilous ridge cliff

While on the perilous ridge I hung
With what strange utterance did the loud
dry wind
Blow through my ears the sky seemed not
of earth & with what motion moved
the clouds
the living beings of the hills
And ye that walk the woods among
By moon or starlight

solitude was did ye

that with the mean of

that with high objects with

With life & nature

the calendar of

{ W
{[?]ith what strange utterance did
                              wind
                  ~~the loud dry~~
Blow through my ears, ~~what colours~~
                        what motion did
        The co      the cloud
        the lou
        the colours of the sky
                          { not
Wh                The sky was { then
                          no sky
Of earth & whith what motion move the cloud,
As on the perilous brink cliff

---

            ridge  cliff              alone
While on the perilous ~~edge~~ I hung
With what strage utterance did the loud
                          dry wind
Blow through my ears the sky seemd not
                        a sky
Of earth, and with what motion moved
        in vain              the clouds
Ah not$_\wedge$ye beings of the hills
And ye that walk the woods and
{ B                      open heaths
{[?]y moon or starlight thus from
                        { wn
        my first da { y
Of childhood did ye love to interweave
The passions
Not with the mean & vullgar works of
                          man
But with high objects with eternal
                          things
With life & nature, purifying thus
The elements of feiling & of thought

---

Continued from Y$^v$; the horizontal line marks a fresh start.

And sanctifying by such discpline
Both pain & fear untill we recognize
A grandeur in the beatings of the heart
      for this
Ah! not ~~in vain~~ ye spirits of the springs
      have your voices in the clouds
And ye that are familiars of the
                 clouds
Through plasant da[?]
Through snow & sunshine & through
               rain & storm
Did ye with such assiduous love
         pursue
Your favourite & your joy did
           ye delight
Thus by the agency of boyish sports
To fix upon the streams the woods the
           hills
To fix upon all forms the character
Of danger & desire & so to [? mak]
   surface of the
The universal earth
With meanings of delight of hope
          and fear
~~Nor belike a~~    ye em
  A vullgar hope was yours when
Such ministry not vainly
       for ye [?knew]
    out[ ? ]

---

Continuation of fair copy from X<sup>v</sup>. Following the third line come draftings toward the passage on W<sup>r</sup>. Two lines from the bottom, "em" seems to be the start of "employed." The final word on the page may be a direction regarding the deletion.

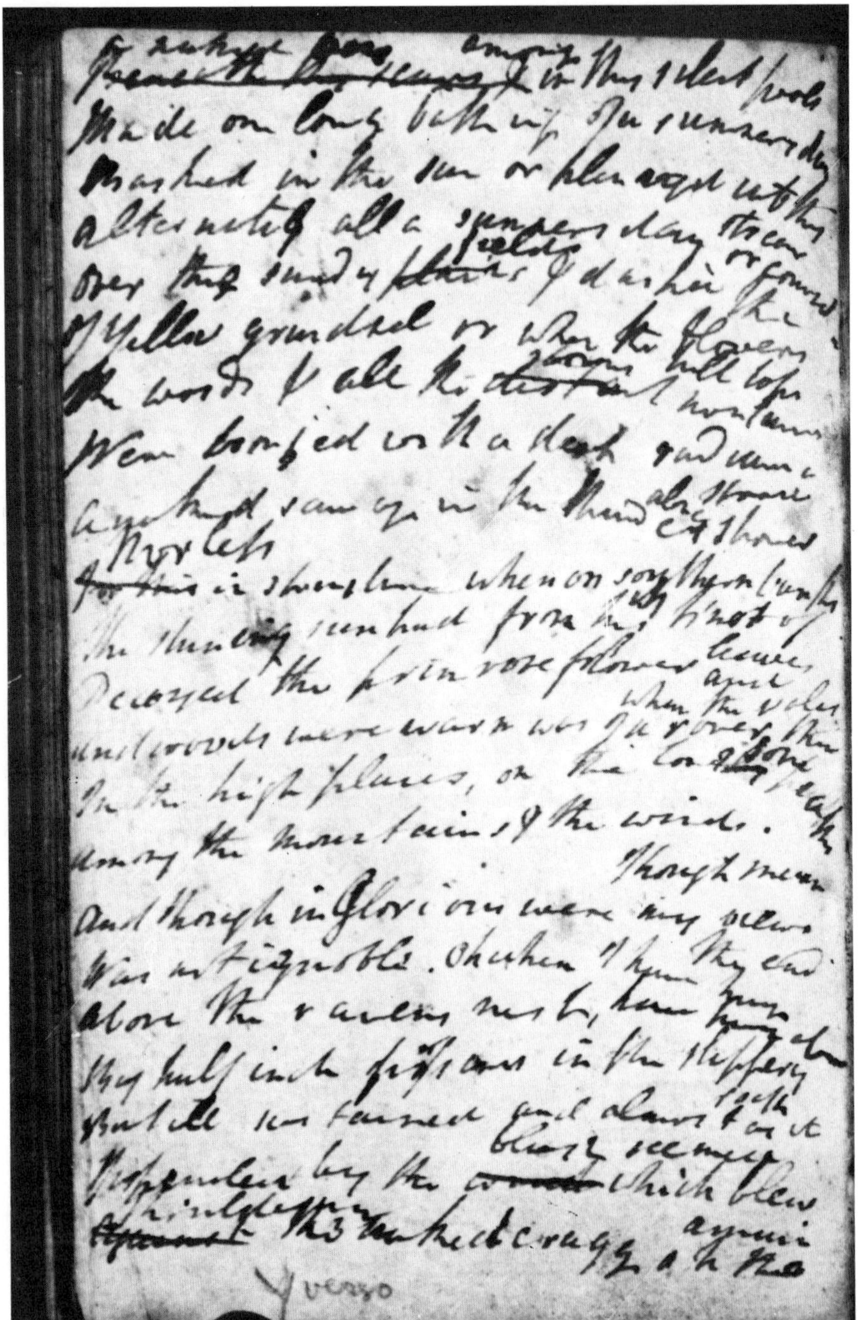

                    a naked boy    among
      ~~Beneath thy scars~~ & in thy silent pools
      Made one long bathing of a summers day
      Basked in the sun or plungd into thy
                  ly                     stream
      Alternate all a summers day, or coursd
               ⌠e              fields
      Over th⌡y sandy ~~plains~~ & dashd the
                                          flowers
      Of Yellow grundsel or when the hill tops
                     glorious
      The woods & all the ~~distant~~ mountains
      Were bronzed with a deep radiance
                                    stood
                           alone
      A naked savage in the thunder shower


            Nor less
      ~~For this~~ in springtime when on southern banks
                              its
      The shining sun had from his knot of
                                 leaves

                        ⌠l
      Decoyed the primrose f⌡rower and


      And woods were warm was I a rover then
                          ⌠esome ⌠eaks
      In the high places, on the lon⌡ely p⌡eak
                                    ~~ely~~
      Among the mountains & the winds.
                              Though mean
      And though inGlorious were my views
                                 the end
      Was not ignoble. Oh when I have hung
      Above the ravens nest, have hung alone
      By half inch fissures in the slippery
                                    rock
      But ill sustained and almost as it
                     blast seemed
      Suspended by the ~~wind~~ which blew
         Shouldering                  amain
      ~~Against~~ the naked cragg ah then

---

Continued from Z^r, facing. Revision of "For this" to "Nor less" (halfway down the page) was probably made when WW decided to insert the trap-robbing episode (on W^v) ahead of the raven's-nest episode, here. Fair copy continues on X^v, where it swiftly breaks down into draft.

[27]                    was it for this

That one, the fairest of all rivers,
                                              loved
To blend his murmurs with my nurse's
And from his alder shades and rocky    my
And from his fords and shallows, sent a
To intertwine my dreams?            a voice
                                             for this
If ... went travelling over ... sides, ... thou
                            didst        my green
... ... ... ... to the
... ... ... ... ... ...
...

...
... ... was was deep ...
                                                  whose
To ... than ...        my thought
Amid the fretful               or gazing ...
to knowledge, a dew ... of ...
... ... falling breathes away
          it for these ... ... word ...
Was for this / now / ... of things
... ... ... ... ...
influent fashioned fondly, to ...
the time of ... was able ...
Was it for this that I a four
                          year child

                        was it for this
            That one, the fairest of all rivers,
                                    loved
            To blend his murmurs with my nurse's song
            And from his alder shades and rocky falls
                                        t⎫
            And from his fords and shallows send⎰
                                    a voice
            To intertwine my dreams, for this
                                    didst thou
            O Derwent—travelling over the green plains
                            didst thou beateus str
            ~~Giving ceaseless music to the~~
            Near my sweet birth-~~place to the night~~
                                    and day
            ~~Give ceaseless music didst thou beauteous~~
                                    stream
            Give ceaseless music to the night & day
            Which with its steady cadence tempering
            Our human waywardness compose
                                    my thought
            To more than infant softness giving me
            Amid the fretful ~~tenements of man~~
                            dwellings of mankind
            A knowledge, a dim earnest of the
            ⎰Which                            calm
            ⎱That [?] Nature breathes among her
                                    woodland h
                        it for these perhaps
            Was for this & now I speak of things
            ~~That have been & that are no gentle dreams~~
            Complacent fashioned fondly to adorn
                        years
            The time of unrememberable being
            Was it for this that I a four
                                    years child

-----

The beginning of fair copy, which runs on to Y<sup>v</sup>. "Didst thou beateus str," in which WW allowed a single "t" to serve for the first two words, is evidently written where it is for want of space below, as the revised ending of the line beginning "Near my sweet birth-place." In the seventh line from the bottom, the comma, in ink, was reinforced in pencil; in the next line "h" was probably the start of "haunts."

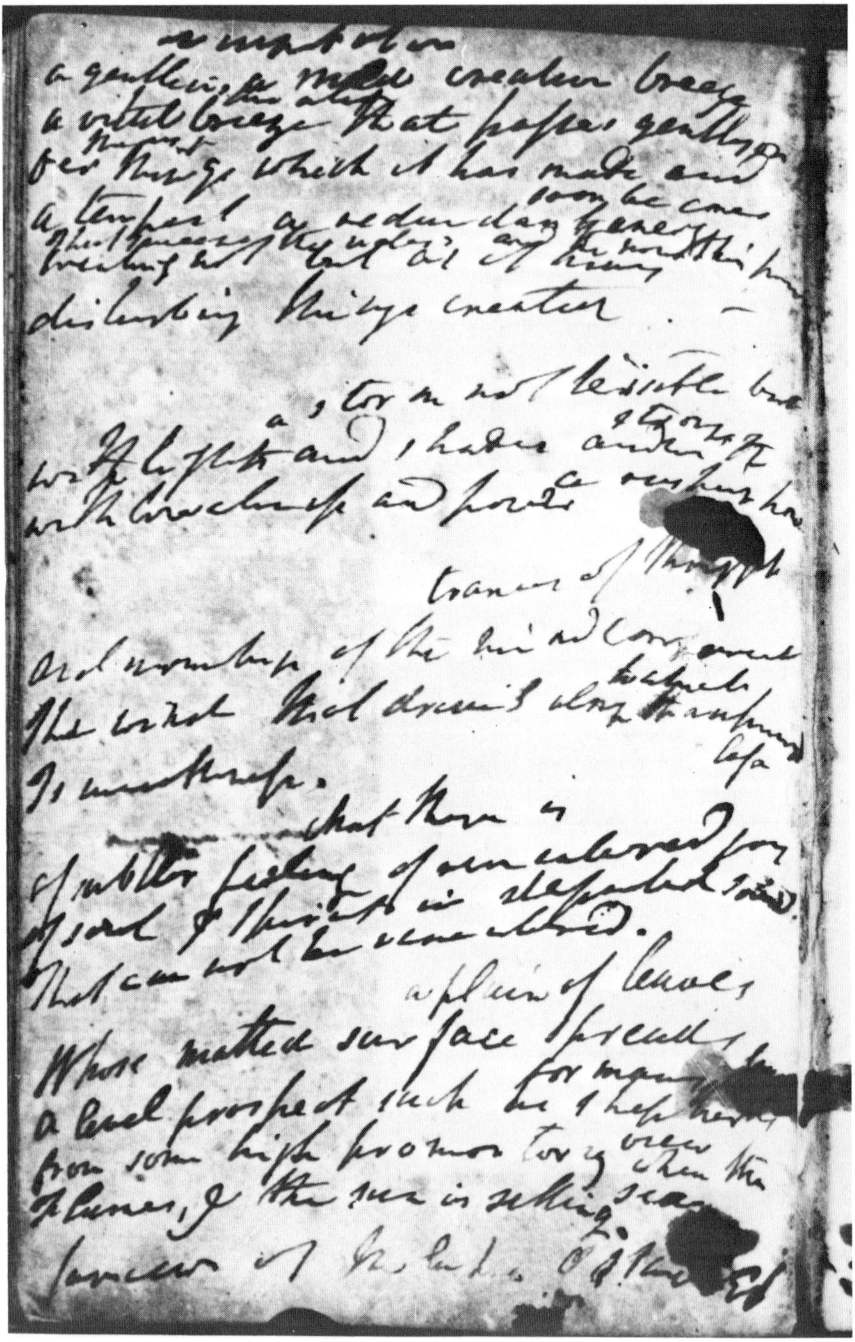

                    inspiration
            a mild creative breeze
        a gentle inspiration
a vital breeze that passes gently on
        the[?]
Oer things which it has made and
                        soon becomes
A tempest a redundant energy
        That sweeps the waters and the [?mountain] [?power]
Creating not but as it may
disturbing things created. —


            a storm not terrible but
                        strong
with lights and shades and with
                    a rushing power
with loveliness and power



                    trances of thought
And mountings of the mind compared
                        to which
The wind that drives along th autumnal
                            lefa
Is meekness.


                what there is
Of subtler feeling of remembered joy
Of soul & spirit in departed sound
That can not be remembered.


                a plain of leaves
Whose matted surface spreads
                    for many [?Leagues]
A level prospect such as shepherds
                    view
from some high promontory when the
                        sea
Flames, & the sun is setting.


familiars of the lakes & stand[?ing]

---

Drafts, presumably toward a preamble. "Inspiration," at the top of the page, was apparently copied above the line after having been crowded in below. The bottom line occurs again on W$^r$.

Almost as silent as the turf they
How often in the silence of the hills
       [?trod]
My eye has travelled on oer three long league
of shining lake an gather'd such [ ? ]
  the
from every [?furlong] of the [?smooth ?expanse]
New pleasure, [?as] a bee among the flowers

[?But] independent of [?collective] [ ? ]
[?Of ?which]

     [ ? ? ]

The mountains & the fluctuating hills

The lines in ink (the second and the last) must have been entered before the other lines, in pencil (most of them connected with work on V$^r$ and V$^v$–W$^r$, where the last line is repeated): the first pencil line had to be split around the first ink line. The isolated "the" above "from every" is also in ink.

## MS. JJ: Reading Text

The text that follows represents an effort to show in a readable form the earliest draft version of *The Prelude*. Manuscript JJ is unusually hard to follow, and the order of its scrambled parts cannot always be fixed. But the order here conjecturally established is a plausible one, and it can be argued for as the likeliest order, for the reasons set down in the Introduction, above; scraps of a preamble are followed by a reasonably coherent passage of verse, which is followed in turn by a series of separate pieces evidently written to be worked in later. The line numbering, in the right-hand margin, is based upon this conjectural order of composition, though it is clear that even as he wrote Wordsworth may have intended certain rearrangements. Spaces mark off sections of composition; short rules mark off sections whose placement is conjectural. In the left-hand margin are indicated the manuscript leaves from which each section of text is taken. Only the earliest readings are shown, except where they are fragmentary or rendered incoherent by readings that follow, or where they consist of drafts that break down and give way to fuller versions, or finally where whole lines important to the sense are inserted in the process of transcription or drafting. Spelling, capitals, and punctuation are unaltered, though a few omitted letters and illegible, incomplete, or missing words are conjecturally supplied in brackets; spaced brackets indicate gaps in the text.

            a mild creative breeze
a vital breeze that passes gently on
Oer things which it has made and soon becomes
A tempest a redundant energy
Creating not but as it may                        [5]
disturbing things created.—

                a storm not terrible but strong
with lights and shades and with a rushing power

                   trances of thought
And mountings of the mind compared to which      [10]
The wind that drives along th[']autumnal [?leaf]
Is meekness.

                 what there is
Of subtler feeling of remembered joy
Of soul & spirit in departed sound                [15]
That can not be remembered.

                 a plain of leaves
Whose matted surface spreads for many [?Leagues]
A level prospect such as shepherds view
from some high promontory when the sea        [20]
Flames, & the sun is setting.

                was it for this
That one, the fairest of all rivers, loved
To blend his murmurs with my nurse's song
And from his alder shades and rocky falls      [25]
And from his fords and shallows sent a voice
To intertwine my dreams, for this didst thou
O Derwent—travelling over the green plains
Near my sweet birth-place didst thou beauteous stream

Give ceaseless music to the night & day                    [30]
Which with its steady cadence tempering
Our human waywardness compose[d] my thought
To more than infant softness giving me
Amid the fretful tenements of man
A knowledge, a dim earnest of the calm                     [35]
That Nature breathes among her woodland h[?aunts]
Was it for this & now I speak of things
That have been & that are no gentle dreams
Complacent fashioned fondly to adorn
The time of unrememberable being                           [40]
Was it for this that I a four years child

[Yᵛ]    Beneath thy scars & in thy silent pools
Made one long bathing of a summers day
Basked in the sun or plungd into thy stream
Alternate all a summers day, or coursd                     [45]
Over thy sandy plains & dashd the flowers
Of Yellow grundsel or when the hill tops
The woods & all the distant mountains
Were bronzed with a deep radiance stood alone
A naked savage in the thunder shower                       [50]

For this in springtime when on southern banks
The shining sun had from his knot of leaves
Decoyed the primrose flower and when the vales
And woods were warm was I a rover then
In the high places, on the lonely peak                     [55]
Among the mountains & the winds. Though mean
And though inGlorious were my views the end
Was not ignoble. Oh when I have hung
Above the ravens nest, have hung alone
By half inch fissures in the slippery rock                 [60]
But ill sustained and almost as it seemed
Suspended by the wind which blew amain
Against the naked cragg ah then

[Xᵛ]    While on the perilous edge I hung alone
With what strange utterance did the loud dry wind          [65]
Blow through my ears the sky seemd not a sky
Of earth, and with what motion moved the clouds

36   The last word is supplied from MSS. U and V.

Ah not in vain ye beings of the hills
And ye that walk the woods and open heaths
By moon or starlight thus from my first day                [70]
Of childhood did ye love to interweave
The passions [                                    ]
Not with the mean & vullgar works of man
But with high objects with eternal things
With life & nature, purifying thus                         [75]
The elements of feiling & of thought

[Y<sup>r</sup>]    And sanctifying by such disc[i]pline
Both pain & fear untill we recognize
A grandeur in the beatings of the heart.


[W<sup>r</sup>]    Ah not in vain ye spirits of the springs         [80]
And ye that have your voices in the clouds
And ye that are familiars of the Lakes
And standing pools, ah not for trivial ends
Through snow & sunshine & the sparkling plains
Of moonlight frost and through the stormy [?day]           [85]
Did ye with such assiduous love pursue

[W<sup>v</sup>]    Your favorite and your joy
                              I may not think
A vulgar hope was your's when ye employd
Such ministry when ye through many a year
Thus by the agency of boyish sports                        [90]
Impressd upon the stream[s] the woods the hill[s]
Impressd upon all form[s] the character
Of danger & desire & thus did make
The surface of the universal earth
With meanings of delight of hope & fear                    [95]
Work like a sea.—


For this when on the witherd mountain slope
The frost and breath of frosty wind had nippd
The last autumnal crocus did I love
To range through half the night among the cliffs           [100]
And the smooth hollows where the woodcocks ran
Along the moonlight turf. In thought and wish

---

72   In MSS. U and V the line reads: "The passions that build up our human soul."
97–117   Possibly written for insertion after l. 50, as in MSS. U and V.

That time my shoulder all with springes hung
I was a fell destroyer
                Gentle power[s],
Who give us happiness & call it peace          [105]

[X^r]    When running on from snare to snare I plied
My anixious visitation hurrying on
Still hurrying hurryin[g] onward, how my heart
Panted: among the lonely eughtrees & the crags
That looked upon me how my bosom beat     [110]
With hope & fear.—Sometimes strong desire
Resistless over came me & the bird
Th[at] was the captive of another's toils
Became my prey, and then [      ] I heard
Low breathings coming after me and sounds   [115]
Of undistinguishable motion steps
Almost as silent as the turf they trod.

[U^r]    Nor while, thou[gh] doubting yet not lost, I tread
The mazes of this argument, and paint
How Nature by collateral interest        [120]
And by extrinsic passion peopled first
My mind with beauteous objects may I well
Forget what might demand a loftier song
How oft the eternal spirit, he that has
His life in unimaginable things         [125]
And he who painting what he is in all
The visible imagery of all the worlds
Is yet apparent chiefly as the soul
Of our first sympathies—Oh bounteous power
In childhood, in rememberable days      [130]
How often did thy love renew for me
Those naked feelings which when thou wouldst form
A living thing thou sendest like a breeze
Into its infant being. Soul of things

[U^v]    How often did thy love renew for me     [135]
Those hallowed & pure motions of the sense
Which seem in their simplicity to own

---

114–115   Revision in JJ leads toward the version of MSS. U and V:
    Became my prey, and when the deed was done
    I heard among the solitary hills
    Low breathings coming after me and sounds

An intellectual charm: that calm delight
Which if I err not surely must belong
To those first born affinities which fit                    [140]
Our new existence to existing things
And in our dawn of being constitute
The bond of union betwixt life & joy.

Yes, I remember when the changeful earth
And twice five seasons on my mind had stampd              [145]
The faces of the changeful year, even then,
A child I held unconscious intercourse
With the eternal beauty drinking in
A pure organic pleasure from the lines
Of curling mist or from the smooth expanse               [150]
Of waters coloured by the cloudless moon

[Vʳ]    The sands of Westmoorland the creeks & bays
Of Cumbria's rocky limits they can tell
How when the sea threw off his evening shade
And to the shepherds hut beneath the craggs              [155]
Did send sweet notice of the rising moon
How I have stood to images like this
A stranger li[n]king with the spectacle
No body of associated forms
And bearing with [me] no peculiar sense                  [160]
Of quietness or peace yet I have stood
Even while my eye has moved oer three long leagues
Of shining water, gathering as it seemd
[                              ]
New pleasure like a bee among the flowers—               [165]
Nor unsubservient even to noblest ends
Are these primordial feeling[s] how serene
How calm those seem amid the swell
Of human passion even yet I feel
Their tranquillizing power                                [170]

[Sʳ]    There was a boy ye knew him well, ye rocks
And islands of Winander & ye green
Peninsulas of Esthwaite many a time
[                         ] When the stars began

---

164    In MSS. U and V the missing line reads: "Through the wide surface of that field of light."
174    In MS. M, where this passage is taken into Book V of the 1805 *Prelude*, the line reads:
"At evening, when the stars had just begun."

To move along the edges of the hills                          [175]
Rising or setting would he stand alone
Beneath the trees or by the glimmering lakes
And through his fingers woven in one close knot
Blow mimic hootings to the silent owls
And bid them answer him. And they would shout      [180]
Across the watry vale & shout again
Responsive to my call with tremulous sobs
And long halloos & screams & echoes loud
Redoubld & redoubld a wild scene
Of mirth & jocund din. And when it chanced        [185]
That pauses of deep silence mockd my skill
Then, often, in that silence while I hung
Listening a sudden shock of mild surprize
Would carry far into my heart the voice
Of mountain torrents: or the visible scene        [190]
Would enter unawares into my mind
With all its solemn imagery its rocks
Its woods & that uncertain heaven rece[i]ved
Into the bosom of the steady lake

[S⁰]   I went alone into a shepherd's boat            [195]
A skiff which to a willow tree was tied
With [        ] it[s] usual home
The moon was up the lake was shining clear
Among the hoary mountains: from the shore
I push'd and struck the oars and struck again      [200]
In cadence and my little boat moved on
Just like a man who walks with stately step
Though bent on speed: A rocky steep uprose
Above the cavern of the willow-tree
And as beseemd a man who proudly rowed             [205]
With his best speed I fixd a steady view
Upon the top of that same shaggy ridge
The bound of the horizon for behind
Was nothing but the stars & the gray sky
She was an elfin pinnace, twenty times             [210]
I dipp'd my oars into the silent lake
And [as] I rose upon the stroke my boat
Went heaving through the water like a swan

197   In MSS. U and V the line reads: "Within a rocky cave, its usual home."

                        It was an act of stealth
            And troubled pleasure not without the voice          [215]
            Of mountain echoes did my boat move on
            Leaving behind [her] still on either side
            Small circles glittering idly in the moon
            Untill they melted all into one track

[Tʳ]        Of sparkling light                                   [220]


[Rᵛ]        When from behind that rocky steep, till then
            The bound of the horizon a huge cliff
            As if with voluntary power instinct
            Uprear'd its head I struck & struck again
            And growing still in stature the huge cliff          [225]
            Rose up between me and the stars & still
            With measured motion like a living thing
            Strode after me. With trembling hands I turnd
            And through the silent water stole my way
            Back to the willow tree, the mooring place           [230]
            Of my small bark
                        Unusual was the power
            Of that strange sight for many day[s] my brain
            Workd with a dim & undetermin'd sense
            Of unknown modes of being in my thought
            There was a darkness call it solitude                [235]
            Or strange desertion no familiar shapes
            Of hourly objects images of trees
            Of sea or sky no colours of green fields
            But huge & mighty forms that do not live
            Like living men moved slowly through my mind         [240]
            By day, and were the trouble of my dreams—


[Rʳ]        The soul of man is fashioned & built up
            Just like a strain of music I believe
            That there are spirits which when they would form
            A favor'd being open out the clouds                  [245]
            As at the touch of lightning seeking him
            With gentle visitation and with such


214–220  Probably meant for insertion at l. 203, above, as in MSS. U and V.
246–247  Taking dictation, DW broke the first line at the wrong place; her capitalization
has been corrected.

Though rarely in my wanderings I have held
Communion    Others too there are who use
Yet haply aiming at the self-same end                    [250]
Severer interventions ministry
Of grosser kind & of their school was I

---

[P<sup>v</sup>]    I would not strike a flower
As many a man would strike his horse; at least
If from the wantonness in which we play                   [255]
With things we love, or from a freak of power
Or from involuntary act of hand
Or foot unruly with excess of life
It eer should chance that I ungently used
A tuft of [        ] or snappd the stem                   [260]
Of foxglove bending oer his native rill
I should be loth to pass along my road
With unreproved indifference I would stop
Self questi[o]ned, asking wherefor that was done
For seeing little worthy or sublime                       [265]
In what we blazon with the names of power
And action I was early taught to love

[Q<sup>r</sup>]    Those unassuming things, that occupy
A Silent station in this beauteous world

---

[Q<sup>v</sup>]    Those beauteous colours of my early years            [270]
Which make the starting-place of being fair
And worthy of the goal to which [?she] tends
Those hours that cannot die those lovely forms
And sweet sensations which throw back our life
And make our infancy a visible scene                      [275]
On which the sun is shining

---

253   In JJ the line first ended "as many a man" but was immediately revised; in MS. 16, where the passage is developed, "I would not strike a flower" is set in as a second half-line, to begin a new paragraph.

260   In MS. 16 "meadow-lillies" is supplied, and "had" inserted before "snapp'd."

272   In the manuscript the line ends "the tends" but "the" is probably a miswriting.

## Letter to Coleridge, December 1798:
## Photographic Reproductions and Transcriptions

This letter is dated by Chester Shaver 14 or 21 December, 1798, and its text is printed in full, *EY*, pp. 235–243. Mark Reed (*Chronology: EY*, p. 260n) has shown that more probable dates are 21 or 28 December. The letter was written out by Dorothy in a rather complicated sequence on a large folded sheet of laid paper, originally measuring 67.8 by 42 centimeters, watermarked with a crown device and crossed palm fronds and countermarked GOSLAR. It is addressed "An der Herrn Coleridge/Ratzeburg" and postmarked "GOSLAR." The letter contains two Lucy poems and a passage from *Nutting* described by Dorothy as "the conclusion of a poem of which the beginning is not written" (her note is mislocated in *EY*, p. 240). At the top of the second page of the folded sheet ($2^r$) Dorothy began the skating scene, and at its close started the boat-stealing scene, which runs over to the back of the leaf ($2^v$). After transcription, Dorothy or William went over the text and added or altered some of the punctuation. It is not always possible to be certain, but punctuation in the following lines appears to have been added: in the skating scene, 152, 154, 159, and 160; in the boat-stealing scene, 88, 91, 104, 116 (the comma), 117 (the second comma), and 124.

Since the sheet, even when folded, is exceptionally large, the facing photographs are much reduced in size, and in the transcriptions of Dorothy's prose headnotes to the two *Prelude* passages line divisions are not preserved. Scraps of non-*Prelude* writing visible in the photographs are not transcribed; line numbers correspond to those of the final text of Part One. In lines 163–165 readings are obscured by a tear in the paper; portions of lines 171–173, where writing shows through a hole in the paper, remain attached to the seal, visible at the right-hand margin, and are printed in their proper place in the lines.

You speak in raptures of the pleasure of skaiting — it must be a delightful exercise, & in the North of England amongst y<sup>e</sup> mountains when we wish to decoy you, you might enjoy it with every possible advantage. A race with William upon his native lakes would read to the heart & the imagination something more dear & valuable than the gay sight of Ladies & countesses whirling along the Lake of Ratzeburg. I will transcribe some lines which are connected with this subject, & of course will be interesting to you now. It is a description of Williams's boyish pleasures.

And in the frosty season when the sun
Was set, and visible for many a mile
The cottage windows through the twilight blazed,
I heeded not the summons: clear and loud
The village clock tolled six, & wheeled about
Proud and exulting like an untired horse
That cares not for his home; All shod with steel
We hissed along the polished ice in games
Confederate, imitative of the chace
And woodland pleasures, the resounding horn,
The pack loud bellowing & the hunted hare.
So through the darkness and the cold we flew
And not a voice was idle: with the din
Meanwhile the precipices rang aloud;
The leafless trees and every icy crag
Tinkled like iron, while the distant hills
Into the tumult sent an alien sound
Of melancholy, not unnoticed while the stars
Eastward, were sparkling clear, & in the west
The orange sky of evening died away,
Not seldom from the uproar I retired
Into a silent bay, or sportively
Glanced sideways leaving the tumultuous throng,
To cut across the shadow of a star
That gleamed upon the ice: and oftentimes
When we had given our bodies to the wind
And all the shadowy banks on either side
Came sweeping through the darkness, spinning still
The rapid line of motion, then at once
Have I, reclining back upon my heels,
Stopped short; yet still the solitary cliffs
Wheeled by me, even as if the earth had rolled
With visible motion her diurnal round;
Behind me did they stretch in solemn train
Feebler & feebler, & I stood & watched
Till all was tranquil as a summer sea &c

I will give you a Lake scene of another kind. I send it to you from the map of what William has written, because it may be easily detached from the rest, & because you can now in a likes daily before your eyes. —
one evening

I went alone into a shepherd's boat,
A skiff, which to a willow-tree was tied
Within a rocky cave, its usual home,
The moon was up, the lake was shining clear
Among the hoary mountains: from the shore
I pushed, and struck the oars, & struck again
In cadence, & my little boat moved on
Just like a man who walks, with stately step
Though bent on speed. It was an act of stealth

We intend to lay out
a little money in
books on our journey
but at would you advise
us to buy?

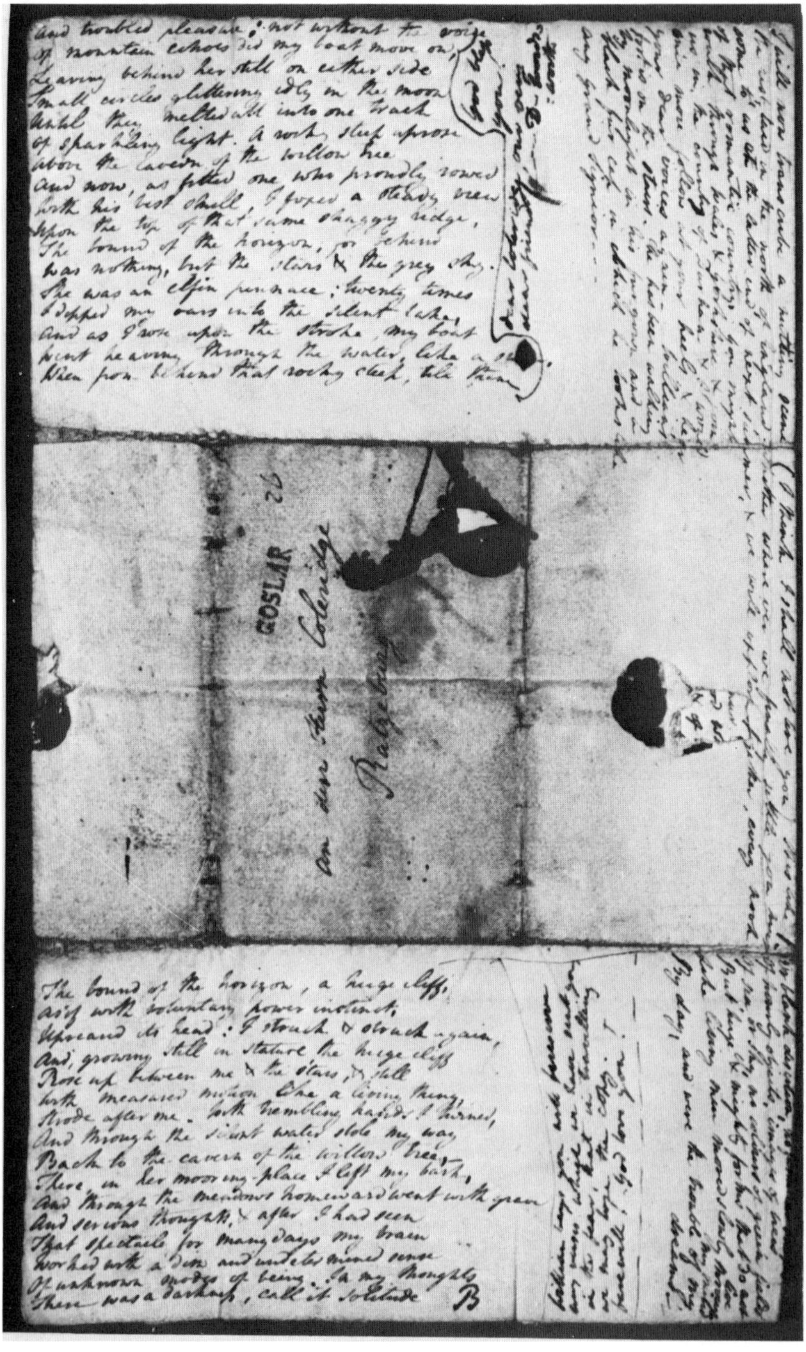

And troubled pleasure; not without the voice
Of mountain echoes did my boat move on,
Leaving behind her still on either side
Small circles glittering idly in the moon
Until they melted all into one track
Of sparkling light. A rocky steep uprose
Above the cavern of the willow tree
And now, as fitted one who proudly rowed
With his best skill, I fixed a steady view
Upon the top of that same shaggy ridge,
The bound of the horizon, for behind
Was nothing but the stars & the grey sky.
She was an elfin pinnace; twenty times
I dipped my oars into the silent lake,
And as I rose upon the stroke, my boat
Went heaving through the water, like a sw[an]
When from behind that rocky steep, till then

GOSLAR 26

Coleridge

Ratzeburg

The bound of the horizon, a huge cliff,
As if with voluntary power instinct,
Upreared its head: I struck & struck again,
And, growing still in stature the huge cliff
Rose up between me & the stars, & still
With measured motion, like a living thing,
Strode after me. With trembling hands I turned,
And through the silent water stole my way
Back to the cavern of the willow tree.
There, in her mooring-place I left my bark,
And through the meadows homeward went with grave
And serious thoughts, & after I had seen
That spectacle for many days my brain
Worked with a dim and undetermined sense
Of unknown modes of being. In my thoughts
There was a darkness, call it solitude
B

[Skating Scene]


*You speak in raptures of the pleasure of skaiting—it must be a delightful exercise, & in*
*the North of England amongst the mountains whither we wish to decoy you, you might*
*enjoy it with every possible advantage. A race with William upon his native lakes would*
*leave* ⎱
[ _?_ ] ⎰ *to the heart & the imagination something more Dear and valuable, than the gay*
*sight of Ladies & countesses whirling along the lake of Ratzeberg. I will transcribe*
*some lines which are connected with this subject, & of course will be interesting to you*
                    *from*
*now. It is*ᴧ*a description of Williams boyish pleasures*


| 150 | *And in the frosty season when the sun* |
|---|---|
| 151 | *Was set, and visible for many a mile* |
| 152 | *The cottage windows through the twilight blazed,* |
| 153 | *I heeded not the summons: clear and loud* |
| 154 | *The village clock tolled six. I wheeled about* |
| 155 | *Proud and exulting like an untired horse* |
| 156 | *That cares not for his home.*⎰ *All shod with steel* |
| 157 | *We hissed along the polished ice, in games* |
| 158 | *Confederate, imitative of the chace* |
| 159 | *And woodland pleasures, the resounding horn,* |
| 160 | *The pack loud bellowing & the hunted hare.* |
| 161 | *So through the darkness and the cold we flew* |
| 162 | *And not a voice was idle: with the din* |
| 163 | *Meanwhile the precipices e[            ]loud,* |
| 164 | *The leafless trees and every [            ]* |
| 165 | *Tinkled like iron—*⎰ *while [         ] trees* |
| 166 | *Into the tumult sent an alien sound* |
| 167 | *Of Melancholy, not unnoticed while the stars,* |
| 168 | *Eastward, were sparkling clear, & in the west* |
| 169 | *The orange sky of evening died away.* |
| 170 | *Not seldom from the uproar I retired* |
| 171 | *Into a silent bay, or sportively* |
| 172 | *Glanced sideways leaving the tumultuous throng* |
| 173 | *To cut across the shadow of a star* |
| 174 | *That gleamed upon the ice. And oftentimes* |
| 175 | *When we had given our bodies to the winds* |
| 176 | *And all the shadowy banks on either side* |
| 177 | *Came sweeping through the darkness, spinning still* |
| 178 | *The rapid line of motion, then at once* |
| 179 | *Have I, reclining back upon my heels,* |
| 180 | *Stopped short; yet still the solitary cliffs* |
| 181 | *Wheeled by me, even as if the earth had rolled* |
| 182 | ⎰*With*  *In visible motion her diurnal round;* |
| 183 | *Behind me did they stretch in solemn train* |
| 184 | *Feebler & feebler, & I stood & watched* |
| 185 | *Till all was tranquil as a summer sea &c—* |

## [Boat-Stealing Scene]

*I will give you ~~a nutting~~ a Lake scene of another kind. I select it from the mass of what*
*William has written, because it may be easily detached from the rest, & because you*
<br>              a⎱
*have now a⎰ lake daily before your eyes—*

| | |
|---|---|
| 81 | ———————— *one evening ~~led by them~~* |
| 82 | *I went alone into a shepherd's boat* |
| 83 | *A skiff, which to a willow-tree was tied* |
| | ⎰W |
| 84 | ⎱*within a rocky cave, its usual home,* |
| 85 | *The moon was up, the lake was shining clear* |
| 86 | *Among the hoary mountains : from the shore* |
| 87 | *I pushed,, and struck the oars, & struck again* |
| 88 | *In cadence, & my little boat moved on* |
| 89 | *Just like a man who walks with stately step* |
| 90 | *Though bent on speed. It was an act of stealth* |

91  { *A* *and troubled pleasure: not without the voice*
92  *Of mountain echoes did my boat move on,*
93  *Leaving behind her still on either side*
94  *Small circles glittering idly in the moon*
95  *Until they melted all into one track*
96  *Of sparkling light. A rocky steep uprose*
97  *Above the cavern of the willow tree*
98  *And now, as fitted one who proudly rowed*
99  *With his best skill, I fixed a steady view*
100 *Upon the top of that same shaggy ridge,*
101 *The bound of the horizon; for behind*
102 *Was nothing, but the stars & the grey sky.*
103 *She was an elfin pinnace: twenty times*
104 *I dipped my oars into the silent lake,*
105 *And as I rose upon the stroke, my boat*
106 *Went heaving through the water, like a swan.*
107 *When from behind that rocky steep, till then*

108 *The bound of the horizon, a huge cliff,*
109 *As if with voluntary power instinct,*
110 *Upreared its head: I struck & struck again,*
111 *And, growing still in stature, the huge cliff*
112 *Rose up between me & the stars, & still*
113 *With measured motion like a living thing,*
114 *Strode after me. With trembling hands I turned,*
115 *And through the silent water stole my way*
116 *Back to the cavern of the willow tree,—*
117 *There, in her mooring-place I left my bark,*
118 *And through the meadows homeward went with grave*
119 *And serious thoughts, & after I had seen*
120 *That spectacle for many days my brain*
121 *Worked with a dim and undetermined sense*
122 *Of unknown modes of being. In my thoughts*
123 *There was a darkness, call it solitude*

124 *Or blank desertion, no familiar shapes*
125 *Of hourly objects, images of trees,*
126 *Of sea, or sky, no colours of green fields*
127 *But huge & mighty forms that do not*
                                    *live*
128 *Like living men moved slowly through*
                                *my mind*
129 *By day, and were the trouble of my*

                    *dreams—*}

Dove Cottage MS. 15. Opening of the First Part:
Photographic Reproduction and Transcription

The manuscript, a pocket notebook known as the *"Christabel* Notebook,"
is described in the Introduction, p. 9, above, and its contents are listed and
analyzed in *Chronology: EY*, Appendix IX (pp. 322–325), and *Chronology:
MY*, Appendix II (pp. 615–616). It seems originally to have had 96 leaves,
gathered in eights, but leaves of a different size containing part of *Christabel*
have been inserted and a number of the original leaves torn out. There remain
114 leaves in the book, and pasted-down end papers. The original leaves
measure 19.6 by 12.3 centimeters, with chain lines at intervals of 2.7 centi-
meters; they are watermarked with a shield device and countermarked
[?]ARING. The inserted *Christabel* leaves are smaller, of wove paper cut to
about 19.2 by 12.2 centimeters.

The only surviving leaf of *Prelude* verse, followed by six stubs, is in Words-
worth's hand. Line numbers in the transcription correspond to those of the
final text of Part One. In line 23, the underlining in the manuscript is ap-
parently a signal of revision.

was it for this

That one the fairest of all rivers loved
To blend his murmurs with my nurse's song
And from his alder shades and rocky falls
And from his fords and shallows sent a voice
That flowed along my dreams. For this didst thou
To interwove my dreams
Oh Derwent travelling over the green plains
Near my sweet birth-place didst thou beauteous Stream
Make ceaseless music night and day.
Which with its steady cadence tempering
Oro human waywardness composed my thoughts
To more than infant softness giving me
Among the fretful dwellings of mankind
A knowledge a dim earnest of the calm
Which nature breathes among her woodland haunts

    Belovèd Derwent fairest of all streams
Was it for this that I a four years child
A naked boy among thy silent pools
Made one long bathing of a summers day
Baskd in the sun to plung'd into thy streams
Alternate all a summer day or coursed
Over the sandy fields and leapd the flowers
Of yellow groundsel or when crag & hill
The woods and all the distant mountain tops
Were bronz'd with a deep radiance stood alone
A naked savage in the thunder showers.

        And afterwards, twas in a later day
Though early when upon the mountain slope
The frost and breath of frosty wind had nipp'd
The last autumnal crocus twas my joy
To wander half the night among the cliffs

1                    was it for this
2    That one the fairest of all rivers loved
3    To blend his murmurs with my nurse's song
4    And from his alders shades and rocky falls
5    And from his fords and shallows sent a voice
          That flowed along my
6    To intertwine my‸dreams. For this didst thou
7    Oh Derwent travelling over the green plains
8    Near my sweet birth-place didst thou beauteous Stream
9    ~~Murmur perpetual music~~ night and day
10    Which with its steady cadence tempering
11    Our human waywardness composed my thoughts
12    To more than infant softness giving me
13    Among the fretful dwellings of mankind
14    A knowledge a dim earnest of the calm
15    Which Nature breathes among her woodland haunts
16          Beloved Derwent fairest of all streams
17    Was it for this that I a four year's child
18    A naked boy among thy silent pools
19    Made one long bathing of a summers day
20    Bask'd in the sun or plung'd into thy streams
21    Alternate all a summer's day or coursed
22    Over the sandy fields and dash'd the flowers
                 crag & hill
23    Of Yellow grundsel or when the hill-tops
24    The woods and all the distant mountain-tops
25    Were bronz'd with a deep radiance stood alone
26    A naked savage in the thunder shower.
27    *      And afterwards, twas in a later day
28     Though early when upon the mountain slope
29    The frost and breath of frosty wind had nipp'd
30    The last autumnal crocus twas my joy
31    To wander half the night among the cliffs

## Dove Cottage MS. 16

The manuscript, a pocket notebook earlier known as 18A, is described in the Introduction, p. 16, above, and in *Chronology: EY*, Appendix IX, pp. 325–328. The leaves measure 12.3 by 19.5 centimeters, with chain lines at intervals of 2.3 centimeters, and are watermarked with a fleur-de-lys. The first surviving leaf of *Prelude* verse, in Wordsworth's hand, preceded by four stubs, is reproduced in two photographs, cut so as to show only the *Prelude* work on the top half of recto and verso. The skating scene, with its trailing passages, is copied in Dorothy's hand on two leaves farther back in the notebook, among a series of disconnected blank-verse fragments which culminate in a version of *Nutting*. Line numbers in the transcriptions correspond to those of the final text of Part One.

At lines 231–233 DW has repeated a phrase and broken the line in the wrong place.

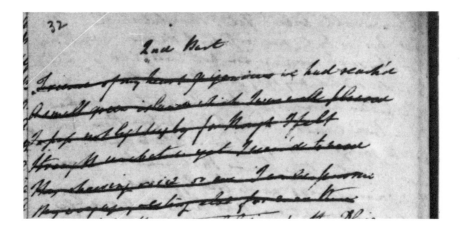

To honourable toil. Yet, should it be
That this is but an impotent desire
That I by such enquiry am not taught
To understand my self, nor how to know
With better knowledge, how the heart was framed
Of him thou lovest; need I dread from thee
Harsh judgements if I am so loth to quit
Those recollected hours that have the charm
Of visionary things and lovely forms
And sweet sensations that throw back our life
And make our infancy a visible scene
On which the sun is shining? ——

            Here we pause

Doubtful, or lingering with a transient trust
Of some rotationary characters
Merely adventurous studious more of peace
And soothing quiet which we here have found. —

[Close of the First Part: Transcription]

| | |
|---|---|
| 453 | To honourable toil. Yet, should it be |
| 454 | That this is but an impotent desire |
| 455 | That I by such enquiry am not taught |
| 456 | To understand myself, nor thou to know |
| 457 | With better knowledge, how the heart was framed |

eed⟩

| | | |
|---|---|---|
| 458 | Of him thou lovest n[?]⟨ I dread from thee | 240 |
| 459 | Harsh judgements if I am so loth to quit | |
| 460 | Those recollected hours that have the charm | |
| 461 | Of visionary things and lovely forms | |
| 462 | And sweet sensations that throw back our life | |
| 463 | And make our infancy a visible scene | |
| 464 | On which the sun is shining? — | 246 |

$$\begin{array}{r} 246 \\ 145 \\ \hline 391 \end{array}$$

    Here we pause
Doubtful; or lingering with a truant heart      400
  Slow & of stationary character
Rarely adventurous studious  more of  peace
And soothing quiet which we here have found.—

[Aborted Opening of the Second Part: Transcription]

     2nd Part

~~Friend of my heart & Genius~~ we had reach'd
~~A small green island which I was well pleased~~
~~To pass not lightly by for though I felt~~
~~Strength unabated yet I seem'd to need~~
~~Thy cheering voice or ere I could pursue~~
~~My voyage, resting else for ever there~~

[Skating Scene with Trailing Passages: Transcriptions]

*Fragment*

---

150  *And in the frosty season when the sun*
151  *Was set, & visible for many a mile*
152  *The cottage windows through the twilight*
                                      *blazed*
153  *I heeded not the summons: clear & loud*
154  *The village clock tolled six. I wheeled about*
155  *Proud & exulting like an untired horse*
156  *That cares not for his home. All shod with steel*
157  *We hissed along the polished ice, in games*
158  *Confederate, imitative of the chace*
159  *And woodland pleasures the resounding horn*
160  *The pack loud bellowing, & the hunted hare*
161  *So through the darkness & the cold we flew*
162  *And not a voice was idle: with the din*
163  *Meanwhile, the precipices rang aloud*
164  *The leafless trees & every icy crag*
165  *Tinkled like iron while the distant hills*
166  *Into the tumult sent an alien sound*

---

[80ᵛ]

167  *Of melancholy, not unnoticed while the stars*
168  *Eastward, were sparkling clear, & in the west*
169  *The orange sky of evening died away.*
170      *Not seldom from the uproar I retired*
171  *Into a silent bay or sportively*
172  *Glanced side-way leaving the tumultuous throng*
173  *To cut across the shadow of a star*
174  *That gleamed upon the ice: and oftentimes*
175  *When we had given our bodies to the wind*
176  *And all the shadowy banks on either side*
177  *Came sweeping through the darkness, spinning still*
178  *The rapid line of motion then at once*
179  *Have I, reclining back upon my heels*
180  *Stopp'd short, yet still the solitary cliffs*
181  *Wheeled by me, even as if the earth had roll'd*
182  *With visible motion her diurnal round*
183  *Behind me did they stretch in solemn train*
184  *Feebler, & feebler, & I stood & watched*
185  *Till all was tranquil as a summer sea*

---

*Redundance*

---

*Not the more*
*Failed I to lengthen out my watch. I stood*
*Within the area of the frozen vale*
*Mine eye subdued & quiet as the ear*
*Of one that listens for even yet the scene*
*Its fluctuating hues & surfaces*
*And the decaying vestiges of forms*
*Did to the dispossessing power of night*
*Impart a feeble visionary sense*

---

[81ʳ]

*Of movement & creation doubly felt*

229          *if the splitting ice*
230    *While it sunk down towards the water sent*
231    *Among the meadows & the hills its long*
232    *Its long and frequent yellings*
233    *Imitative some, of wolves that howl along the Both-*
                                          *-nic main*

# Texts Contributing
# to the Second Part

## The Alfoxden Notebook (two leaves):
## Photographic Reproductions and Transcriptions

The Alfoxden Notebook (DC MS. 14) is a small leather-bound notebook which originally contained 36 leaves in gatherings of six; all but 21 (4 of them blank) have been cut or torn out. The leaves measure 9.4 by 16 centimeters, with chain lines at intervals of 2.6 centimeters; no watermark is visible. The contents of the notebook are given in *Chronology: EY*, pp. 321–322.

On the third surviving leaf (originally the twelfth) and on the fifth (the fifteenth) are entered drafts in WW's hand later worked up into fair copy for *The Pedlar*, MS. D, lines 1–20; see the text in Jonathan Wordsworth's *The Music of Humanity* (London, 1969), p. 172. On 12$^v$ the second paragraph (lines 7–10, deleted) was probably drafted first, followed by the first paragraph (lines 1–6) and then lines 11–19. On 15$^v$ the first line was probably added when the deletion in line 3 was made. Line numbers which appear in the transcriptions that follow correspond to those of the final text of the 1798–1799 *Prelude*, Part Two.

~~There would he~~ wander ~~in the~~ storm and there
         Would feel
354     ~~He felt~~ whateer there is of power in sounds
355     To breathe an elevated mood—by form
         Or image unprofaned of sounds that
                                              are
358     The ghostly language of the antient earth
359     Or make their dim abode in distant
                                              winds


354     Not for whateer there is of power in sounds
359     That make their dim abode in distant
355     To breathe an elevated mood by form
         Or imaged unprofaned.
                              [?]
         Oh listen listen how ~~sounds~~ that wind
                                        away
         While the last touch they le[?vae] upon the sense
         Tells they [?have]
                                   the [?firs]
         ~~Hush they are coming—they have passd~~
         ~~And [?]~~          There would he stand
                     still
         ~~Beneath~~ In the ~~warm~~ covert of some [?lonesome]
                                              rock
            Or
         Would gaze upon the moon untill its
                                        light
         Fell like a strain of music on his soul
         And seem'd to sink into his very heart

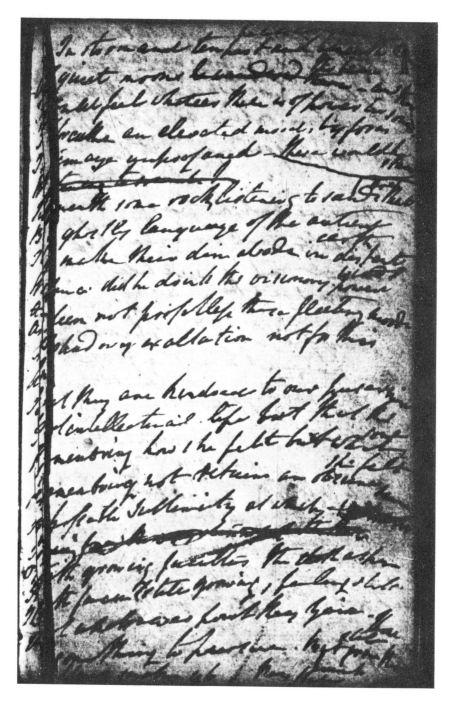

                              he wanderd there
352       In storm and tempest and beneath
                                      the beam
353       Of quiet moons ~~he wandered there~~—and there
354       Would feel whateer there is of power in sound,
355       To breathe an elevated mood, by form
356       Or image unprofaned—there would he
                                          stand

          ~~Listening to sounds [?]~~
                                      ⌐ are
357       Beneath some rock, listening to sounds that
358       The ghostly language of the antient
                                      earth
359       Or make their dim abode in distant
                                      winds
360       Thence did he drink the visionary power
361       I deem not profitless those fleeting moods
362       Of shadowy exaltation not for this

363       That they are kindred to our purer mind
364       And intellectual life but that the
                                      soul
365       Remembring how she felt but what
                                      she felt
366       Remembring not retains an obscure sense
367       Of possible sublimity at which her [—?—]
          ~~Een from the very dimness of the [?things]~~
                              ⌠s  ⌠doth
368       With growing faculties ⌡the ⌡[  ?  ] aspire
369       With facult still growing, feeling still
370       That whatsoever point they Gain, There
                                      still
371       Is something to pursue. But from these
                                      haunts
              Have something to    they still

*The Pedlar*, in Dove Cottage MS. 16:
Transcriptions of Lines 1–20 and Lines 204–222

The manuscript is described in the Introduction, above, p. 16, and in
*Chronology*: *EY*, pp. 325–328. The two excerpts from *The Pedlar* here tran-
scribed, the first of them developed from the Alfoxden Notebook fragments,
the second crossed out in pencil, are lines 1–20 and 204–222 of MS. D (see
Jonathan Wordsworth's text, *The Music of Humanity* [London, 1969], pp.
172ff.), in Dorothy's hand. Line numbers correspond to those of the final
text of Part Two of *The Prelude* of 1798–1799.

*Fragment*

352   *In storm and tempest and beneath the beam*
353   *Of quiet moons*                    *and there*
354   *Whate'er there is of power in sound*
355   *To breathe an elevated mood, by form*
356   *Or image unprofan'd there would he stand*
357   *Beneath some rock listening to sounds that are*
358   *The ghostly language of the ancient earth*
359   *Or make their dim abode in distant winds*
360   *Thence did he drink the visionary power*
361   *I deem not profitless these fleeting moods*
362   *Of shadowy exaltation, not for this*
363   *That they are kindred to our purer mind*
364   *And intellectual life but that the soul*
365   *Remembering how she felt, but what she felt*
366   *Remembering not, retains an obscure sense*
367   *Of possible sublimity at which*
368   *With growing faculties she doth aspire*
369   *With faculties still growing, feeling still*
370   *That whatsoever point they gain there still*
371   *Is something to pursue.*

[63ᵛ]

446   *From Nature, & her overflowing soul*
447   *He had received so much that all his thoughts*

[64ʳ]

448   *Were steeped in feeling. He was only then*
449   *Contented, when with bliss ineffable*
450   *He felt the sentiment of being, spread*
451   *O'er all that moves, & all that seemeth still*
452   *O'er all which lost beyond the reach of thought*
453   *And human knowledge to the human eye*
454   *Invisible, yet liveth to the heart*
455   *O'er all that leaps & runs, & shouts, & sings*
456   *Or beats the gladsome air, o'er all that glides*
457   *Beneath the wave, yea in the wave itself*
458   *And mighty depth of waters. Wonder not*
459   *If such his transports were for in all things*
460   *He saw one life & felt that it was joy*
461   *One song they sang and it was audible*
462   *Most audible then when the fleshly ear,*
463   *O'ercome by grosser prelude of that strain,*
464   *Forgot its functions, & slept undisturbed.*

Dove Cottage MS. 33 (four passages):
Photographic Reproductions and Transcriptions

This manuscript, which contains the second version of *Peter Bell*, is a small notebook bound in boards which seems to have been made up of 96 leaves in gatherings of 16; some of the leaves have been cut out and only 71 remain, several of them now loose. The leaves measure 9.7 by 15 centimeters; the paper is watermarked with an image of Britannia under the legend PRO PATRIA, with chain lines at intervals of 2.8 centimeters. Besides *Peter Bell*, the notebook contains Wordsworth's prose explication of *To Joanna* (*PW*, II, 487) and several passages of verse in Wordsworth's hand, some associated with *The Ruined Cottage*, *The Brothers*, the now lost "Somersetshire Tragedy," and other poems.

The first four of these verse passages, on what were leaves 49 and 50, touch upon the pains and the labor of composition, and the "false secondary power by which / In weakness we create distinctions," and the fourth passage was drawn upon for the Second Part of the 1798–1799 *Prelude* as it first stood in MS. RV. The RV passage (on 10$^v$ and 11$^r$) was dropped when the final version of 1799 was put together, but a marginal addition on RV 5$^v$, containing four of the lines from DC MS. 33, was preserved as lines 251–254 of Part Two of the 1798–1799 *Prelude*.

It is not clear how the four passages were meant to be connected. De Selincourt, when he published the first two of them, *Prel.*, lvi n, conjectured, persuasively, that between the passages the argument requires a thought such as "When I reviewed this random and desultory verse I saw its worthlessness, and came to realize that an artist reveals his true power only . . . ."

In the second passage, the last line appears to be a revision of the fourth line. Line numbers in the left-hand margin of the transcription of the fourth passage correspond to those of the final text of Part Two; in the right-hand margin are indicated the leaves of MS. RV which carry the lines.

nor had my voice

Been silent oftentimes had I burst forth
In verse which with a strong and random light
Touching an object in its prominent parts
Created a memorial which to me
Was all sufficient and to my own mind
Recalling the whole picture seemed to speak
An universal language: Scattering thus
In passion many a desultory sound
I deemed that I had adequately cloathed
Meanings at which I had but dimly hinted thoughts
And forms of which I scarcely had produced
A monument and arbitrary sign

To that considerate and laborious work
In that matures which not mingling nor reply'd
slow creation doth impart to speech
Outline & substance even till it has given
A function kindred to organic power
The vital spirit of a perfect form

                    nor had my voice
Been silent often times had I burst forth
In verse which with a strong and random light
Touching an object in its prominent parts
Created a memorial which to me
Was all sufficient and to my own mind
Recalling the whole picture seemed to speak
An universal language: Scattering thus
In passion many a desultory sound
I deemed that I had adequately cloathed
                            rd⎫
Meanings at which I hadl⎰ly hinted thoughts
And forms of which I scarcely had produced
A monument and arbitrary sign


      that considerate and laborious work
    In That patience which admitting no neglect
⎰By              ⎰doth
⎱That slow creation ⎱which imparts to speach
Outline & substance even till it has give
A function kindred to organic power
The vital spirit of a perfect form
                        resting not till
                                it has
                                givn

                              I knew not then
What fate was mine nor that the day would
When after loathings damps of discontent  come
Returning ever like the obstinate pains
Of an uneasy spirit with a force
Inexorable would from hour to hour
For ever seem now my exhausted mind

—Iseemed   to learn                         of
           that what we see of                  images
Which float along our minds & what we feel
Of active or recognizable thought
Prospectiveness or intellect or will
Not only is not worthy to be deemed
Our being, to be prized as that we are
But is the very littleness of life
Such consciousness I deem but accidents
Relapses from that one interior life
That lives in all things sacred from
Of that false secondary power by which
In weakness we create distinctions, this is
Beleive that our puny boundaries are
Which we perceive and not which we have made
—In which all beings live with god themselves
Are god existing in one mighty whole
As undistinguishable as the cloudless
at noon is from the cloudless west when
The hemisphere is one cerulean blue

                    I knew not then
        What fate was mine nor that the day would
                                        come
        When after loathings damps of discontent
        Returning ever like the obstinate pains
        Of an uneasy spirit, with a force
        Inexorable would from hour to hour
        For ever summon my exhausted mind


                        see [?note]
        I seemed to learn
            Individual              of          & forms
        That what we see of forms and images                    [RV 10<sup>v</sup>]
        Which float along our minds & what we feel
        Of active or recognizable thought
        Prospectiveness or intellect or will
        Not only is not worthy to be deemed
        Our being, to be prized as what we are
        But is the very littleness of life
        Such consciousness I deem but accidents
                        ⌠e
        Relapses from th⌡at one interior life
                        far beyond
        That lives in all things sacred from the
                                        touch
  251   Of that false secondary power by which                  [RV 5<sup>v</sup>]
  252   In weakness we create distinctions, then
                    all      ⌠   y
  253   Believe that our pun⌡[?ie] boundaries are things
  254   Which we perceive and not which we have
                                        made
        —In which all beings live with god themselves           [RV 10<sup>v</sup>]
        Are god existing in one mighty whole
        As undistinguishable as the cloudless east              [RV 11<sup>r</sup>]
        At noon is from the cloudless west when
                                        all
        The hemisphere is one cerulean blue

MS. RV: Photographic Reproductions and Transcriptions

Manuscript RV was made up by folding 18 sheets of heavy accountant's paper into a booklet of 36 leaves, then stitching the leaves at the fold (see Introduction, pp. 27–28). The sheets measured exactly $12\frac{1}{2}$ by 8 inches, and the leaves of the booklet therefore measure $6\frac{1}{4}$ by 4 inches. They are watermarked with varying designs: an emblem of Britannia within two double circles surmounted by a partial crown, and an emblem of a warrior similarly framed. The countermark is a crown above a diamond containing the letters OI.

The first 13 leaves of the booklet contain a reasonably fair copy—interspersed with some drafts and marginal insertions—of the Second Part of the 1798–1799 *Prelude* in the hands of WW, DW, and MH. The text originally began on the inside front cover—that is, on the verso of the first leaf—with the booklet turned sideways, so that the writing descends line by line from the outer margin down to the center fold then outward to the lower margin of the next leaf. Each successive pair of facing pages was filled in the same manner. For one long addition at the beginning of the text, WW turned back and used the cover of the booklet (the recto of the first leaf) so that the revised text now begins there at the inner margin. Line numbers running in twenties were entered irregularly, probably by WW, and two line-number summaries or calculations mark stopping places in copying or composition.

In the transcription which follows, line numbers of the final text of 1798–1799 are shown in the running head of each leaf, corresponding to the lines entered on the leaf. Marginal insertions which are fair copy are treated as extensions of the base text, not as revisions, hence are shown in larger type.

[ ¿ ] [?at; ?promises] who man a than Less
[ ¿ ] [?spectacle] the with I am Nor

Thus far my Friend have we retraced the way
Through which I travelled when I first began
To love the woods and fields: the passion yet
Was in its birth sustained as might befall
By nourishment that came unsought for still
From week to week from month to month we lived
A round of tumult: duly were our games
Prolonged in summer till the daylight failed
The village .        were empty fast asleep
The labourer and the aged man who sat
A later lingerer yet the revelry
Continued and the  .        uproar: at last
When all the ground was dark and the huge clouds
Were edged with twinkling stars to bed we went
With weary joints and with a beating mind.
Ah! is there one who ever has been young
And needs a monitory voice to tame
The pride of virtue and of intellect
And is there one the wisest and the best
Of all mankind who does not sometimes wish
For things which cannot be who would not give
If so he might to duty and to truth
The eagerness of infantine desire.
Even there where sorrow is not time brings on
Its own composing weight
A tranquillizing spirit presses now
On my corporeal frame so wide appears
The vacancy between me & those days
Which yet have such self presence in my heart
That some times when I think of them I seem
Two consciousnesses, conscious of myself
And of some other being. A grey stone
Of native rock left midway in the square
Of our small market village was the home

Revised opening, written after the first 292 lines had been copied; the first 5 lines are the original opening lines. Page number, title, and line numbers visible on the photograph were written on later by WW's twentieth-century editors, as were similar numbers throughout the manuscript. The two lines scrawled at the top of the page are in pencil.

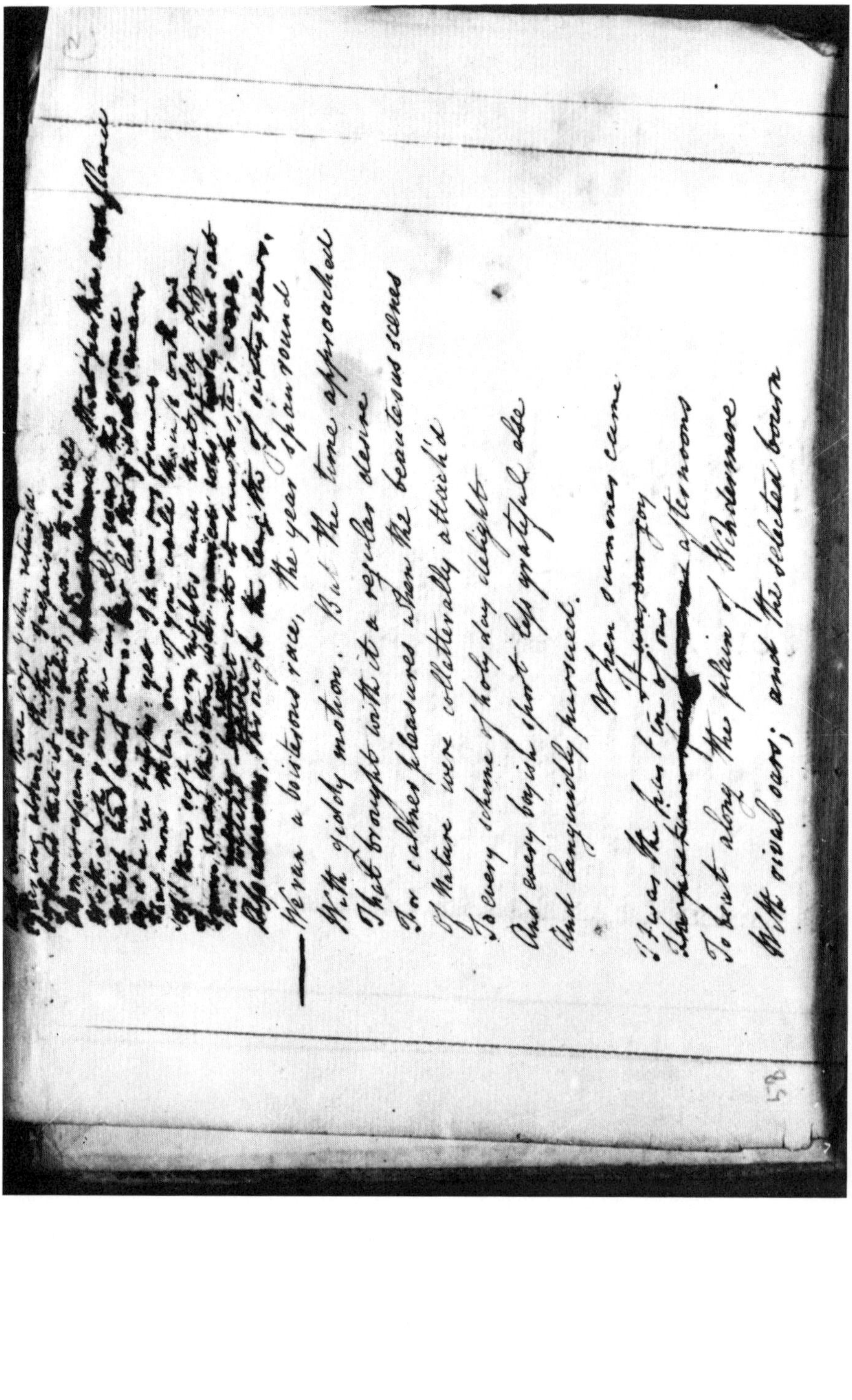
We ran a boisterous race, the year span round
With giddy motion. But the time approach'd
That brought with it a regular desire
For calmer pleasures when the beauteous scenes
Of Nature were collaterally attach'd
To every scheme of holyday delight
And every boyish sport less grateful else
And languidly pursued.
When summer came
To beat along the plain of Windermere
With rival oars; and the selected bourn

And centre of these joys & when return'd
After long absence thither I repaired
I found that it was split, & gone to build
       that perk'd and flared

A smart assembly room [?which] & flared
With wash & rough-cast elbowing the ground
Which had been ours. But let the fidde scream
And be ye happy : yet I know my friends
That more than one of you will think with me
Oft those soft starry nights and that old dame
From whom the stone was named who there had sat
   her
And held her basket with its huckster's ware,
  watched   table
Assiduous, through the length of sixty years.
— We ran a boisterous race, the year span round
With giddy motion. But the time approached
That brought with it a regular desire
For calmer pleasures when the beauteous scenes
Of Nature were collatterally attach'd
To every scheme of holy day delight
And every boyish sport less grateful else
And languidly pursued.
     When summer came
      It was our joy
   It was the pastime of our
The pastime of our summer afternoons
To beat along the plain of Windermere
With rival oars; and the selected bourn

---

Continuation of the revised opening; the original 5 lines have been erased and written over, and the dash in the margin marks the sixth original line. "Oft" in line 9 appears to be a miswriting of "Of."

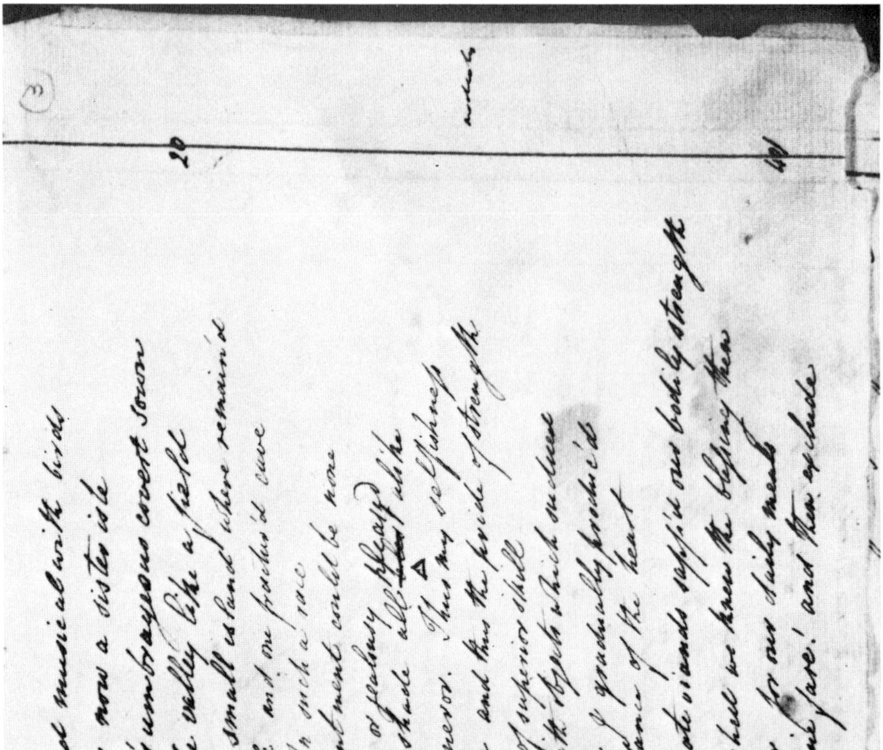

modesty

20

40/

Was now an island musical with birds
That sang for ever now a sister isle
Beneath the oak's umbrageous covert sown
With lillies of the valley like a field
And now a third small island where remain'd
An old stone table and one fractur'd cave
A hermits history. In such a race
So ended disappointment could be none
Uneasiness or pain or jealousy
                      pleased
We rested in the shade all blest alike
                        △
Conquer'd or conqueror. Thus my selfishness
Was mellow'd down and thus the pride of strength
And the vain-glory of superior skill
Were interfused with objects which sudued
And tempered them & gradually produc'd
A quiet independance of the heart
   No delicate viands sapp'd our bodily strength
More than we wished we knew the blessing then
Of vigourous hunger for our daily meals
Were frugal, Sabine fare! and then exclude

          *

The self-sufficing power of solitude.
And I was taught to feel perhaps too much
A modesty and diffidence ensued
Unapprehensive of reproof, that hence
x  And to my {friend who knows me I may add
              {F

WW's line numbers commence here, with 20 and 40; the marginal insertion here is the only
one in the manuscript included in these line counts; "modesty" in the margin is clearly related to,
possibly the origin of, the inserted lines, which are located by asterisks.

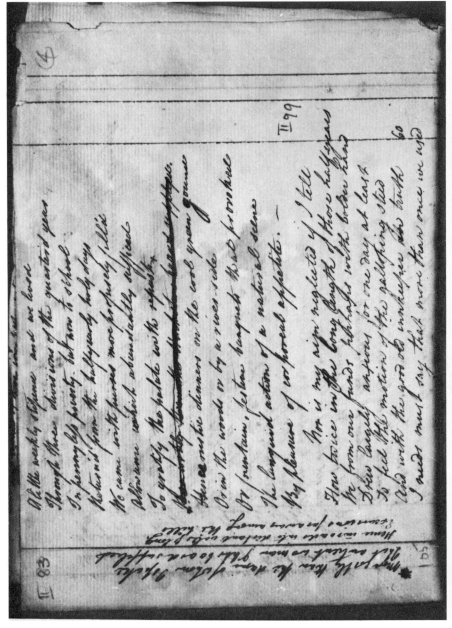

60

A litte{e weekly stipend and we lived
Through three divisions of the quarter'd year
In pennyless poverty—but now to school
Return'd from the half-yearly holy days
We came with purses more profusely fill'd
       {wh
Allowance {wiich abundantly sufficed
To gratify the palate with repasts,
                     {fied
More costly than the Hucksters board suppl{y.
Thence rustic dinners on the cool green gound
Or in the woods or by a river-side
Or fountain, festive banquets that provoked
The languid action of a natural scene
By pleasure of corporeal appetite.—

*

   *Nor is my aim neglected if I tell*
*How twice in the long length of those half-years*
*We from our funds perhaps with bolder hand*
*Drew largely anxious for one day at least*
*To feel the motion of the galloping steed*
                   *{in*
*And with the good old innkeeper {at truth*
*I needs must say that more than once we used*

* More costly than the dame of whom I spake
That antient woman & her board supplied
Hence inroads into distant vales & long
Excursions far away among the hills

---

Asterisks locate the marginal insertion. MH's hand begins with the second paragraph.

Fit audience for the intended sound ...
Of the day's journey was too distant far
For any cheerful inn a structure famed
Beyond its neighbourhood the antique walls
Of a large abbey with its precincts each
Bellying and buttressed and living trees
A holy scene! Along the smooth green turf
Our horses grazed. No more than island here
left by the waters that overflows the vale
In that sequestered ruin trees and towers
Both silent and both motionless alike
Hear all day long the murmuring sea that beats
Incessantly upon the craggy shore

Our steeds remounted and the summons given
with which and there we through the gateway [passe]
In uncouth race; and left the cross-legged knight
and the stone abbot and that single wren
which one day sang so sweetly in the nave
Of the old church; that though from recent showers, &c
The earth was comfortless and touch'd by faint
Internal tidings from the earthy walls
The shuddering ivy dripped large drops yet still

80

Sly subterfuge for the intended bound
Of the days journey was too distant far
For any cautious man a structure fam'd
Beyond its neighbourhood the antique walls
Of a large abbey with its fractured arch
Belfrey and images and living trees
A holy scene! Along the smooth green turf

Our horses grazed; in more than in {land peace
Left by the winds that overpass the vale
In that sequestered ruin trees and towers
Both silent and both motionless alike
Hear all day long the murmuring sea that beats
Incessantly upon the craggy shore
      Our steeds remounted and the summons given
With whip and spur we through the gateway flew
In uncouth race; and left the cross-legged knight
And the stone abbot and the single wren
Which one day sang so sweetly in the nave
Of the old church that though from recent showers
The earth was comfortless and touch'd by faint
Internal breezes from the roofless walls
The shuddering ivy dripp'd large drops yet still

So mutely and the gloom the invisible bird
Sang its still tale there I could have made
My dwelling place and long for ever there
To hear such music Might the willow flee
And dear my eyes ... but ... ... ...
... ... ... and through length and smooth
The sunshine's homeward O ye earth and streams
And that still shout of the evening air

... ... ... ... ... ...
... ... ... ... ... ...
... ... ... ... ... ...
Your hovered ... ... with slackened step we breathed
Along the sides of the steep hills, or when
Lightened by gleams of moonlight from the sea
We beat with thundering hoofs the level sand.

Upon the eastern shore of Windermere
Above the crescent of a pleasant bay
There was an inn no homely-featured shed
Brother of the surrounding cottages
But that a splendid place the door then                    110
With chearly ... rooms and liveries and within
Decanter, glasses and the blooded wine
In ancient times or ere the hall was built
On the proud island it had been a ... ... ...

153

So sweetly mid the gloom the invisible bird
Sang to itself that there I could have made
My dwelling place and lived for ever there
                    Through the walls we flew

To hear such music.
And down the valley —+—      and a circuit made
                [?A]}nd through rough and smooth
In wantonness of heart —
                                joyous
We scamper'd homeward. O ye rocks and streams
And that still spirit of the evening air
What wonder if I then had other joys

        Even in this happy time I sometimes felt
Then what ye give. Yet did I sometimes feel
Your presence when with slackened step we breathed
Along the sides of the steep hills, or when
Lighten'd by gleams of moonlight from the sea
We beat with thundering hoofs the level sand.
        Upon the eastern shore of Windermere
Above the crescent of a pleasant bay
There was an inn no homely-featured shed
Brother of the surrounding cottages
But 'twas a splendid place the door beset
With chaises, grooms and liveries and within
Decanters, glasses and the blood-red wine
In antient times or 'ere the hall was built
                        s}                had the dwelling been
On the large il}land it had been a place

100

more worthy of a poet's love a hut

Stood of its one bright face and sycamore shade

But through the shaggier were gone which once encircled

The Husband and large golden characters

On the blue front eight-hand had wrought

The place of the old time in contempt

And mocking of the rustic painter's hand

Yet to this shew the girls to me is dear

With all its foolish pomp. The garden lay

Upon a slope surmounted by the sheer

Of a small bowling-green beneath us stood

A grove, with plants of water through the trees

And over the blue tops; nor did we want

Refreshment, strawberries and mellow cream

And there through half an afternoon we played

On the smooth platform and the shouts we sent       124

Made all the mountains ring        But ere the fall

Of night, when in our pinnace, we returned

Over the dusky lake and to the beach

Of some small island steered our course with one

The minstrel of our troop, and left him there

ATT. VII: between the 11th of my music

More worthy of a poet's love a hut
Proud of its one bright fire and sycamore shade
But though the rhymes were gone which once inscribed
The threshold and large golden characters
On the blue frosted sign-board had usurp'd
The place of the old lion in contempt
And mockery of the rustic painter's hand
Yet to this hour the spot to me is dear
With all its foolish pomp. The garden lay
Upon a slope surmounted by the plain
Of a small bowling-green beneath us stood
A grove, with gleams of water through the trees
And over the tree-tops; nor did we want
Refreshment, strawberries and mellow cream
And there through half an afternoon we play'd
On the smooth plat-form and the shouts we sent
Made all the mountains ring. But 'ere the fall
Of night, when in our pinnace we returned
Over the dusky lake and to the beach
Of some small island steered our course with one
The minstrel of our troop, and left him there

120

175  And came off gently while he blew his flute
Alone upon the lake; oh then the calm
And dead still water lay upon my mind
Even with a weight of pleasure and the sky
Never before so beautiful sank down
Into my heart and held me like a dream

Thus day by day my sympathies increased
And thus the boundless range of visible things
Grew dear to me: already I began
To love the sun: a boy I loved the sun
Not as I since have loved him as a pledge
And surety of my earthly life, a light
Which while I view I feel I am alive
But for this cause that I had seen him lay
His beauty on the morning hills had seen
The western mountain touch his setting orb
In many a thoughtless hour when from excess
Of happiness my soul appeared to flow
With its own pleasure and I breathed with joy

And rowed off gently while he blew his flute
Alone upon the rock; oh then the calm
And dead still water lay upon my mind
Even with a weight of pleasure and the sky
Never before so beautiful sank down
Into my heart and held me like a dream

   Thus day by day my sympathies encreased

And thus the common ran {[?]e of visible things
Grew dear to me: already I began
To love the sun: a boy I loved the sun
Not as I since have loved him as a pledge
And surety of my earthly life, a light
Which while I vied} I feel I am alive

But for this cause that I ha{ve seen him lay
His beauty on the morning hills had seen
The western mountain touch his setting orb
In many a thoughtless hour when from excess
Of happiness my blood appeared to flow
With its own pleasure and I breathed with joy

140

And from like feelings humble through interior
To habitual and Domestic love
Analogous the more to me was dear
And I would dream away my burghers
Looking to both repeating while she hung
Midway between the hills as if she fallen
No other region but belongs to her
Yea abandoned by a higher right
To thee and thy grey huts my native vale

These incidental charms which first attached
My heart to rural object day by day
Grew weaker and I harken on to title
New nature intervenient till this time
And evening how at length was wrought
For her mind sake.—    But who shall parcel out
His intellect by geometric rule
Split like a hobbins into round square
Who knows the individual hour in which
His habits were first sown even are read
Who that shall point my course around play
This for two of the higher of my mind

And from like feelings humble though intense
To patriotic and domestic love
Analogous the moon to me was dear
And I would dream away my purposes
Standing to look upon her while she hung
Midway between the hills as if she knew
No other region but belonged to thee
Yea appertained by a peculiar right
To thee and thy grey huts my native vale
 Those incidental charms which first attached
My heart to rural objects day by day
Grew weaker and I hasten on to tell
How nature intervenient till this time
And secondary, now at length was sought
For her own sake. ——   But who shall parcel out          160
His intellect by geometric rules
Split like a province into round & square
Who knows the individual hour in which
His habits were first sown even as a seed
Who that shall point as with a wand & say
This portion of the river of my mind

Came from yon fountain⟩< If to thee my Friend
The unity of ⌐      hath been revealed
Then wilt thou doubt with me less aptly skill'd
Than many are to class the cabinet
Of their sensations & in voluble phrase
Run through the history and birth of each
As of a single independent thing.
Hard task to analyse a soul in which
Not only general habits and desires
But each most obvious and particular thought
Not in a mystical & idle sense
But in the words of reason deeply weigh'd
{Ha
{[?]th no beginning.—      Bless'd the infant babe
(For with my best conjectures I would trace
                        {B
The progress of our {being} blest the Babe
{N {M
[?P]urs'd in his {mother's arms the Babe who sleeps
Upon his Mother's breast who when his soul
Claims manifest kindred with an earthly soul

180

thoughts
Came from yon fountain Thou, my Friend art one
More deeply read in thy own mind no slave
Of that false secondary power by which
In weakness we create distinctions then
Believe that our puny boundaries are things
Which we perceive & not which we have made
To thee unblinded by these outward shews
The unity of all have been rvealed

The X in the margin and the smeared X with a tail in the first line locate the marginal insertion.

Such feelings press into his torpid life
Like an awakening breeze and here his men
Even in the first trouble of its powers
So prompt and ~~wakeful~~ eager to combine

Such feelings pass into his torpid life
Like an awakening breeze and hence his min
Even in the first trial of its powers
Is prompt and ~~active~~ — eager to combine
              wakeful

200

Doth gather passion from his Mothers eye.
This passion is the awakening breeze of life
Thus stirred in the first trial of its powers
~~His mind is~~
~~Stir'd up by constant sensibility~~
~~His mind~~            is prompt and eager to combine
    n
I[?]}  one appearance all the elements
And parts of the same object else detach'd
And loath to coalesce. Thus day by day
{Subj
{[?] ected to the discipline of love
His organs and recipient faculties
Are quicken'd are more vigourous his mind spreads
Tenacious of the forms which it receives.
In one beloved presence nay, and more
In that most apprehensive habitude
And those sensations which have been derived
F}
Th}rom       beloved presence        there exists
A virtue which irradiates and exalts
All objects through all intercourse of sense.
              bewilder'd
No outcast He ~~abandon'd~~ & depress'd
Along his infant veins are interfused
The gravitation & the filial bond
Of Nature that connect him with the world.

The marginal draft replaces lines 2–4.

220

Emphatically such a Being lives
An inmate of this active universe.
From Nature largely he receives nor so
  s
I } satisfied but largely gives again
  For feeling has to him imparted strength
For powerful in all sentiments of grief
  And
Of exultation fear & joy his mind
Even as an agent of the one great mind
Creates, creator & receiver both
  Acting but in alliance with
Working but in the spirit of the works
Which it beholds. —— Such verily is the first
Poetic Spirit of our human life
By uniform control of after years
In most abated & suppress'd, in some
Through every change of growth or of decay
Preeminent till death. From early days,
Beginning not long after that first time
In which a babe by intercourse of touch
I held mute dialouges with my Mothers heart
I have endeavour'd to display the means
  Whereby
By which this infant sensibility,

WW probably did not mean to delete "Working" in the ninth line, for it is the reading of later manuscripts.

Hence a countless store
With which my memory daily was impressed
Of modes and temporary qualities
Else undiscover'd hence a register
Of permanent relations else unknown

                                                        ⎰hence
Hence life & change and beauty, knowledge ⎰[  ?  ]
And gentle agitations of the mind
                        distinctions
From manifold ~~impressions~~ difference
Perceived in things where to the common eye
No difference is: and hence from the same source
Sublimer joy

Hence modes & qualities
difference & [?distinct—]
endless [?combinations]

      o
2[?]  o

Great birthright of our being, was in me
      Augmented
Extended & sustained. Yet is a path
        difficult
difficult  More [?obdurate] before me & I fear
That in its broken windings we shall need
The Chamois sinews & the eagle's wing
For now a trouble came into my mind
From ~~obscure~~ causes: I was left alone
Seeking this visible world nor knowing why
The props of my affections were removed
And yet the building stood as if sustained
By its own spirit. All that I beheld
Was dear to me & from this cause it came
That now to Nature's finer influxes
              more exact
My mind lay open to that
    And intimate communion
~~More curious & attentive~~ which our hearts
                              properties
Maintain with the minuter ~~qualities~~
Of objects which already are belov'd
And of those only.* I would walk alone
In storm & tempest or in starlight nights
        *Turn over

---

    In the seventh line, no alternative reading was thought of for "obscure," deleted; U reads "obscure," V leaves a blank, and M reads "unknown." Marginal drafts in the upper right-hand corner probably represent the first effort toward the insertion at the asterisk, next-to-bottom line; the second effort, from which only the last 2½ lines were finally taken, is found across the top of the page, and the third effort on 7$^v$ continued on 8$^r$.

Beneath the quiet heavens and at that time.
Would feel whate'er there is of power in sound
To breathe an elevated mood by form
Or image unprofaned; and I would stand,
Beneath some rock listening to sounds that are
The ghostly language of the ancient earth
Or make their dim abode in distant winds.
Thence did I drink the visionary power;
. . . [I] profitably those fleeting moods
Of shadowy exultation, not for this
That they are kindred (to our purer mind)
And intellectual life but that the soul
Remembering how she felt but what she felt
Remembering not, retains an obscure sense
Of possible sublimity, to which
With growing faculties she doth aspire
With faculties still growing, feeling still
That whatsoever point they gain they still

260

Beneath the quiet heavens and at that time
Would feel what e'er there is of power in sounds
To breathe an elevated mood by form
Or image unprofaned: and I would stand
Beneath some rock listening to sounds that are
The ghostly language of the antient earth
Or make their dim abode in distant winds.
Thence did I drink the visionary power.
I deem not profitless these fleeting moods
Of shadowy exaltation, not for this
That they are kindred to our purer mind
And intellectual life but that the soul
Remembering how she felt but what she felt
Remembering not, retains an obscure sense
Of possible sublimity to which
With growing faculties she doth aspire
With faculties still growing feeling still
That whatsoever point they gain they still

Which but for this most watchful power of love
Of modes and temporary qualities
And every season brought a countless store
And sorrow is not there. The seasons came
Of knowledge when all knowledge is delight
When every hours brings palpable access
Of youth but oh what happiness to live
Many are the joys

DW's hand begins in the eleventh line.

280

*Have something to pursue.*
          *And not alone*
*In grandeur and in tumult but no less*
*In tranquil scenes that universal power*
*And fitness in the latent qualities*
*And essences of things by which the mind*
*Is moved with feelings of delight to me*
*Came strengthened with a superadded soul*
*A virtue not its own. My morning walks*
*Were early, oft before the hours of school*
*I travelled round our little lake five miles*
*Oft pleasant wandering : happy time more dear*
  *F*
⌊*for this that one was by my side, a friend*
*Then passionately loved. With heart how full*
*Will he peruse these lines this page perhaps*
*A blank to other men, for many years*
*Have since flowed in between us, and our minds*
*Both silent to each other, at this time*
*We live as if those hours had never been.*
*Nor seldom did I lift our cottage latch*

From manifold distinctions difference
And gentle agitations of the mind
            silent unobtrusive
By silent pleasures ~~tranquil~~ sympathies
Society made sweet as solitude
More active even than best society
Hence life and change & beauty solitude
Of permanent relations else unknown.
Had been neglected left a register

Far warbling, and before the vernal thrush
Was audible, among the hills I sate
Alone, upon some jutting eminence,
At the first hour of morning when the vale
Lay quiet in an utter solitude.
How shall I trace the history, where seek
The origin of what I then have felt?
Oft in those moments such a holy calm
Did overspread my soul, that I forgot
The agency of sight & what I saw
Appeared like something in myself, a dream
a prospect in my mind. — Twas summer & to tell
Whatsoever of autumn would the winter — more
But what the summer shade that fancy sought
And the morning . . . . . . . .
The evening . . . . . . .
But . . . let my words . . . . . . . . .
That . . . of religion . . . . . . . . .
In all . . . in its silence, that let them at least
. . . . . forget this . . . . .
Why . . . . . . . . . .
That . . . by this regular . . . of this world

335

292
43
—
335

Far earlier, and before the vernal thrush
Was audible among the hills I sate
Alone upon some jutting eminence
At the first hour of morning when the vale
Lay quiet in an utter solitude.
How shall I trace the history where seek
The origin of what I then have felt
Oft in those moments such a holy calm
Did overspread my soul that I forgot
The agency of sight & what I saw
Appeared like something in myself—a dream
A prospect in my mind. Twere long to tell
What spring & autumn what winter-snows
And what the summer shade what day & night
The evening and the morning what my dreams
                                              nurse
And what my waking hours did bring to feel
                             in
                    u
                 s[?]pplied
That Spirit of religious love with which
I walked with nature. But let this at least
Be not forgotten that I still retained
My first creative sensibility
That by the regular action of the world

To his summary line count WW evidently adds here the lines that make up the new opening on 1ʳ and 1ᵛ. See the Introduction, pp. 30–31.

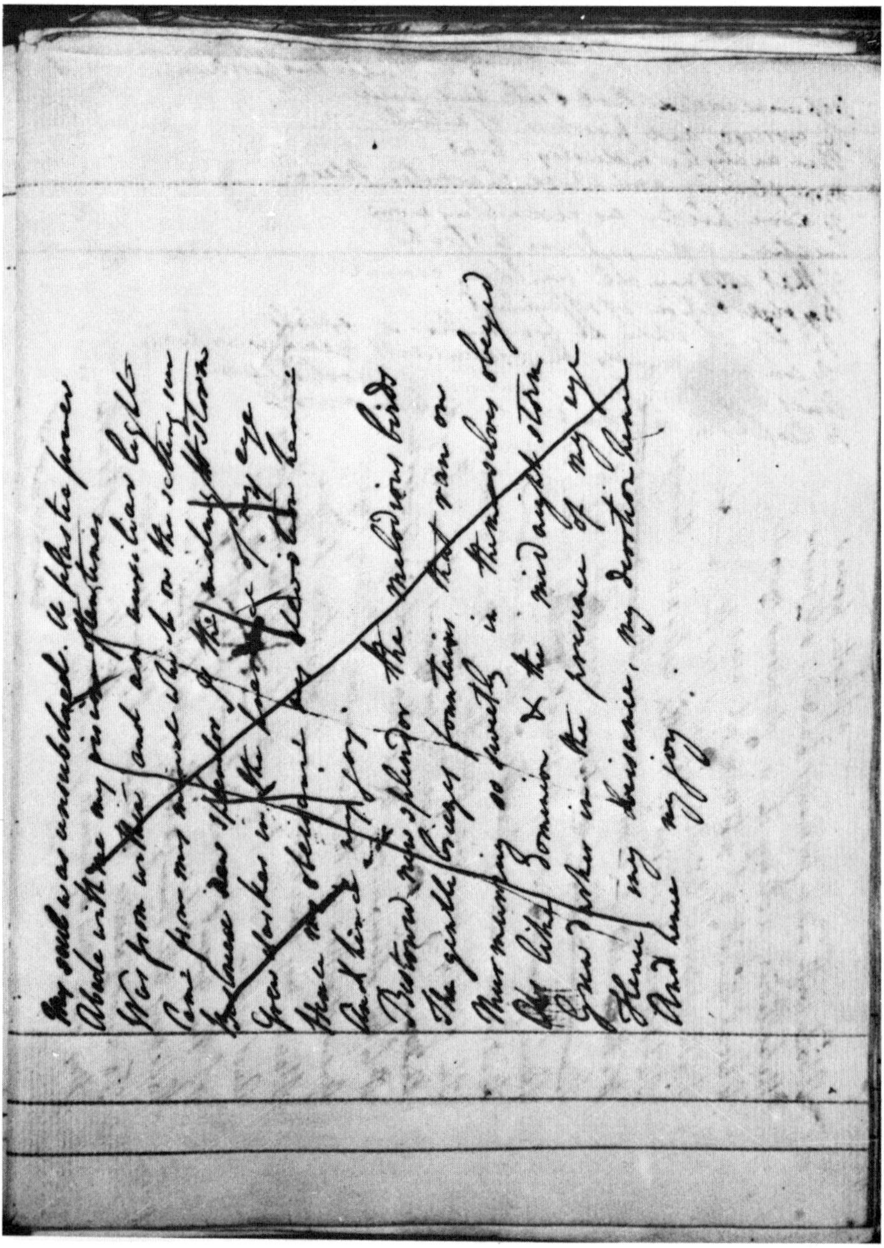

My soul was unsubdued. A plastic power
Abode with me my vision often times
Was from within and an auxiliar light
Came from my mind which on the setting sun
Bestowed new splendor & the midnight storm
Grew darker in the presence of my eye
Hence my obeisance my devotion hence
And hence my joy.
*Bestowed new splendor the melodious birds*
*The gentle breezes fountains that ran on*
*Murmuring so sweetly in themselves obeyed*
*{A*
*{Ob like dominion & the midnight storm*
*Grew darker in the presence of my eye*
*Hence my obeisance, my devotion hence*
*And hence my joy.*

---

The second paragraph is in DW's hand. The entire page, except for the first half-line, is replaced by fair copy on 9ᵛ.

& nor should this perchance
perhaps unrecorded that a state had lower
the exercise and produce of a toil
Than analytic industry. to me
more pleasing and whose character I deem
Is more poetic as resembling more
Creative agency, I mean to speak
Of that interminable building reared
By observation of affinities
In objects where no brotherhood exists
Is common minds: their seventeenth year was come
And whether from this habit rooted now
So deeply in my mind    or from excess

a plastic power
Abode with me, a forming hand, at times
Rebellious, acting in a devious mood
A local spirit of it's own at war
With general tendency but for the most
Subservient strictly to the external things
With which it communed. them my own enthusiastic
joy from within an auxiliar light
Came from my mind which on the setting sun
Bestowed new splendour; the melodious birds
The gentle breezes, fountains that ran on
murmuring so sweetly in themselves, obey'd
A like dominion, and the midnight storm
Grew darker in the presence of my eye.
Hence my obeisance my devotion hence
And hence my transport. Wherefore from
Of this great consummate principle of life
Obeying all things with it's sympathy
To unorganic natures transferred
my own enjoyments, or the power of truth

                              ˣNor should this perchance
Pass unrecorded that I still had loved
The exercise and produce of a toil
Than analytic industry, to me
More pleasing and whose character I deem
Is more poetic as resembling more
Creative agency, I mean to speak
Of that interminable building reared

By ob⸨se⸩jervation of affinities
In objects where no brotherhood exists
To common minds: ⸨M⸩my seventeenth year was come

And wheth[?]⸨e⸩r from this habit rooted now
So deeply in my mind or from excess

                    a plastic power
Abode with me, a forming hand, at times
Rebellious, acting in a devious mood
A local spirit of its own at war
With general tendency but for the most
Subservient strictly to the external things
With which it communed. Hence my vision oft
Was from within and an auxiliar light
Came from my mind which on the setting sun
Bestowed new splendour, the melodious birds,
The gentle breezes, fountains that ran on
Murmuring so sweetly in themselves, obey'd
A like dominion, and the midnight storm
Grew darker in the presence of my eye.
Hence my obeisance my devotion hence
And hence my transport Whether, from excess
Of the great social principle of life,
Coercing all things into sympathy,
To unorganic natures I transferre'd
My own enjoyments, or, the power of truth

360

Coming in revelation, I conversed
With things that really are, I at this time
Saw blessings spread around me like a sea.
    Thus did my days pass on
My seventeenth year was come and now at length
From Nature and her overflowing soul
I had received so much that all my thoughts
Were steep'd in feeling, I was only then
Contented, when with bliss ineffable
I felt the sentiment of being spread
O'er all that moves, and all that seemeth still,
Oer all which lost beyond the reach of thought
And human knowledge, to the human eye
Invisible, yet liveth to the heart,

forms
Oer all which leaps and ⎰r ⎱ and ⎰s ⎱ and shouts & sings
Or beats the gladsome air oer all which Glides
Beneath the wave yea in the wave itself
And mighty depth of waters: wonder not
If such my transports were for in all things

---

The line number 360, coming 30, not 35, lines after 335, may represent a miscount or WW's belated recognition that he had counted the first 5 lines of Part Two twice (see the Introduction, p. 31). Revision of the fourth line was made necessary by WW's having used the deleted words in his long addition on 9ᵛ. In the fourteenth line WW converted "and" (a miswriting) to "runs" by the alterations shown and by letting the original "a" serve as a "u."

380

I saw one life and felt that it was joy
One song they sang and it was audible
Most audible then when the fleshly ear
Oercome by grosser prelude of that strain
Forgot its functions & slept undisturb'd.

By such communion I was early taught
That what we see of forms and images
Which float along our minds and what we feel
Of active or recognizable thought
Prospectiveness intelligence or will

Not{[?]nly is not worthy to be deemed
Our being, to be prized as what we are
But is the very littleness of life
Such consciousnesses seemed but accidents
Relapses from the one interior life
Which is in all things from that unity
In which all beings live with god, are lost
In god & nature in one mighty whole

290

Come to began held as the clouds part
At even as from the cloudless west, when all
The landscape is one circular theme.
Of this (I ever and another faith
Cannot accept to the inward mind
That now I grossly destitute of all
These human interests which make this earth
To us... if I should fail with grateful voice
To speak of you... ye mountains! & ye lakes
And sounding cataracts. ye mists and winds
That dwell among the hills where I was born
If in my youth I have been pure in heart
If mingling with the world content
With... my own modest pleasures & her view,
With God and Nature communing, removed
From little enmities & low desires

398

As undistinguishable as the cloudless east
As} noon is from the cloudless west, when all
The hemisphere is one cerulean blue.

If this be error and another faith
Find easier access to the pious mind
Yet}
Then} were I grossly destitute of all
Those human sentiments which make this earth

                                                voice
So dear: if I should f[?]} l with grateful soul
To speak of you, ye mountains! & ye lakes
And sounding cataracts, ye mists and winds
That dwell among the hills where I was born
If in my youth I have been pure in heart
If mingling with the world I am content

With my own modest pleasures & have los}ved,
With {god and Nature communing, removed
From little enmities & low desires

---

The summary line count suggests a pause in composition, or transcription, after which DW's hand begins.

The gift is yours — in these times of fear
This unheralded work of hopes betrayed
If mind indifference and apathy
And wicked exultation when good men
On every side fall off we know not how
To refreshing disguises in gentle themes
Of peace & quiet, & domestic love
Yet mingled not unwillingly with sweets
On ordinary minds, if in this hour
Of revelation and so may I yet
Of revelation and nature but retain
Despair not of our nature but retain
A more than Roman confidence a faith
That fails not, in all sorrows my support
The blessing of my life the gift is yours
Ye mountains! thine O Nature. thou hast fed

waste

420

*The gift is yours if in these times of fear*
*This melancholy world of hopes o'erthrown*
*If 'mid indifference and apathy*
*And wicked exultation when good men*
*On every side fall off we know not how*
*To selfishness disguised in gentle names*
*Of peace, & quiet, & domestic love*
*Yet mingled not unwillingly with sneers*
*On visionary minds, if in this time*
*Of dereliction and dismay I yet*
*Despair not of our nature but retain*
*A more than Roman confidence a faith*
*That fails not, in all sorrow my support*
*The blessing of my life the gift is yours*
*Ye mountains; thine O Nature! thou hast fed*

Alongside the second line, "waste" in the margin is an alternate, later adopted, for "world."

430

*My lofty speculations and in thee*
*For this uneasy heart of ours I find*
*A never-failing principle of joy*
*And purest passion—* Thou my Friend wast bred
In the great city mid far other scenes

But we by different roads at length have gained
             from this cause
The self-same bourne. And speaking thus to thee
I speak unapprehensive of contempt
I neither dread aversion nor contempt
The insinuated scoff of coward tongues
  With      unworthy   And all that silent
Nor all that mask of silent language which
In conversation betwixt man & man
Blots from the human countenance all trace
         {hast sought
Of beauty & of love. For thou {art one
The truth in solitude and thou art one
The most intense of natures worshippers
In many things my brother chiefly here
In this my deep devotion. Fare thee well
Be happy seeking oft the haunts of men
But yet more often living with thy self

so oft

The summary line count (WW had been counting in twenties) at the end of the fair copy marks another stopping-place.

reared

Health and the quiet of a healthy mind
Attend thee seeking of the haunts of men
            yet
But more often living with thy self
And for thyself, so, haply, shall thy days
Be many, & a blessing to mankind

                    Thou my Friend wast bred

In the great city mid far other scenes
But we by different roads at length have gained
The selfsame bourne. And from this cause to thee
I speak unapprehensive of contempt
The insinuated scoff of coward tongues
And all that silent language which so oft
In conversation betwixt man & man
Blots from the human contenance all trace
Of beauty & of love. For thou hast sought
The Truth in solitude & thou art one
The most intense of nature's worshippers
In many things my brother chiefly here
In this my deep devotion

DW's hand resumes at the second paragraph.

End of the second Part

*Fare thee well!*
                                    ful
*Health & the quiet of a healthy mind*
*Attend thee! seeking oft the haunts of men*
*But yet more often living with thyself,*
*And for thyself, so haply shall thy days*
*Be many & a blessing to mankind. . . . . . . .*

*End of the second Part*

                        rustic spot
                Twas a ~~small domain~~
The town in which we dwelt a small domain
Less populous with houses than with trees
And there each evening duly were our games
Prolong      &c
No chair remained before the doors the bench
And threshold steps were empty fast asleep
The labourer & the old [?man] man who had sat

WW's revision of the opening lines on 1ʳ is in pencil.

# MSS. U and V

Photographic Reproductions and Transcriptions of MS. V,
with Readings of MS. U in an *Apparatus Criticus*

MS. U (DC MS. 22) is a vellum-bound notebook containing 92 leaves. The leaves measure exactly $6\frac{1}{8}$ by $7\frac{1}{2}$ inches, with chain lines at intervals of 2.6 centimeters; the watermark is a large circle surmounted by a crown, containing an image of Britannia; the countermark is the date 1796. The notebook is completely filled by fair copies of three works. *The Borderers* with its preface takes up the first 72 leaves; its underlying fair-copy text was revised by Mary Wordsworth in preparation for the play's first publication in 1842. Parts One and Two of the 1798–1799 *Prelude* follow, also in the hand of Mary (then Mary Hutchinson), followed by *The Beggar* in a hand that is probably SH's, running right to the end of the notebook.

MS. V (DC MS. 23) is a smaller notebook now taken apart; only 19 leaves survive, along with 1 additional loose leaf of a smaller size inserted at the front. The original leaves, which were in gatherings of two, measure 14.9 by 20.5 centimeters and are countermarked CURTEIS & SONS 1798 and watermarked with a design showing Britannia seated within an oval frame surmounted by a crown; chain lines are at intervals of 2.4 centimeters. The loose single leaf measures 15 by 18.9 centimeters, with chain lines 2.5 centimeters apart. Since it is no longer possible to see exactly how the notebook was originally put together, or to find all the stubs, only the surviving leaves are counted in the numbering.

Fair copy of the two-part *Prelude* in DW's hand begins at the top of the first surviving original leaf of V and runs through 3 leaves before being broken off owing to DW's failure to insert the skating episode, which had to be brought in from another manuscript than the one she was following. The poem then runs in fair copy right to the end, but the leaf which contained the opening $52\frac{1}{2}$ lines of the second part has been torn out. In the transcription which follows, these lines are supplied from U with facing photographs which give a representative idea of that manuscript. All other readings of U, with the exception of single-letter miswritings corrected by the copyist, are given (in roman type) in the *apparatus criticus*.

Line numbers running by twenties, visible in some of the photographs of V, were penciled in by DW or WW, and are shown in the transcriptions alongside the running line numbers which correspond to the final text of 1799. Most of the revisions which can be seen on V were made between 1801 and 1804 in the course of extending the poem to five books, and are therefore not given line numbers.

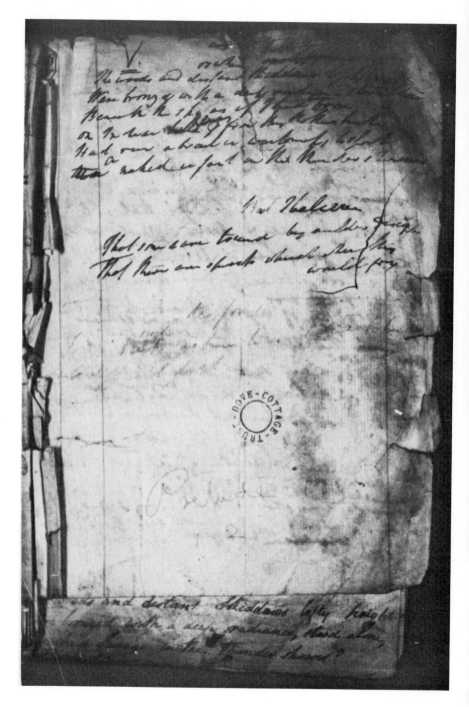

crg & hill
                *hill & rock*
or when rock & plain

The woods and distant Skiddaws lofty height
                                             ⌠lone
Were bronzd with a deep radiance stood a⌡bove
                             been
Beneath the sky as if I had born
                   plains
On Indian ~~hills~~ & from My Mothers hut
Had run abroad in wantonness to sport
              A
⌠ ~~An~~
⌡[?An] naked infant in the thunder showwer


But I believe

That some are traind by milder discipline
⌠T
⌡that there are spirits which when they
                         would [?form]


the [?forms]
              such
To [ ? ] such as have been [  ?  ] to [  ?  ]
A different part

---

At the top of the leaf "hill & rock" are in DW's hand. The first group of lines develops ll. 23–26 of Part One toward the version of 1805; the second and perhaps the third group (the third mostly illegible) appear to run over from revisions on 1ᵛ. The "V" at the top of the leaf and the inscription "Prelude 1 2," visible at the bottom, were added by a twentieth-century editor.

The apprehensons [?]
                                                          the breath
          The mind of man is fram'd even like a song
And                            There is
     Or harmony of music    Tis a dark
                         ip⟩
Invisible workmansh[?]⟩ that reconciles
Discordant elements & makes them move
In one society Ah me that all
The terrors All the early miseries
     The medly of aversions & desires
Regrets, vexations lassitudes that all
The the thoughts & feelings which have
                    mind              been infus'd
Into my mind life should ever have made up
The calm existence that is mine When I
When I am wor
Am worthy of myself—Praise to the end
          milder            but some are [?traind]
Thanks likewise for the means but I believe
     By other discipline & I [?believe]
                         milder
That some are train'd by other discipline
That there are spirits which when they would
                              very dawn form
A favor'd being from his earliest dawn
             do⟩
Of Infancy to⟩ open out the clouds
As at the touch of lightning seeking him
With gentle visitation quiet powers [ ?retird ]
     Retired & seldom recognised yet kind
And seld And to the very meanest not unknown
Retired with me thou' rarely in my boyish days
They communed for as I have said there are
                    of
Teachers who work by different character who [?are]
     ⟨ply
Yet ha⟨ppily using

---

The hand is DW's. The passage develops ll. 67–80 toward their 1805 form.

271-304

[...A Nature of the lowlier...]
[...]
[...]
[... I rose the ...... what it ... for this]
That one the fairest of all rivers, loved
To blend his murmurs with my Nurse's song,
And from his alder shades, and rocky falls,
And from his fords and shallows, sent a voice
That flowed along my dreams? For this didst thou
O Derwent, travelling o'er the green plains
Near my "sweet birth-place," didst thou beauteous Stream
Make ceaseless music through the night and day,
Which with its steady cadence, tempering
Our human waywardness, composed my thoughts
To more than infant softness, giving me,
Among the fretful dwellings of mankind,
        Knowledge, a dim earnest of the calm
Which Nature breathes among the fields and groves.
        Beloved Derwent! fairest of all Streams!
Was it for this that I, a four years' child,
A naked Boy, among thy silent pools
Made one long bathing of a summer's day?
Basked in the sun, or plunged into thy streams,
Alternate, all a summer's day, or coursed
O'er the sandy fields, and dashed the flowers
Of yellow grunsel, or when crag and hill,
The woods and distant Skiddaw's lofty height
[...with a deep radiance, stood alone]
[...]

That Nature often times when she would frame
⎰T           not the less
⎱though haply aiming at the self same end
~~Does~~ it delight her to employ
[?Oftime]    & so she dealt with me

1    *Was it for this*

2    *That one, the fairest of all rivers, loved*

⎰N
3    *To blend his murmurs with my* ⎱*nurse's song,*

4    *And from his alder shades, and rocky falls,*
                                        ,⎱
5    *And from his fords and shallows* ⎰*sent a voice*
⎰T ⎰at                          ?⎱
6    ⎱*Wh*⎱*ich flowed along my dreams* ⎰*For this didst thou*
                    ,⎱
7    *O Derwent* ⎰*travelling over the green plains*
                            ,⎱
8    *Near my "sweet birth-place"⎰" didst thou beauteous Stream*
                                            .⎱
9    *Make ceaseless music through the night and day* ⎰

10   *Which with its steady cadence tempering*
                        ,⎱
11   *Our human waywardness* ⎰*composed my thoughts*
                            ,⎱        ,⎱
12   *To more than infant softness* ⎰*giving me* ⎰
                                    ,⎱
13   *Among the fretful dwellings of mankind* ⎰
                ,⎱
14   *A knowledge* ⎰*a dim earnest of the calm*
                                            .⎱
15   *Which Nature breathes among the fields and groves* ⎰
                                            !⎱
16   *Beloved Derwent! fairest of all Streams* ⎰
                                            ,⎱
17   *Was it for this that I, a four year's child* ⎰

18   *A naked Boy, among thy silent pools*
                                    ?⎱
19   *Made one long bathing of a summer's day* ⎰

---

⎰N
3   ⎱nurses    *no comma*
4   falls,] falls
6   That     dreams.
9   *first five words missing*
        d⎱
13  manking⎰,
14  earnest *first four letters written over erasure*
15  groves *written over erasure*
18  boy

---

Fair copy begins in DW's hand. Line numbers written in here and elsewhere which correspond to those of 1805 or 1850 are, of course, added by a twentieth-century editor, as are page numbers. WW's (or DW's) line numbers are in pencil, running by twenties (the first one is present here; many have been rubbed away). Lines of draft at the top of the page are connected with drafts on the facing verso.

20 20 *Basked in the sun, or plunged into thy streams*

21    *Alternate, all a summer's day or coursed*     ✕

22    *Over the sandy* fields *and dashed the flowers*

23    *Of yellow grunsel or when crag and hill*
24    *The woods and* distant Skiddaw's lofty height

25    *Were bronzed with a deep radiance stood alone,*

26    [ ]*naked Savage in the thunder shower.*

22  Over thy  e⟩  fields, *written over* plains, *erased*
24  *no erasure*
25  radience
26  A     Savage,

26  The first word, "A," is worn away.

Nor what hereford. self reproach can I

And afterwards, twice in a later day

the cave to mind was in a later day

Though early, when upon the mountain-slope

The frost and breath of frosty wind had snipped

The last autumnal crocus, 'twas my joy

To wander half the night among the cliffs

And the smooth hollows, where the woodcocks ran

Along the open turf. In thought and wish,

That time, my shoulder all with springes hung

I was a fell destroyer. gentle powers, on the heighth

Yf

I did when from snare to snare I piled

My anxious visitation, hurrying on,

Still hurrying hurrying onward,                Moon & stars

Were shining o'er my head, I was alone

and seem'd to be a trouble to the peace

That was among them: a of they troubled me

with expectation sometimes strong desire

did it befoly that a strong desire

o'erpowered my better reason & the bird

Which was the captive of another's toils

Became my prey; and when the deed was done

I heard among the solitary hills

Low breathings coming after me, and sounds

Of undistinguishable motion, steps

Almost as silent as the turf they trod.

      Nor less, in spring-time, when on southern banks

The shining sun had from his knot of leaves

Decoyed the primrose flower, and when the vales

And woods were warm, was I a rover then

|    | Nor without kindred self reproach can I |
|----|-----------------------------------------|
| 27 | *And afterwards, twas in a later day* |
|    | Recall to mind how in a later day |
| 28 | *Though early, when upon the mountain-slope* |
|    |             ⎰sna |
| 29 | *The frost and breath of frosty wind had* ⎱*nipped* |
| 30 | *The last autumnal crocus* ⎱ *'twas my joy* |
| 31 | *To wander half the night among the cliffs* |
| 32 | *And the smooth hollows* ⎱ *where the woodcocks ran* |
|    |        open |
| 33 | *Along the ~~moonlight~~ turf. In thought and wish* ⎱ |
| 34 | *That time, my shoulder all with springes hung,* |
|    |                 ⎰O |
|    |      ~~When alone~~ ⎱on the heights |
| 35 | *I was a fell destroyer. ~~Gentle Powers!~~* |
| 36 | *~~Who give us happiness and call it peace~~* ⎱ |
|    |     Scudding away |
| 37 | *~~When scudding on~~ from snare to snare I plied* |
| 38 | *My anxious visitation, hurrying on* ⎱ |
|    |                  Moon & stars |
| 39 | *Still hurrying hurrying onward,* ⎱ *~~how my heart~~* |
|    |     Were shining oer my head, I was alone |
| 40 | *~~Panted,~~* ⎱ *~~among the scattered yew-trees,~~* ⎱ *~~and the crags~~* |
|    |     And seem'd to be a trouble to the peace |
| 41 | *~~That looked upon me~~* ⎱ *~~how my bosom beat~~* |
|    |     That was among them; and they troubled me |
| 42 | *~~With expectation. Sometimes strong desire~~* |
|    |     Sometimes did it befal that strong desire |
| 43 | *~~Resistless~~* ⎱ *~~overpowered me, and the bird~~* |
|    |     Oerpowerd my better reason & the bird |
| 44 | *Which was the captive of another's toils* |
| 45 | *Became my prey,* ⎱*and when the deed was done* |
| 46 | *I heard among the solitary hills* |
| 47 | *Low breathings coming after me* ⎱ *and sounds* |
| 48 | *Of undistinguishable motion, steps* |
| 49 | *Almost as silent as the turf they trod* ⎱ |
| 50 | *Nor less* ⎱ *in spring-time* ⎱ *when on southern banks* |
| 51 | *The shining sun had from his knot of leaves* |
| 52 | *Decoyed the primrose* ⎱*flower, and when the vales* |
|    |              plunderer |
| 53 | *And woods were warm* ⎱ *was I a rover then* |

---

| 27 | 'twas | th *erased following* day | 40 | Panted; | yew-trees,] yew-trees |
|----|-------|---------------------------|----|---------|------------------------|
| 29 | snapped | | 43 | *no erasure* | |
| 30 | crocus, | | | | ⎰ren |
| 35 | *no exclam point* | | 50 | south⎱ern | |
| 39 | *no punct* | | | | |

In the high places, on the lonesome peaks,    337–72
Among the mountains and the winds. Though mean
~~The maxx but had neither lodge~~ Rough were
~~And though inglorious were~~ yet ~~hony~~ end
~~Was not~~ ignoble. Oh, when I have hung
Above the raven's nest, by knots of grass,
Or half-inch fissures in the slippery rock,
But ill sustained, and almost, as it seemed,
Suspended by the blast which blew amain
Shouldering the naked crag, oh at that time,
While on the perilous ridge I hung alone,
With what strange utterance did the loud dry wind
Blow through my ears, the sky seemed not a sky
Of earth, and with what motion moved the clouds
The mind of man is fashioned & built up
Even as a strain of music: I believe
That there are spirits, which, when they would form
A favored being, from his very dawn
Of infancy do open out the clouds
As at the touch of lightning, seeking him
With gentle visitation: quiet Powers!
Retired and seldom recognized, yet kind,
And to the very meanest not unknown;
With me, though rarely, in
They communed: others too there are who use,
Yet haply aiming at the self-same end,
Severer interventions, ministry
More palpable, and of their school was I

54   *In the high places, on the lonesome peaks*
        Whereer
55   *Among the mountains and the winds.* ~~Though mean~~
        The Mother bird had built her lodge though mean

56   ~~And though inglorious were my views~~ ~~the end~~
        My object and inglorious yet the end

57   *Was not ignoble. Oh when I have hung*

58   *Above the raven's nest   by knots of grass*

59   *Or half-inch fissures in the slipp'ry rock*

60  60 *But ill sustained   and almost, as it seemed,*
61   *Suspended by the blast which blew amain*
62   *Shouldering the naked crag, oh at that time,*

63   *While on the perilous ridge I hung alone*
64   *With what strange utterance did the loud dry wind*
65   *Blow through my ears, the sky seemed not a sky*
66   *Of earth, and with what motion moved the clouds*[  ]
67        *The mind of man is fashioned & built up*

68   *Even as a strain of music   I believe*

69   *That there are spirits   which   when they would form*

70   *A favored being   from his very dawn*
71   *Of infancy do open out the clouds*

72   *As at the touch of lightning   seeking him*

73   *With gentle visitation*[  ] *quiet Powers*

74   *Retired and seldom recognized, yet kind*

75   *And to the very meanest not unknown*

---

59   Or] And          slippe⎰ry
62   time,] time
66   clouds!
67   &] and
68   of] in
70   very dawn] earliest day
                    n⎱
72   lighten⎰ing
73   visitation;          Powers] Powers:
74   *no punct*

---

57   The X, presumably connected with the deletion, is in pencil, as is the comma after "Oh."
66   Punctuation at the end of the line is worn away.
73   Punctuation is obscured by the ink blot.

76  With me } though rarely } in my early

77  They commu_ned } others too there are who use }

78  Yet haply aiming at the self-same end }
79  Severer interventions, ministry

80  8o  More palpable, and of their school was I. }

---

77  communed,
78  *no hyphen*

---

76  The added half-line is in pencil; the last word is probably worn away.

They quietted me: one evening, led by them
I went alone into a shepherds boat,
A skiff that to a willow-tree was tied
Within a rocky cave, its usual home;
The moon was up, the lake was shining clear
Among the hoary mountains: from the shore
I pushed, and struck the oars and struck again
In cadence, and my little Boat moved on
Just like a man who walks with stately step
Though bent on speed. It was an act of stealth
And troubled pleasure; nor without the voice
Of mountain-echoes did my boat move on,
Leaving behind her still on either side
Small circles glittering idly in the moon,
Until they melted all into one track
Of sparkling light. A rocky steep uprose
Above the cavern of the willow-tree,
And now, as suited one who proudly rowed
With his best skill, I fixed a steady view
Upon the top of that same craggy ridge,
The bound of the horizon, for behind
Was nothing but the stars and the grey sky.
— — She was an elfin pinnace; twenty times
I dipped my oars into the silent lake,
And as I rose upon the stroke, my Boat
Went heaving through the water, like a swan.
When from behind that rocky steep, till then

One Evening, She was     s usual

81  *They guided me: one evening ⎬ led by them,*
⎰Evening
One ⎱night, (surely She was then my Guide

82  *I went alone into a Shepherd's boat ⎬*
bound

83  *A skiff that to a willow-tree was tied*

84  *Within a rocky cave, its usual home;*

⎰sh    ⎰ing
85  /  *The moon was up ⎬ the lake was ⎱[ ? ]in⎱g   clear*

86  *Among the hoary mountains: from the shore*

87  *I pushed, and struck the oars and struck again*

88  *In cadence, and my little Boat moved on*

Even as
89  *Just like a man who walks with stately step*

90  *Though bent on speed. It was an act of stealth*

r
91  *And troubled pleasure; not without the voice*

92  *Of mountain-echoes did my boat move on ⎬*

93  *Leaving behind her still on either side*

94  *Small circles glittering idly in the moon*

95  *Until they melted all into one track*

96  *Of sparkling light. A rocky steep uprose*

97  *Above the cavern of the willow tree ⎬*

98  *And now, as suited one who proudly rowed*

99  *With his best skill ⎬ I fixed a steady view*

100  *Upon the top of that same craggy ridge,*

101  *The bound of the horizon, for behind*

⎰ s
102  *Was nothing ⎯⎬ but the ⎱[ ? ]tars and the grey sky.*

103  *————She was an elfin pinnace; twenty times*

104  *I dipped my oars into the silent lake ⎬*        .

---

81  *indented as para*     *no comma*
83  that] which
85  up:    shining
87  oars] oars,
97  willow tree] willow-tree
98  proudly *first five letters written over* rowed
99  skill,
102  stars
103  pinnace,

---

85  The vertical mark probably shows where lines from 5ʳ were to be inserted.
91  Deletion is in pencil and ink, revision in ink.

105    *And, as I rose upon the stroke* } *my Boat*

106    *Went heaving through the water* } *like a swan* }

107    *When from behind that rocky steep* } *till then*

---

105    And,] And          stroke,
107    steep,

The bound of the horizon, a huge Cliff    406–434

As if with voluntary power instinct,

Upreared its head. I struck, and struck again,

And, growing still in stature, the huge cliff

Rose up between me and the stars, and still

With measured motion like a living thing,

Strode after me. With trembling hands I turned,

And through the silent water stole my way

Back to the cavern of the willow tree.

There, in her mooring-place I left my bark,

And through the meadows homeward went with grave

And serious thoughts: and after I had seen

That spectacle, for many days my brain

Worked with a dim and undetermined sense

Of unknown modes of being: in my thoughts

There was a darkness, call it solitude

Or blank desertion, no familiar shapes

Of hourly objects, images of trees,

Of sea or sky, no colours of green fields:

But huge and mighty forms, that do not live

Like living men, moved slowly through my mind

By day, and were the trouble of my dreams.    427

     Ah not in vain ye Beings of the hills!

And ye that walk the woods and open heaths

By moon or star-light, thus from my first dawn

Of childhood did ye love to intertwine

The passions that build up our human soul

108   The bound of the horizon, a huge {C ,}{cliff}

109   As if with voluntary power instinct}

110   Upreared its head: I struck'} and struck again'}

111   And'} growing still in stature'} the huge cliff
112   Rose up between me and the stars, and still

113   With measured motion, like a living thing'}

114   Strode after me. With trembling hands I turned'}
115   And through the silent water stole my way
116   Back to the cavern of the willow-tree.

117   There, in her mooring-place I left my bark'}

118   And through the mea{d}[ ?]ows homeward went with grave
119   And serious thoughts: and after I had seen

120 120  That spectacle, for many days m[ ?]{y} brain
121   Worked with a dim and undetermined sense
122   Of unknown modes of being: in my thoughts

123   There was a darkness'} call it solitude or

124   Or blank des{e}[ ?]rtion, no familiar shapes

125   Of hourly objects, images of trees'}
126   Of sea or sky, no colours of green fields:

127   But huge and mighty forms'} that do not live

128   Like living men'} moved slowly through my mind

129   By day'} and were the trouble of my dreams'}

130        Ah! not in vain ye Beings of the hills'}
131   And ye that walk the woods and open heaths
132   By moon or star light, thus from my first dawn
133   Of childhood did ye love to intertwine
134   The passions that build up our human soul

---

108  Cliff
116  willow-tree.] willow-tree
118  meadows      homeward *inserted with caret*
120  my
121  un{determined sense}{known sense}
123  darkness,     solitude or] solitude

124  desertion;
126  *no colon*
128  slo{wly}{ly}
129  day,
132  star-light,
133  ye] you

Not with the mean and vulgar works of man
But with high objects, with eternal things
With life and nature purefying thus
The elements of feeling and of thought
And sanctifying by such discipline
Both pain and fear until we recognise
A grandeur in the beatings of the heart.

              Ye Powers of earth, ye Genii of the springs!
And ye that have your voices in the clouds
And ye that are familiars of the lakes
And standing pools— ah not for trivial ends
Through snow and sunshine through the sparkling plains
Of moonlight frost and in the stormy day
Did ye with such assiduous love pursue
Your favorite and your joy. I may not think
A vulgar hope was yours when ye employed
Such ministry, when ye through many a year
Thus by the agency of boyish sports
On caves and trees, upon the woods and hills
Impressed upon all forms the characters
Of danger or desire and thus did make
The surface of the universal earth
With meanings of delight, of hope, and fear
Work like a sea.

              Not uselessly employed
I might pursue this theme through every change
Of exercise and sport to which the year

[135]  *Not with the mean and vulgar works of man*
[136]  *But with high objects, with eternal things*
[137]  *With life and nature purifying thus*
[138]  *The elements of feeling and of thought*
[139]  *And sanctifying by such discipline*
[140]  *Both pain and fear until we recognise*
[141]  *A grandeur in the beatings of the heart.*
[186]          *Ye Powers of earth, ye Genii of the springs!*
[187]  *And ye that have your voices in the clouds*
[188]  *And ye that are familiars of the lakes*
                    ~~Ye know if there be aught~~
       *And standing pools.  ah! not for trivial ends*
                        {[?those]
       ~~Of cause for faith that I in~~ {  ?  } [pursuits]
       ~~Through snow and sunshine, through the sparkling plains~~
          ~~Was your peculiar care~~          *plains*
       ~~Of moonlight frost and in the stormy day~~
       *Did ye with such assiduous love pursue*
       *Your favorite and your joy. I may not think*
[190]  *A vulgar hope was yours when ye employed*
[191]  *Such ministry, when ye through many a year*
[192]  *Thus by the agency of boyish sports*
[193]  *On caves and trees, upon the woods and hills*
[194]  *Impressed upon all forms the characters*
[195]  *Of danger or desire, and thus did make*
[196]  *The surface of the universal earth*
[197]  *With meanings of delight, of hope, and fear*
[198]  *Work like a sea.*
                    *Not uselessly employed*
[199]  *I might pursue this theme through every change*
[200]  *Of exercise and sport to which the year*

---

188/190   DW first wrote "plains" at the end of the line, then erased it and rewrote it below. All other revisions and deletions are in pencil, apparently in the hand of STC. At the end of this page DW broke off, to recommence on 5ᵛ, doubling back to the beginning of the page; hence the repeated line numbers here are bracketed. The second time through she inserted the skating episode, together with its eight-line introduction (ll. 142–149) for which space had been left in U. For readings of MS. U, see *app. crit.* on pp. 247, 251, and 253.

Twas by the shore of Patterdale a vale
When I was a stranger, thither came
My chance in travel to my father's house

If I on the village thou had wandered for
the purpose of this small vessel in the care
had embarked to Row along the

by some shady fountain while soft airs

ye thought that travel round the world like
the hours of

                            surely I was led by her
Twas by the shores of Paterdale,—a vale
When I was as a stranger, thither come
By chance in travel to my fathers house
~~I from~~      I from the village Inn had wanderd forth
   ~~Alone I f~~
And finding this small vessel in its cave
I had embarked without the owners leave
A⌉And in                     ⌠is the
~~U⌡nder~~ the [?cavern] finding th⌡ese small skiff

Or by some shady fountain while soft airs
Among the leaves were stirring & the sun
Unfelt, shone sweetly round us in our peace

                             mighty thoughts
Ye thoughts that travel round the world like winds
         ⌠Joy
         ⌡[?of]
         ⌠~~d~~
Motions of ⌡[?]~~eli~~

The first passage was inserted before l. 84. The second develops revisions drafted in the margins of 13ᵛ and 14ʳ. The third passage may have been intended for the apostrophe on the facing verso (ll. 186ff.).

Not with the mean and vulgar works of man,  435
But with high objects, with eternal things,
With life and nature; purifying thus
The elements of feeling and of thought,
And sanctifying by such discipline
Both pain and fear, until we recognise
A grandeur in the beatings of the heart.

       Nor was this fellowship vouchsafed to me
With stinted kindness. In November days,
When vapours, rolling down the valleys, made
A lonely scene more lonesome; among woods
At noon, and mid the calm of summer nights
When by the margin of the trembling lake
Beneath the gloomy hills I homeward went
In solitude, such intercourse was mine
Twas ever at the seasons took their...
...when the stars...
Has set, and, visible for many a mile,
The cottage windows through the twilight blazed,
I heeded not the summons: clear and loud
The village clock toll'd six; I wheel'd about
Proud and exulting like an untired horse
That cares not for its home — All shod with steel
We hiss'd along the polish'd ice, in games
Confederate, imitative of the chace
And woodland pleasures, the resounding horn
The pack loud bellowing, and the hunted hare.
So through the darkness and the cold we flew,
And not a voice was idle; with the din,
Meanwhile, the precipices rang aloud,
The leafless trees and every icy crag

135    *Not with the mean and vulgar works of man* ⸜

136    *But with high objects, with eternal things* ⸜

137    *With life and nature* ⸝ *purifying thus*

138    *The elements of feeling and of thought* ⸜
139    *And sanctifying by such discipline*

140    *Both pain and fear* ⸜ *until we recognise*
141    *A grandeur in the beatings of the heart.*
142        *Nor was this fellowship vouchsafed to me*
143    *With stinted kindness. In November days,*

144    *When vapours* ⸜ *rolling down the valleys* ⸜ *made*

145    *A lonely scene more lonesome,* ⸝ *among woods*
146    *At noon, and mid the calm of summer nights*
147    *When by the margin of the trembling lake*
148    *Beneath the gloomy hills I homeward went*

149    *In solitude* ⸜ *such intercourse was mine* ⸝
        Twas mine among the fields both day & night
        And by the waters all the summer long
150        *And in the frosty season when the sun*

151    *Was set, and* ⸜ *visible for many a mile* ⸜

152    *The cottage windows through the twilight blazed* ⸜
                            ⸝ twas indeed
153    *I heeded not the summons* ⸝ₐ*clear and loud*
154    *The village clock toll'd six; I wheel'd about*
155    *Proud and exulting like an untired horse*

156    *That cares not for its home* ⸝ *All shod with steel*
157    *We hiss'd along the polish'd ice, in games*
158    *Confederate, imitative of the chace*
159    *And woodland pleasures, the resounding horn,*

Right margin (vertical text):

And by the waters all the summer long
We·I heeded not the summons twas indead
A happy time for all ⸝[⸝?]f us, to me   o
It was a time of rapture clear & loud

---

138  feelings
139  dicipline
140  fear,        recognize
141  *no punct*
142–149  *missing in U with 8-line gap*
153  summons:
154  tolled        six;] six        wheeled
156  home.
157  hissed        polished

---

The marginal insertion came in following l. 153.

160     *The pack loud bellowing, and the hunted hare.*
161     *So through the darkness and the cold we flew,*

162     *And not a voice was idle : with the din* ⎫

163     *Meanwhile, the precipices rang aloud* ⎫
164     *The leafless trees and every icy crag*

---

160   *no comma*
161   *no punct*

Tinkled like iron while the distant hills
Into the tumult sent an alien sound
Of melancholy not unnoticed while the stars
Eastward, were sparkling clear, and in the west
The orange sky of evening died away.

— Not seldom from the uproar I retired

Into a silent bay, or sportively
Glanced sideway leaving the tumultuous throng
To cut across the shadow of a star
That gleamed upon the ice: and oftentimes
When we had given our bodies to the wind
And all the shadowy banks on either side
Came sweeping through the darkness spinning still
The rapid line of motion then at once
Have I reclining back upon my heels,
Stopped short, yet still the solitary cliffs
Wheeled by me, even as if the earth had roll'd
With visible motion her diurnal round
Behind me did they stretch in solemn train
Feebler and feebler, and I stood and watched
Till all was tranquil as a summer sea

| | | |
|---|---|---|
| 165 | | *Tinkled like iron while the distant hills* |
| 166 | | *Into the tumult sent an alien sound* |
| 167 | | *Of melancholy not unnoticed while the stars,* |
| 168 | | *Eastward, were sparkling clear, and in the west* |
| 169 | | *The orange sky of evening died away.* |
| 170 | | *—Not seldom from the uproar I retired* |
| 171 | | *Into a silent bay, or sportively* |
| 172 | | *Glanced side-way leaving the tumultuous throng* |
| 173 | | *To cut across the shadow of a star* |
| 174 | | *That gleamed upon the ice : and oftentimes* |
| 175 | | *When we had given our bodies to the wind* |
| 176 | | *And all the shadowy banks on either side* |
| 177 | | *Came sweeping through the darkness spinning still* |
| 178 | | *The rapid line of motion then at once* |
| 179 | | *Have I, reclining back upon my heels,* |
| 180 | | *Stopped short, yet still the solitary cliffs* |
| 181 | | *Wheeled by me, even as if the earth had roll'd* |
| 182 | | *With visible motion her diurnal round* |
| 183 | | *Behind me did they stretch in solemn train* |
| 184 | [?180] | *Feebler and feebler, and I stood and watched* |
| 185 | | *Till all was tranquil as a summer sea.* |

*Ye presences that are among the clouds* (marginal, vertical)

                   a ⎱
     Ye winds ye voices that we⎰re in the clouds
186     ~~Ye Powers of earth! ye Genii of the springs!~~
              & ye Souls
     Ye visions of the mountains Virtues, powers
187     ~~And ye that have your voices in the clouds~~
       ~~And influences never may I think~~
188     ~~And ye that are Familiars of the lakes and~~
       of the
[189]    ~~And ₍standing pools, ah not for trivial ends~~
       the
      ~~of [?mountain] pools~~
     ~~Did ye with such assiduous love pursue~~
      [?moun]

---

165  iron,
167  melancholy,
169  *no punct*
170  *no dash*
172  side-way] sideway
179  I,] I
181  roll'd] rolled
182  round.
185  summer] summer's
188  lakes and] lakes
188/190  *for these three lines U has* And of the standing pools I may not think

---

184  If the penciled line count is 180, WW (or DW) would have to have been counting on 4ᵛ, where four lines are deleted, not on 5ᵛ which replaced it.

188/190  On this, her second, time through this passage, DW left out two of the lines that had stood in her first version, on 4ᵛ (this version had included the lines inscribed in the margin of MS. 16—see the Introduction, pp. 22–23). At the bottom of the page, the distinctive diagonal deletion strokes, in brown ink, appear occasionally in U (they can be seen on U 80ʳ), and the lines they delete here are not in U. Line 189 is also deleted in pencil.

Of lonely places ~~never may ye think~~ [struck]
~~Knew you [illegible]~~ ~~you think~~
A vulgar hope was yours when ye employed
Such ministry, when ye through many a year
Thus by the agency of boyish sports
On caves and trees, upon the woods and hills,
Impressed upon all forms the characters
Of danger or desire, and thus did make
The surface of the universal earth
With meanings of delight of hope and fear
Work like a sea.

                    Not uselessly employed
I might pursue this theme through every change
Of exercise and sport to which the year
Did summon us in its delightful round
We were a noisy crew; the sun in heaven
Beheld not vales more beautiful than ours
Nor saw a race in happiness and joy
More worthy of the fields where they were sown
I would record with no reluctant voice
Our home amusements by the warm peat fire
At evening, when with pencil and with slate
In square divisions parcelled out, and all
With crosses and with cyphers scribbled o'er
We schemed & puzzled, heads opposed to heads
In strife too humble to be named in verse
Around the naked table, snow-white deal
Cherry or maple [illegible]
[illegible] to the combat Loo or Whist led on

Of lonely places never may I think
[189]    ~~Pursue your favorite and your joy. I may not think~~
190    *A vulgar hope was yours when ye employed*
191    *Such ministry, when ye through many a year*
192    *Thus by the agency of boyish sports*
193    *On caves and trees, upon the woods and hills,*
194    *Impressed upon all forms the characters*
195    *Of danger or desire, and thus did make*
196    *The surface of the universal earth*
197    *With meanings of delight, of hope and fear*
                    Following this theme will[?]
198    *Work like a sea.*          [?allow]
                    *Not uselessly employed*
199    *I might pursue this theme through every change*
200    *Of exercise and sport to which the year*
201    *Did summon us in its delightful round*
202    *—We were a noisy crew; the sun in heaven*
203    *Beheld not vales more beautiful than ours*
204    *Nor saw a race in happiness and joy*
205    *More worthy of the fields where they were sown*
206    *I would record with no reluctant voice*
207    *Our home amusements by the warm peat fire*
208    *At evening, when with pencil,* {*and with slate*
209    *In square divisions parcelled out, and all*
210    *With crosses and with cyphers scribbled o'er*
211    We schemed & puzzled } head *opposed to* head
212    *In strife too humble to be named in verse*
213    *Or* round *the naked* table } *snow* {white deal
214    *Cherry or maple* sate *in close* array
215    *And to the combat L û or Whist led on*

Right margin (vertical text):
*Eager & never weary we pursued*
*Our simple pastimes & c.*

*of lonely places &*      *I*
                          { ye visions of the mountains &
                          { ye souls
*ye visions of the mountains &*

---

193    hills,] hills
198    *no punct*
201    us] *as corrected to* us
202    *indented as para*
206    *indented as para*
         {peat fire
207    {[?fire ?side]
208    pencil,] pencil
209    *no punct*
211    *no erasure*
212    verse.
213    snow-white      *no erasure*
214    *no erasure*
215    Lû] Lu

---

The first of the marginal revisions must have been meant for ll. 202 or 205, where there are marks in the margin, but it was never used; the second is connected with revision at the foot of 6ʳ.

A thick ribbed army, not as in the world
Discarded and ungratefully thrown by
Even for the very service they had wrought
But husbanded through many a long campaign
Oh with what echoes on the board they fell
Ironic diamonds, ~~hearts of sable~~
Queens gleaming through their splendour's last decay
Knaves wrapt in one assimilating gloom
And Kings indignant at the ~~slow~~
By royal visages. Meanwhile abroad
The heavy rain was falling or the frost
Raged bitterly, with keen and silent tooth
And interrupting the impassioned game
~~From~~ the neighbouring lake the splitting ice
While it sank down towards the water sent
Among the meadows and the hills its long
And ~~solemn~~ yellings like the noise of wolves
~~on~~ the Bothnic main. 570
Nor with less willing heart would I rehearse
The woods of autumn and their hazel bowers
With milk-white clusters hung; the rod and line
True symbol of the foolishness of hope,
Which with its strong enchantment led us on
By rocks, and pools where never summer star
Impressed its shadow, to forlorn cascades
Among the windings of the mountain-brooks
The kite, in sultry calms from some high hill
Sent up, ascending thence till it was lost
Among the fleecy clouds; in gusty days
Launched from the grounds, and suddenly

                 [ ? ? ? ? ] [?delights]

216   *A thick-ribb'd army, not as in the world*
217   *Discarded and ungratefully thrown by*
218   *Even for the very service they had wrought*
219   *But husbanded through many a long campaign*
220   *Oh with what echoes on the board they fell*
                black funereal hearts
221   *Ironic diamonds, ~~hearts of sable hue~~*
222   *Queens gleaming through their splendour's last decay*
223   *Knaves wrapt in one assimilating gloom*
                     wrongs sustained
224   *And Kings indignant at the ~~shame incurr'd~~*
225   *By royal visages. Meanwhile abroad*
226   *The heavy rain was falling or the frost*
227   *Raged bitterly with keen and silent tooth*
228   *And interrupting the impassioned game*
           From Esthwaites
229   *~~Oft from the~~ neighbouring lake the splitting ice*
230   *While it sank down towards the water sent*
231   *Among the meadows and the hills its long*
            dismal         like the noise of wolves
232   *And ~~frequent~~ yellings ~~imitative some~~*
            When they are howling round
233   *~~Of wolves that howl along~~ the Bothnic main.*
         [?When] a [ ? ? ]
234   *Nor with less willing heart would I rehearse*
                  hazel
235   *The woods of autumn and their ~~hidden~~ bowers*
236   *With milk-white clusters hung ; the rod and* line,

237   *True symbol of the foolishness of hope* },
                           us
238   *Which with its strong enchantment led ~~me~~ on*

239   *By rocks* }, *and pools where never summer-star*
240   *Impressed its shadow, to forlorn cascades*
241   *Among the windings of the mountain-brooks*
242   *The kite, in sultry calms from some high hill*
243   *Sent up, ascending thence till it was lost*
244   *Among the fleecy clouds ; in gusty days*
245   *Launched from the l[ ]r grounds, and suddenly*

---

216   thick ribbed
223   assimulating
226   falling,
228   *second* r *left out of* interrupting *then inserted*
234   *indented as para*
236   milk white     line] line,
         { c
243   as { sending
245   lower grounds, *inserted with caret*

---

245   The middle letters of "lower" are worn away.

Dash'd headlong— and rejected by the storm          529
All these and ~~more~~ more with rival claims deman
Grateful acknowledement. It were a song
Venial, and such as if I rightly judge
I might protract unblamed but I perceive
That much is overlooked, and we should ill
Attain our object if from delicate fears
Of breaking in upon the unity
Of this my argument I should omit
To speak of such effects as cannot here
Be regularly classed, yet tend no less
To the same point, the growth of mental power
And love of nature's works.          Ere I had seen
Eight summers (and 'twas in the very week
When I was first transplanted to thy vale
Beloved Hawkshead! when thy paths, thy shores
And brooks were like a dream of novelty
To my half infant mind) I chanced to cross
One of those open fields which (shaped like ears)
Make green peninsulas on Esthwaite's lake
Twilight was coming on, yet through the gloom
I saw distinctly on the opposite shore
Beneath a tree and close by the lake side
A heap of garments as if left by one
Who there was bathing: half an hour I watched
And no one owned them: meanwhile the calm lake
Grew dark with all the shadows on its breast
And now and then a leaping fish disturb'd
The breathless stillness. The succeeding day
There came a company, & in their boat
Sounded with iron hooks and with long poles

246     *Dash'd headlong—and rejected by the storm*
                                       demand

247     *All these and ~~many~~ more with rival claims*

       ⌠Grateful         ⌡
248     ⌡*Demand acknowledement* ⌠ *It were a song*

249     *Venial, and such as if I rightly judge*

250     *I might protract unblamed but I perceive*

251     *That much is overlooked, and we should ill*

252     *Attain our object if from delicate fears*

253     *Of breaking in upon the unity*

254     *Of this my argument I should omit*

255     *To speak of such effects as cannot here*

256     *Be regularly classed, yet tend no less*

257     *To the same point, the growth of mental power*

                         ⌠N
258     *And love of* ⌡*nature's works.*
                                    *Ere I had seen*

259     *Eight summers (and 'twas in the very week*

260     *When I was first transplanted to thy vale*

261     *Beloved Hawkshead! when thy paths, thy shores*

262     *And brooks were like a dream of novelty*

                  *l*⌠
263     *To my haf*⌡*f infant mind) I chanced to cross*

264     *One of those open fields which,*⌡ *shaped like ears)*

265     *Make green peninsulas on Esthwaite's lake*

266     *Twilight was coming on, yet through the gloom*

267     *I saw distinctly on the opposite shore*

268     *Beneath a tree and close by the lake side*

269     *A heap of garments as if left by one*

270     *Who there was bathing: half an hour I watched*

271     *And no one owned them: meanwhile the cal m lake*

272     *Grew dark with all the shadows on its breast*

273     *And now and then a leaping fish disturb'd*

274     *The breathless stillness. The succeeding day*

275     *There came a company, & in their boat*

276     *Sounded with iron hooks and with long poles*

---

246   storm.
247   All these and more with rival claims demand
248   Acknowledgement *erased and overwritten* Grateful Acknowledgement *with* A *altered to* a
250   unblamed;
256   *semicolon deleted to comma*
258   Nature's      *no period*      'Ere
263   half
264   *no comma, no closing paren*
269   garments,
271   calm] still
273   then *inserted with caret*      disturbed
275   &] and

---

247–248    For comment on the revision, see the Introduction, p. 23.
264    The extra parenthesis is a mistake.
268    The "a" may first, mistakenly, have been written "at."
271    It looks as though WW converted "still" to "calm" by erasing all but the first "l" then writing "ca" ahead of it and "m" after it.

At length the dead man mid that beauteous scene
Of trees and hills and water bolt upright
Rose with his ghastly face. I might advert
To numerous accidents in flood, or field
Quarry or moor, or 'mid the winter snows
Distresses and disasters, tragic facts
Of rural history that impressed my mind
With images to which in following years
Far other feelings were attached; with forms
That yet exist with independent life
And, like their archetypes, know no decay.

There are in our existence spots of time
Which with distinct pre-eminence retain
A fructifying virtue, whence, depressed
By trivial occupations and the round
Of ordinary intercourse, our minds,
(~~that are the soul~~)
(~~Especially the imaginative power~~)
Are nourished, and invisibly repaired.
Such moments chiefly seem to have their date
In our first childhood. I remember well
(~~That once~~ ~~while yet~~ ~~I was a little child~~)
While I was yet an urchin, one who scarce
Could hold a bridle, with ambitious hopes
I mounted, and we rode towards the hills;
We were a pair of horsemen; honest James
Was with me, my encourager and guide.
We had not travelled long ere some mischance
Disjoined me from my comrade and through fear
Dismounting, down the rough and stony moor

277 *At length the dead man 'mid that beauteous scene*
278 *Of trees, and hills, and water bolt upright*
279 *Rose with his ghastly face. I might advert*
280 *To numerous accidents in flood, or field*
281 *Quarry or moor, or 'mid the winter snows*

282 *Distresses and disasters* ⎰ *tragic facts*
283 *Of rural history that impressed my mind*
284 *With images, to which in following years*
285 *Far other feelings were attached; with forms*
286 *That yet exist with independent life*
287 *And, like their archetypes, know no decay.*
288 *There are in our existence spots of time*
289 *Which with distinct pre-eminence retain*
290 280 *A fructifying virtue, whence, depressed*
291 *By trivial occupations and the round*
292 *Of ordinary intercourse, our minds,*
        *But more than all*
293 *(Especially the imaginative power)*
294 *Are nourished, and invisibly repaired.*
295 *Such moments chiefly seem to have their date*
296 In our first childhood. I remember well
297 (Tis of an early season that I speak
298 The twilight of rememberable life,)
299 While I was yet an urchin, one who scarce
300 *Could hold a bridle, with ambitious hopes*
301 *I mounted, and we rode towards the hills;*

302 *We were a pair of horsemen* ⎰ *honest James*
303 *Was with me, my encourager and guide.*
304 *We had not travelled long ere some mischance*
305 *Disjoined me from my comrade and through fear*
306 *Dismounting, down the rough and stony moor*

---

278 hills,] hills
                    r⎱
280 *no punct*   of⎰
281 *no apostrophe*
282 disasters, *comma perhaps inserted later, as in V*
287 archetypes,] archetypes     *no period*
289 preeminence
291 occupations,

292 intercource,
294 *no comma*
296 well,
297–298 *not in U*
299 While I was yet] While yet
                            ⎱H
302 horsemen honest] horsemen: ⎰honest
305 comrade,

---

290 The penciled line count here falls ten behind. Perhaps the likeliest of the various possible explanations is that WW or DW made an error while counting in twenties.
293 The revision is in pencil.
297–298 After the line counts were entered WW erased ll. 296 and 299 and recopied them, inserting in parentheses the two new lines, which were later in turn deleted, as the photograph shows, both in pen and in pencil. There survive fragments of illegible pencil draft, probably for the new lines, ll. 293/294 and 294/295.

XI.
288-352

tied my horse and, stumbling on, at length
Came to a bottom where in former times
A ~~murderer~~ who had hung ~~the murderer of his wife, was hung~~
was hung
In irons, mouldered was the gibbet mast
The bones were gone, the iron and the wood
Only a long green ridge of turf remained
Whose shape was like a grave. I left the spot,
And, reascending the bare slope, I saw
A naked pool that lay beneath the hills,
The beacon on the summit, and more near
A girl who bore a pitcher on her head
And seemed with difficult steps to force her way
Against the blowing wind. It was in truth
An ordinary sight but I should need
Colours and words that are unknown to man
To paint the visionary dreariness
Which, while I looked all round for my lost guide,
Did at that time, invest the naked pool
The beacon on the lonely eminence
The woman and her garments vexed and tossed
By the strong wind. Nor less I recollect
(Long after, ~~though my childhood had not ceased~~)
Another scene which left a hundred power
Implanted in my mind.
                One Christmas time
The day before the holidays began
Feverish, and tired and restless, I went forth
Into the fields, impatient for the sight
Of those three horses which should bear us home
My Brothers and myself. There was a crag
An eminence which from the meeting point.

307 *I led my horse and, stumbling on, at leng⌈th*
308 *Came to a bottom where in former times*
       a murderer
309 *~~A man, the murderer of his wife, was hung~~*
310 *In irons, mouldered was the gibbet mast*
311 *The bones were gone, the iron and the wood*
312 *Only a long green ridge of turf remained*
313 *Whose shape was like a grave. I left the spot,*
314 *And, reascending the bare slope, I saw*
315 *A naked pool that lay beneath the hills,*
316 *The beacon on the summit, and more near*
317 *A girl who bore a pitcher on her head*

318 *And seemed with difficult steps to forc[?]⌉ her way*
319 *Against the blowing wind. It was in truth*
320 *An ordinary sight but I should need*
320 *Colours and words that are unknown to man*
322 *To paint the visionary dreariness*
323 *Which, while I looked all round for my lost guide,*
324 *Did, at that time, invest the naked pool*
325 *The beacon on the lonely eminence*
326 *The woman and her garments vexed and tossed*
327 *By the strong wind. Nor less I recollect*
328 *~~(Long after, though my childhood had not ceased)~~*
329 *Another scene which left a kindred power*
330 *Implanted in my mind.*
                  *One Christmas time*
331 *The day before the holidays began*
332 *Feverish, and tired and restless, I went forth*
333 *Into the fields, impatient for the sight*
334 *Of those three horses which should bear us home*
335 *My Brothers and myself. There was a crag*
336 *An eminence which from the meeting point*

---

307  horse,    on, *written over comma*    length
314  And,] And    rea⌈sscending
318  force
322  dreary⌈ness
323  guide,] guide
324  *no punct*
330  *no punct*

---

The penciled X appears to mark the miswriting of "force." On a stub conjugate with the leaf now numbered 8 appears a faintly penciled line of verse in DW's hand; it begins "~~Such~~ This Intercourse"; the rest is illegible. See l. 149 on 5ʳ.

Of two highways ascending overlooked
At least a long halfmile of those two roads,
By each of which the expected steeds might come,
The choice uncertain. Thither I repaired
Up to the highest summit; 'twas a day
Stormy, and rough, and wild, and on the grass
I sate, halfsheltered by a naked wall
Upon my right hand was a single sheep
A whistling hawthorn on my left, and there
Those two companions at my side I watched
With eyes intensely straining as the mist
Gave intermitting prospects of the wood
And plain beneath. Ere I to school returned
That dreary time, ere I had been ten days
A dweller in my Father's house, he died
And I and my two Brothers, orphans then,
Followed his body to the grave. The event
With all the sorrow which it brought appeared
A chastisement, and when I called to mind
That day so lately passed when from the crag
I looked in such anxiety of hope
With trite reflections of morality
Yet with the deepest passion I bowed low
To God, who thus corrected my desires
And afterwards the wind, and sleety rain
And all the business of the elements
The single sheep, and the one blasted tree

337    *Of two highways ascending overlooked*

338    *At least a long half-mile of those two roads*

339    *By each of which the expected steeds might come*

340    *The choice uncertain⎰ Thither I repaired*
341    *Up to the highest summit ; 'twas a day*
342    *Stormy, and rough, and wild, and on the grass*
343    *I sate, half-sheltered by a naked wall*
344    *Upon my right hand was a single sheep*
345    *A whistling hawthorn on my left, and there*
346    *Those two companions at my side I watched*
347    *With eyes intensely straining as the mist*
348    *Gave intermitting prospects of the wood*
349    *And plain beneath. Ere I to school returned*
350    *That dreary time, ere I had been ten days*
351    *A dweller in my Father's house, he died,*

352 ⎰3 ⎱240 *And I and my two Bro⎰t⎱fhers, orphans then,*
353    *Followed his body to the grave. The event*
354    *With all the sorrow which it brought appeared*
355    *A* chastisement, and when *I called to mind*
356    *That day so lately passed when from the crag*
357    *I looked in such anxiety of hope*
358    *With trite reflections of morality*
359    *Yet with the deepest passion I bowed low*
360    *To God, who thus corrected my desires*
361    *And afterwards the wind, and sleety rain*
362    *And all the business of the elements*
363    *The single sheep, and the one blasted tree*

---

338    roads,
339    come,
340    uncertain.
341    summit:
345    whiste⎰t⎱ling
349    'Ere
350    'ere
352    Brothers,
355    *no erasure*
358    reflexions
361    *no punct*

And the bleak music of that old stone wall
The noise of wood and water and the mist
Which on the line of each of those two roads
Advanced in such indisputable shapes
All these were spectacles and sounds to which
I often would repair, and thence would drink
As at a fountain, and I do not doubt
That in this later time when storm and rain
Beat on my roof at midnight or by day
When I am in the woods, unknown to me
The workings of my spirit thence are brought.

                    Nor scrupulous to trace

                                                    187.

How Nature by collateral interest
And by extrinsic passion peopled first
My mind with forms or beautiful or grand
And made me love them may I well forget
How other pleasures have been mine, and joys
Of subtler origin how I have felt
Not seldom, even in that tempestuous time
Those hallowed and pure motions of the sense
Which seem in their simplicity to own
An intellectual charm, that calm delight
Which, if I err not, surely must belong
To those first-born affinities that fit
Our new existence to existing things
And in our dawn of being constitute
The bond of union betwixt life and joy

364  *And the bleak music of that old stone wall*
365  *The noise of wood and water and the mist*
      *That*
366  *~~Which~~ on the line of each of those two roads*
367  *Advanced in such indisputable shapes*
368  *All these were spectacles and sounds to which*
      { *I often would*
369  { *To which repair, and thence would drink*
370  *As at a fountain, and I do not doubt*
371  *That in this later time when storm and rain*
372  *Beat on my roof at midnight or by day*
373  *When I am in the woods, unknown to me*
374  *The workings of my spirit thence are brought.*

[375]             *Nor sedulous to trace*
      {N
376  *How* {*nature by collateral interest*
377  *And by extrinsic passion peopled first*
378  *My mind with forms, or beautiful or grand*
379  *And made me love them may I well forget*
380  *How other pleasures have been mine, and joys*
381  *Of subtler origin how I have felt*
382  *Not seldom, even in that tempestuous time*
383  *Those hallowed and pure motions of the sense*
384  *Which seem in their simplicity to own*
385  *An intellectual charm, that calm delight*
386  *Which, if I err not, surely must belong*
387  *To those first-born affinities that fit*
388  *Our new existence to existing things*
389  *And in our dawn of being constitute*
390  *The bond of union betwixt life and joy*

---

366  Which] That
367  shape
369  *first read* I often would repair, and drink as at a fountain *then last five words overwritten* thence would drink
372  midnight, or by
374  spirit *possibly first written* spirits *with final s erased*   *no punct*
[375]  *gap of one or two lines*
376  nature    *second l of* collateral *inserted*
      {tl
381  sub{lter
387  first born

---

366  Deletion and revision in pencil.
369  As can be seen, DW used some letters from the original reading in making her correction.
372  A large penciled X marks the word to be altered.
375  The pencil addition appears to be in Coleridge's hand.

586
614

Yes I remember when the changeful earth
And twice five seasons on my mind had stamped
The faces of the moving year, even then,
A Child, I held unconscious intercourse
With the eternal Beauty drinking in
A pure organic pleasure from the lines
Of curling mist or from the level plain
Of waters coloured by the steady clouds.
        The sands of Westmoreland, the creeks and bays
Of Cumbria's rocky limits, they can tell
How when the sea threw off his evening shade
And to the Shepherds hut beneath the crags
Did send sweet notice of the rising moon
How I have stood to images like these
A stranger, ~~xxxx~~ linking with the spectacle
No body of associated forms
And bringing with me no peculiar sense
Of quietness or peace, yet I have stood
Even while my eye has moved o'er three long leagues
Of shining water, gathering, as it seemed
Through the wide surface of that field of light
New pleasure, like a bee among the flowers
            Thus often in those fits of vulgar joy
Which through all seasons on a childs pursuits
Are prompt attendants mid that giddy bliss
Which like a tempest works along the blood
And is forgotten, even then I felt
Gleams like the flashing of a shield the earth

391             *Yes, I remember when the changeful earth*
392 380  *And twice five seasons on my mind had stamped*
393             *The faces of the moving year, even then,*
394             *A Child, I held unconscious intercourse*
395             *With the eternal Beauty drinking in*
396             *A pure organic pleasure from the lines*
397             *Of curling mist or from the level plain*
398             *Of waters coloured by the steady clouds.*
399             *The sands of Westmoreland, the creeks and bays*
400             *Of Cumbria's rocky limits, they can tell*
401             *How when the sea threw off his evening shade*
402             *And to the Shepherds hut beneath the crags*
403             *Did send sweet notice of the rising moon*
404             *How I have stood to images like these*
405             *A stranger, ~~and~~ linking with the spectacle*
406             *No body of associated forms*
407             *And bringing with me no peculiar sense*
408             *Of quietness or peace, yet I have stood*
409             *Even while my eye has moved o'er three long legu[ ]*
410             *Of shining water, gathering, as it seemed*
411             *Through the wide surface of that field of light*
412 400  *New pleasure, like a bee among the flowers*
413                 *Thus often in those fits of vulgar joy*
414             *Which through all seasons on a child's pursuits*
415             *Are prompt attendants 'mid that giddy bliss*
416             *Which like a tempest works along the blood*
417             *And is forgotten, even then I felt*
418             *Gleams like the flashing of a shield, the earth*

---

391  *no punct*
399  Westmorland,
402  Shepherd's
405  stranger, linking      spectacle *first four letters written over erasure*
409  leagues
412  flowers.

---

409  The ending of "leagues" is worn away.

I 615-642

and common face of nature spake to me
Remembrable things: sometimes 'tis true
By quaint associations yet not vain
Nor profitless if haply they impressed
Collateral objects and appearances
Albeit lifeless then, and doomed to sleep
Until maturer seasons called them forth
To impregnate and to elevate the mind.
— And if the vulgar joy by its own weight
Wearied itself out of the memory
The scenes which were a witness of that joy
Remained, in their substantial lineaments
Depicted on the brain and to the eye
Were visible, a daily sight: and thus
By the impressive agency of fear.
By pleasure and repeated happiness
So frequently repeated, and by force
Of obscure feelings representative
Of joys that were forgotten these same scenes
So beauteous and majestic in themselves
Though yet the day was distant did at length
Become habitually dear, and all
Their hues and forms were by invisible links
Allied to the affections.
                    I began
My story early, feeling, as I fear,
The weakness of a human love, for days

419   *And common face of nature spake to me*
420   *Rememberable things: sometimes 'tis true*
421   *By quaint associations yet not vain*
422   *Nor profitless if haply they impressed*
423   *Collateral objects and appearances*
424   *Albeit lifeless then, and doomed to sleep*
425   *Until maturer seasons called them forth*
426   *To impregnate and to elevate the mind.*
427   *——And if the vulgar joy by its own weight*
428   *Wearied itself out of the memory*
429   *The scenes which were a witness of that joy*
430   *Remained, in their substantial lineaments*
431   *Depicted on the brain and to the eye*
432   *Were visible, a daily sight: and thus*
433   *By the impressive agency of fear*
434   *By pleasure and repeated happiness*
435   *So frequently repeated, and by force*
436   *Of obscure feelings representative*
437   *Of joys that were forgotten these same scenes*
438   *So beauteous and majestic in themselves*
439   *Though yet the day was distant did at length*
440   *Become habitually dear, and all*
441   *Their hues and forms were by invisible links*
442   *Allied to the affections.*
                              *I began*
443   *My story early, feeling, as I fear,*
444   *The weakness of a human love, for days*

---

426   *no punct*
431   were visible *erased at end of line*
432   *comma after* sight *apparently altered to colon*
437   forgotten,
442   *no punct*
444   human *last two letters written over erasure*

Disowned by memory, ere the birth of Spring
Planting my snowdrops among winter snows.
Nor will it seem to thee, my Friend so prompt
In sympathy that I have lengthened out
With fond and feeble tongue a tedious tale.
Meanwhile my hope has been that I might fetch
Reproaches from my former years, whose power
May spur me on, in manhood now mature,
To honourable toil. Yet, should it be
That this is but an impotent desire
That I by such inquiry am not taught
To understand myself, nor thou to know
With better knowledge how the heart was fram
Of him thou lovest need I dread from thee
Harsh judgements if I am so loth to quit
Those recollected hours that have the charm
Of visionary things, and lovely forms
And sweet sensations that throw back our life
And make our infancy a visible scene
On which the sun is shining. — — — —

lovely cottage in which we dwell
...itation of your own was yours
...city a ... for love
I forget you being as ye were
beautiful among the ... fields
such ye ... two or ... forget
... homely ...
...out your ...

445              Disowned by memory, ere the birth of spring
446              Planting my snowdrops among winter snows.
447              Nor will it seem to thee, my Friend so prompt
448              In sympathy that I have lengthened out
449              With fond and feeble tongue a tedious tale.
450              Meanwhile my hope has been that I might fetch
451              Reproaches from my former years, whose power
452  440         May spur me on, in manhood now mature,
453              To honourable toil. Yet, should it be
454              That this is but an impotent desire
455              That I by such inquiry am not taught
456              To understand myself, nor thou to know
457              With better knowledge how the heart was fram[  ]
458              Of him thou lovest need I dread from thee
459              Harsh judgments if I am so loth to quit
460              Those recollected hours that have the charm
461              Of visionary things, and lovely forms
462              And sweet sensations that throw back our life
463              And make our infancy a visible scene

464              On which the sun is shining ⎱ ———————  452

*(left margin, vertical:)*
pleasures
Your own dear pastimes & your own delights
The Kite[?s] sent up among the driving clouds
And breasting the strong wind [?the ?wind ? ] —

                 Ye lowly cottages in which we dwelt
                 A ministration of your own was yours
                 A sanctity a presence & a love
                 Can I forget you being as ye were
                 So beautiful among the pleasant fields
                 In which ye stood or can I here forget
                 The plain & homely countenance with wh[  ]
                 Ye dealt out your plain comforts yet
                                          had ye

---

445   'ere
446   snow-drops
453   honorable
455   enquiry
457   framed
             ⎧st
458   love⎨d[?],
459   judgements
*MS. U concludes with* End of the First Part

---

457   The last two letters of "framed" are worn away, as are the last letters of "which," at the bottom of the page.

The passages in the margin and at the foot of the page are late additions to lines on 7$^r$ and 7$^v$, toward 1805, I, 520ff.

a common tale of woe

nor am I not resigned
That I have need of candour, and of mild
Indulgence as a man who treads in fear
a difficult road

to thee
I science appears but what in truth she is
Not as our glory and our absolute boast
But as a succedaneum & a prop
to our infirmity          thou art so slaves

It was a motley host of which no few
Had changed their parts sometimes, plebeian cares,
Which gate beyond the promise of their birth
that honoured calling them to represent
the persons of departed potentates.

the black funereal heads
heads of the    funereal heads

                    nor am I not informed
That I have need of candour, and of mild
Indulgence as a man who treads in fear
A difficult road

        ⌠ence                    to thee
Sci⌡[ ? ] appears but what in truth she is
Not as our glory and our absolute boast
But as a succedaneum & a prop
Of our infirmity
                    Thou art no slave

It was a motley host of which no few
                            , ⎫
Had changed their functions ⎰some, plebeian cards,
⌠W
⌡which fate beyond the promise of their birth
        glorified & called
Had honoured calling them to represent
The persons of departed potentates.

                        th
                    [?Or] black funereal hearts
                    heart of dull funereal hue

---

   The first passage, not used, may have been meant for ll. 316–318 of Part Two (on 18ʳ); the second expands ll. 249–250 (on 16ᵛ). The third passage was drafted for insertion following l. 219 of Part One; the fourth revises l. 221 (on 7ʳ).

Second Part

Thus far my friend, have we retraced the way
Through which I travelled when I first began
To love the woods and fields; the passion yet
Was in its birth, sustained as might befit
By nourishment that came unsought, for still
From week to week, from month to month we lived
A round of tumult. ~~this~~ ~~~~
~~~~
~~~~ duly were our games
Prolong'd in summer till the day light fail'd
No chair remain'd before the door, the benches
and threshold steps were empty, fast asleep
The labourer and the old man who had sate
A later lingerer, yet the revelry
Continued and the loud uproar at last
When all the ground was dark and the huge clouds
Were edged with twinkling stars to bed we went
With weary joints and with a beating mind --
Ah! is there one who ever has been young
And needs a monetary voice to tame
The pride of virtue and of intellect
And is there one the wisest and the best
Of all mankind who does not sometimes wish
For things which cannot be, who would not give
If so he might, to duty and to truth
The eagerness of infantine desire?
A tranquillizing spirit presses now
On my corporeal frame, so wide appears
The vacancy between me and those days

*Second Part*

1    *Thus far my Friend, have we retraced the way*
2    *Through which I travelled when I first began*
3    *To love the woods and fields : the passion yet*
4    *Was in its birth, sustain'd as might befal*
5    *By nourishment that came unsought for still*
6    *From week to week, from month to month we lived*
[7]   *A round of tumult. 'Twas a rustic spot*
      *The town in which we dwelt a small domain*
[7]   *And there each evening duly were our games*
8    *Prolong'd in summer till the day-light fail'd*
9    *No chair remain'd before the doors, the bench*
10   *And threshold steps were empty, fast asleep*
11   *The labourer and the old man who had sate*
12   *A later lingerer yet the revelry*
13   *Continued and the loud uproar : at last*
                                  *{and the*
14   *When all the ground was dark, {to bed huge clouds*
15   *Were edged with twinkling stars to bed we went*
16   *With weary joints and with a beating mind.*
17   *Ah! is there one who ever has been young*
18   *And needs a monitory voice to tame*
19   *The pride of virtue and of intellect*
20   *And is there one the wisest and the best*
21   *Of all mankind who does not sometimes wish*
22   *For things which cannot be, who would not give,*
23   *If so he might, to duty and to truth,*
24   *The eagerness of infantine desire?*
25   *A tranquillizing spirit presses now*
26   *On my corporeal frame, so wide appears*
27   *The vacancy between me and those days*

---

6/8   The deletion marks may be compared to those visible on 6ʳ and 6ᵛ of MS. V. The lines deleted here were made up from drafts at the end of RV; they are included in the V line count, which shows up at l. 78, but must have been deleted from V at the same time.

Which yet have such self-presence in my heart
That sometimes when I think of them I seem
Two consciousnesses, conscious of myself
And of some other being. A grey stone
Of native rock, left midway in the square
Of our small market village, was the home
And centre of these joys, and when returned
After long absence, thither I repaired
I found ~~that it was split and~~ gone to build
A ~~smart~~ ~~of~~ ~~the~~ ~~were~~ ~~that~~ ~~had~~ ~~disregarded~~
With wash and rough-cast ~~elbowing the grounds~~
Which had been ours. But let the fiddle scream
And be ye happy! yet I know, my Friends,
That more than one of you will think with me
Of those soft starry nights and that old dame
From whom the stone was named who there had sate
And watch'd her table with its huckster's wares
Assiduous, for the length of sixty years.

——— We ran a boisterous race, the year span round
With giddy motion. But the time approach'd
That brought with it a regular desire
For calmer pleasures when the beauteous scenes
Of nature were collaterally attach'd
To every scheme of holiday delight
And every boyish sport less grateful else
And languidly pursued

                    When summer came
It was the pastime of our afternoons
To beat along the plain of Windermere
With rivals and the selected bower

28    *Which yet have such self-presence in my heart*
29    *That sometimes when I think of them I seem*
                    ⎰ sn
30    *Two consciou⎱[ ? ]esses, conscious of myself*
31    *And of some other being. A grey stone*
32    *Of native rock, left midway in the square*
33    *Of our small market-village, was the home*
34    *And centre of these joys, and when, returned*
35    *After long absence, thither I repaired*
36    *I found that it was split and gone to build*
37    *A smart assembly-room that perk'd and flared*
38    *With wash and rough-cast elbowing the ground*
39    *Which had been ours. But let the fiddle scream*
40    *And be ye happy! yet I know, my Friends,*
41    *That more than one of you will think with me*
                                      ⎰ l
42    *Of those soft starry nights and that o⎱fd dame*
43    *From whom the stone was named, who there had sate*
44    *And watch'd her table with its huckster's wares*
45    *Assiduous, for the length of sixty years.*
46    *——We ran a boisterous race, the year span round*
47    *With giddy motion. But the time approach'd*
48    *That brought with it a regular desire*
49    *For calmer pleasures when the beauteous scenes*
50    *Of nature were collaterally attach'd*
51    *To every scheme of holiday delight*
52    *And every boyish sport less grateful else*
53    *And languidly pursued*
                              *When summer came*
[54]  *It was the pastime of our afternoons*
[55]  *To beat along the plain of Windermere*
                 oars
[56]  *With rival�; and the selected bourn*

---

53   *MS. U resumes with the second half of the line*

When summer came                    l. 551

It was the pastime of our after-noons
To beat along the plain of Windermere
With rival oars; and the selected bourn
Was now an island musical with birds
That sang for ever; now a sister isle
Beneath the oak's umbrageous covert sown
With lilies of the valley like a field
And now a third Small island where remain'd
An old stone table and one moulder'd cave
A hermit's history. In such a race
So ended disappointment would be none
Uneasiness, or pain or jealousy
We rested in the shade all pleased alike
Conquer'd or conqueror. Thus our selfishness
Was mellow'd down, and thus the pride of strength
And the vain-glory of superior skill
Were interfus'd with objects which subdu'd
And temper'd them, & gradually produc'd
A quiet independence of the heart.
And to my Friend who knows me I may add
Unapprehensive of reproof, that hence
Ensued a diffidence and modesty,
And I was taught to feel, perhaps too much,
The self-sufficing power of solitude

        No delicate viands sapp'd our bodily strength
More than we wish'd we knew the blessing then

53              *When summer came*
54    *It was the pastime of our afternoons*
55    *To beat along the plain of Windermere*
56    *With rival oars; and the selected bourn*
57    *Was now an island musical with birds*
58    *That sang for ever; now a sister isle,*    60
59    *Beneath the oak's umbrageous covert sown*
60    *With lilies of the valley like a field*
61    *And now a third small island where remain'd*
62    *An old stone table and one* moulder*'d cave*
63    *A hermit's history. In such a race*
64    *So ended disappointment could be none*
65    *Uneasiness, or pain, or jealousy*
66    *We risted in the shade all pleased alike*
67    *Conquer'd or conqueror. Thus our selfishness*
68    *Was mellow'd down, and thus the pride of strength*
69    *And the vain-glory, of superior skill*
70    *Were interfus'd with objects which subdu'd*
71    *And temper'd them, & gradually produc'd*
72    *A quiet independence of the heart.*
73    *And to my Friend who knows me I may add*
74    *Unapprehensive of reproof, that hence*
75    Ensued a di*ff*idence and mo*desty,*
76    *And I was taught to feel, perhaps too much,*
77    *The self-sufficing power of solitude*
78  80    *No delicate viands sapp'd our bodily strength*
79    *More than we wish'd we knew the blessing then*

56  oars *inserted with caret*
58  *no comma*
59  the] an
62  moulder'd] fractured
63  Hermit's
66  rested
67  or conqueror.] and conquerer.
71  &] and
75  *no erasure, no punct*
76  much,] much
77  solitude.
79  wished

Of vigorous hunger, for our daily meals
Were frugal, Sabine fare! and then, exclude
A little weekly stipend, and we lived
Through three divisions of the quarter'd year
In pennyless poverty. But now to school
Return'd from the half yearly holidays
We came with purses more profusely fill'd
Allowance which abundantly suffic'd
To gratify the palate with repasts
More costly than the Dame of whom I spake
That ancient woman and her board supplied
Hence inroads into distant vales, and long
Excursions far away among the hills
Hence rustic dinners on the cool green ground
                    new
Or in the woods or by a river-side
Or fountain, festive banquets that provok'd
The languid action of a natural scene.
By pleasure of corporeal appetite.

        Nor is my aim neglected if I tell
How twice in the long length of those half years
We from our funds perhaps with bolder hand
Drew largely; anxious for one day at least
To feel the motion of the galloping steed
And with the good old Innkeeper in truth
I needs must say that sometimes we have used
Thy subterfuge, for the intended bound
If the day journey was too distant far

80    *Of vigorous hunger, for our daily meals*
81    *Were frugal, Sabine fare! and then exclude*

82    *A little weekly stipend* ⌐ *and we lived*
83    *Through three divisions of the quarter'd year*
          ⌠ *ss*        .⌐ ⌠ B
84    *In pennyle*⌊[ ? ] *s poverty!*⌡ ⌊*but now to school* [ ? ]
85    *Return'd from the half yearly holidays*
86    *We came with purses more profusely fill'd*
                                 ⌠ *ced*
87    *Allowance which abundantly suffi*⌊[ ? ]
88    *To gratify the palate with repasts*
          ⌠ M
89    ⌊[*Th*]*ore costly than the Dame of whom I spake*
90    *That ancient woman and her board supplied*
91    *Hence inroads into distant vales, and long*
92    *Excursions far away among the hills* /
93    *Hence rustic dinners on the cool green/ground*
                                    near
94    *Or in the woods or* ~~by~~ *a river-side*
                  by some shady fountain while soft airs
                                    soft airs
95    ~~Or fountain, festive\banquets that provoked~~
96    ~~The languid action of~~ *a natural scene*
97    *By pleasure of corporeal appetite.*
98                *Nor is my aim neglected if I tell*        100
99    *How twice in the long length of those half years*
100   *We from our funds perhaps with bolder hand*
101   *Drew largely, anxious for one day at least*
102   *To feel the motion of the galloping steed*
                      ⌠ n
103   *And with the good old In*⌊*kkeeper in truth*
104   *I needs must say that* sometimes we have *used*
105   *Sly subterfuge, for the intended bound*
106   *Of the day's journey was too distant far*

*(right margin, vertical:)*
⌠ by
⌊[?Or] [?shady] [?fount] ~~meanwhile~~ gentle airs, meanwhile
Were stirring ⌠on the branches
               ⌊in
[?amon] the leaves were [ ? ]

---

84    pennyless poverty. But
85    holidays *last five letters written over erasure*
86    fill'd,
         ⌠sufficed
87    ⌊fu[?]
89    More
90    woman,        supplied *last three letters written over erasure*
94    river's side *altered to* river-side
103   Innkeeper
104   sometimes we have] more than once we

---

The revision in the margin, developed in the margin of the facing recto (14ʳ), was to go in at the X, l. 93 or 94.

For any cautious man, a structure framed
Beyond its neighbourhood, the antique walls
Of a large Abbey with its fractured arch
Belfry, and images, and living trees
A holy scene! Along the smooth green turf
Our horses grazed: in more than inland peace
Left by the winds that overpass the vale
In that sequester'd ruin trees and towers
Both silent, and both motionless alike
Hear all day long the murmuring sea that beats
Incessantly upon a craggy shore.

    Our steeds remounted, and the summons given
With whip and spur we by the Chantry flew
In uncouth race; and left the trespass'd knights
And the stone Abbot, and that single wren
Which one day sang so sweetly in the nave
Of the old church that, though from recent showers
The earth was comfortless, and touch'd by faint
Internal breezes from the roofless walls
The shuddering ivy dripp'd large drops yet still
So sweetly 'mid the gloom the invisible bird
Sang to itself that there I could have made
My dwelling-place & lived for ever there
To hear such music. Through the walls we flew
And down the valley and, a circuit made
In wantonness of heart, through rough & smooth

| | |
|---|---|
| 107 | *For any cautious man, a Structure famed* |
| 108 | *Beyond its neighbourhood, the antique walls* |
| 109 | *Of a large Abbey with its fractured arch* |
| 110 | *Belfry, and images, and living trees* |
| 111 | *A holy scene! Along the smooth green turf* |
| 112 | *Our horses grazed: in more than inland peace* |
| 113 | *Left by the winds that overpass the vale* |
| 114 | *In that sequester'd ruin trees and towers* |
| 115 | *Both silent, and both motionless alike* |
| 116 | *Hear all day long the murmuring sea that beats* |
| 117 | *Incessantly upon a craggy shore.* |
| 118  120 | *Our steeds remounted, and the summons given* |
| 119 | *With whip and spur we by the Chantry flew* |
| 120 | *In uncouth race; and left the cross-legg'd Knight* |
| 121 | *And the stone Abbot, and that single wren* |
| 122 | *Which one day sang so sweetly in the nave* |
| 123 | *Of the old church that, though from recent showers* |
| 124 | *The earth was comfortless, and touch'd by faint* |
| 125 | *Internal breezes from the roofless walls* |
| 126 | *The shuddering ivy dripp'd large drops yet still* |
| 127 | *So sweetly mid the gloom the invisible bird* |
| 128 | ⎰th |
| 129 | *Sang to itself that ⎰here I could have made* |
| 130 | *My dwelling-place, & lived for ever there* |
| 131 | *To hear such music. Through the walls we flew* |
| 132 | *And down the valley and, a circuit made* |
| | *In wantonness of heart, through rough & smooth* |

*(left margin, vertical interlineations)*

Among the leaves were stirring & the sun
⎰on
Unfelt sh⎰in sweetly round us in our joy

festive banquets with soft airs
while
our joy

---

|  |  |  |
|---|---|---|
| 107 | fam⎰e⎰'d | |
| 110 | Belfrey, | |
| 114 | sequestered | ruin *written over erasure* |
| 117 | a] the | |
| 119 | by the Chantry] through the gateway | |
| 121 | abbot, | knight |
| 123 | church, | from *inserted with caret* |
| 126 | drops, | |
| 127 | 'mid | |
| 128 | itself, | there |
| 129 | *no hyphen* | &] and |
| 131 | and a | |
| 132 | &] and | |

We scamper'd homeward. O ye rocks and streams
And that still spirit of the evening air
Even in this joyous time I sometimes felt
Your presence when with slacken'd step we breathe
Along the sides of the steep hills or when,
Lighten'd by gleams of moonlight from the sea, [ ]
We beat with thundering hoofs the level sand.

       There was a row of ancient trees, since fallen
That on the margin of a jutting land
Stood near the lake of Coniston and made
With its long boughs above the water stretch'd
A gloom through which a boat might sail along
As in a cloister. An old Hall was near
Grotesque and beautiful, its gavel end
And huge round chimneys to the top o'ergrown
With fields of ivy. Thither we repair'd,
'Twas even a custom with us to the shore
And to that cool piazza. They who dwelt
In the neglected mansion-house supplied
Fresh butter, tea-kettle, and earthen-ware,
And chafing-dish with smoking coals, and so
Beneath the trees we sate in our small boat
And in the court eat our delicate meal
Upon the calm smooth lake. It was a joy
Worthy the heart of one who is full grown
To rest beneath those horizontal boughs

133   *We scamper'd homeward. O ye rocks and streams*
134   *And that still spirit of the evening air*
135   *Even in this joyous time I sometimes felt*

136   *Your presence when with slacken'd step* [ *?* ]} *breathed*
                                    *we*}
137   *Along the sides of the steep hills or when,*

138   *Lighten'd by gleams of moonlight from the sea*}     140
139   *We beat with thundering hoofs the level sand.*
140       *There was a row of ancient trees, since fallen*
141   *That on the margin of a jutting land*
142   *Stood near the lake of Coniston and made*
143   *With its long boughs above the water stretch'd*
144   *A gloom through which a boat might sail along*
145   *As in a cloister. An old Hall was near*

146   *Grotesque and beautiful*} *its gavel end*
147   *And huge round chimneys to the top o'ergrown*

148   *With fields of ivy. Thither we repair'd*}

149   *'Twas even a custom with us*} *to the shore*
150   *And to that cool, piazza. They who dwelt*
151   *In the neglected mansion-house supplied*
152   *Fresh butter, tea-kettle, and earthern-ware,*

153   *And chafing-dish with smoking coals*} *and so*
154   *Beneath the trees we sate in our small boat*
155   *And in the covert eat our delicate meal*
156   *Upon the calm smooth lake. It was a joy*
157   *Worthy the heart of one who is full grown*
158   *To rest beneath those horizontal boughs*

---

133  scampered
136  presence,      slackened *with first* e *inserted*     we
137  hills or when,] hills, or when
140  *no punct*
146  beautiful,
148  repaired
150  *no comma*
152  *no comma after* tea-kettle     earthern-ware,] earthen-ware
153  coals,
156  *punct obscured by ink blot*

---

140ff.  This and the following paragraph, which were not in RV, were dropped by 1804, as the cross-outs show. Doubtless the marginal revision of ll. 173–174 on 15ʳ was made before 1804, though a version of these lines did make a reappearance by 1850 in Book VIII, ll. 474–475.

And mark the radiance of the setting sun
Himself unseen, reposing on the top
Of the high eastern hills. And there I said,
That beauteous sight before me, there I said,
(Then first beginning in my thoughts to mark
That sense of dim similitude which links
Our moral feelings with external forms)
That in whatever region I should close
My mortal life I would remember you
Fair scenes! that dying I would think on you
My soul would send a longing look to you:

Even as that setting sun while all the vale
Could nowhere catch one faint memorial gleam
Yet with the last remains of his last light
Still linger'd, and a farewell lustre threw
On the dear mountain-tops where first he rose.

'Twas then my fourteenth summer & these words
Were utter'd in a casual access
Of sentiment, a momentary trance
That far outran the habit of my mind.

Upon the eastern shore of Windermere,
Above the crescent of a pleasant Bay,
There was an Inn, no homely-featured shed
Brother of the surrounding cottages
But 'twas a splendid place, the door beset
With chaises, grooms, & liveries & within

159　　　　　　And mark the radiance of the setting sun
160　　　　　　Himself unseen, reposing on the top
161　　　　　　Of the high eastern hills. And there I said ⸗

162　　　　　　That beauteous sight before me, there I said,
163　　　　　　( Then first beginning in my thoughts to mark
164　　　　　　That sense of dim similitude which links
165　　　　　　Our moral feelings with external forms )
166　　　　　　That in whatever region I should close
167　　　　　　My mortal life I would remember you
168　　　　　　Fair scenes! that dying I would think on you
169　　　　　　My soul would send a longing look to you:
170　　　　　　Even as that setting sun while all the vale
171　　　　　　Could nowhere catch one faint memorial gleam
172　　　　　　Yet with the last remains of his last light
173　　　　　　Still linger'd, and a farewell lustre threw
174　　　　　　On the dear mountain-tops where first he rose.
175　　　　　　　　'Twas then my fourteenth summer & these words
176　　　　　　Were utter'd in a casual access
177　　　　　　Of sentiment, a momentry trance
178　　　　　　That far outran the habit of my mind.
179　　　　　　　　　　Upon the eastern shore of Windermere,
180　　　　　　Above the crescent of a pleasant Bay,
181　　　　　　There was an Inn, no homely-featured shed
182　　　　　　Brother of the surrounding cottages
183　　　　　　But 'twas a splendid place, the door beset
184　　　　　　With chaises, grooms, & liveries, & within

*Left margin (vertical):* light
*low*
*Is dark and shadowy thr[ough] a farewell gleam*
*On the dear mountain tops where first he rose*

161　said,
163　mark) *with paren erased*
171　no where
173　lingered,
174　*no period*
175　fourtenth　　&] and
176　uttered
177　momentary
178　out-ran　　*no period*
179　*no punct*
180　Bay,] bay
183　'twas *first two letters written over deletion*
184　and liveries and

Decanters, glasses, and the bloodred wine.
In antient times or ere the Hall was built
On the large island had the dwelling been
More worthy of a poet's love, a hut
Proud of its one bright fire and sycamore shade
But though the rhymes were gone which once inscrib'd
The threshold and large golden characters
On the blue frosted sign-board had usurp'd
The place of the old Lion in contempt
And mockery of the rustic painter's hand
Yet to this hour the spot to me is dear
With all its foolish pomp. The garden lay
Upon a slope surmounted by the plain
Of a small bowling-green beneath us stood
A grove, with gleams of water through the trees
And over the tree tops nor did we want
Refreshment, strawberries, and mellow cream
And there through half an afternoon we play'd
On the smooth platform and the shouts we sent
Made all the mountains ring. But ere the fall of night
Of night, when in our pinnace we return'd
Over the dusky lake, and to the beach
Of some small island steer'd our course with one,
The minstrel of our troop, and left him there
And row'd off gently while he blew his flute
Alone upon the rock; oh then the calm
And dead still water lay upon my mind

185  *Decanters, glasses, and the blood-red wine.*
186  *In antient times or ere the Hall was built*
187  *On the large island had the dwelling been*
188  *More worthy of a poet's love, a hut*
189  *Proud of its one bright fire and sycamore shade*
190  *But though the rhymes were gone which once*
                                      *inscrib'd*
191  *The threshold and large golden characters*
192  *On the blue frosted sign-board had usurp'd*
193  *The place of the old Lion in contempt*
194  *And mockery of the rustic painter's hand*
195  *Yet to this hour the spot to me is dear*
196  *With all its foolish pomp. The garden lay*
197  *Upon a slope surmounted by the plain*            160
198  *Of a small bowling-green beneath us stood*
199  *A grove, with gleams of water through the trees*
200  *And over the tree tops nor did we want*
201  *Refreshment, strawberries, and mellow cream*
202  *And there through half an afternoon we play'd*
203  *On the smooth platform and the shouts we sent*
204  *Made all the mountains ring. But ere the fall of night*
205  *Of night, when in our pinnace we return'd*
206  *Over the dusky lake, and to the beach*
207  *Of some small island steer'd our course with one,*
208  *The minstrel of our troop, and left him there*
209  *And row'd of gently while he blew his flute*
210  *Alone upon the rock; oh then the calm*
211  *And dead still water lay upon my mind*

---

185  glasses,] glasses
186  ancient       'eve
187  island,
190  incribed
192  blue-frosted
198  bowling-green,
200  tree tops,
201  strawberries,] strawberries
202  an] the
203  platform,
204  'ere        of night *erased*
205  returned
208  troop,] troop
209  of] of *corrected to* off

---

190  DW made a false start on a word following "once" then erased it.
197  The penciled line count excludes the two canceled paragraphs on 14ᵛ and 15ʳ. Commencing with the sharp, clear "140" on 14ᵛ, a new series of penciled counts appears to have been added, after the cancellation.
204  DW picked up two words from the following line and left them uncanceled.

Even with a weight of pleasure, and the sky,
Never before so beautiful, sank down
Into my heart and held me like a dream.

    Thus day by day, my sympathies increas'd
And thus the common range of visible things
Grew dear to me: already I began      *180*
To love the sun, a Boy I loved the sun
Not as I since have loved him, as a pledge
And surety of my earthly life; a light
Which while I view I feel I am alive
But for this cause that I had seen him lay
His beauty on the morning hills had seen
The western mountain touch his setting orb
In many a thoughtless hour when from excess
Of happiness my blood appeared to flow
With its own pleasure and I breathed with joy

And from like falings, humble though intense
To patriotic and domestic love
Analogous the moon to me was dear
For I would dream away my purposes
Standing to look upon her while she hung
Midway between the hills as if she knew
No other region but belong'd to thee
Yea, appertain'd by a peculiar right
To thee and thy grey huts my      *202*

212    *Even with a weight of pleasure, and the sky,*
213    *Never before so beautiful, sank down*
214    *Into my heart and held me like a dream.*
215         *Thus day by day, my sympathies increas'd*
216    *And thus the common range of visible things*
217    *Grew dear to me: already I began*                    180
218    *To love the sun, a Boy I loved the sun*
219    *Not, as I since have loved him, as a pledge*
220    *And surety of my earthly life, a light*
221    *Which while I view I feel I am alive*
                              d⎱
222    *But for this cause that I have*⎰ *seen him lay*
223    *His beauty on the morning hills had seen*
224    *The western mountain touch his setting orb*
225    *In many an thoughtless hour when from excess*
226    *Of happiness my blood appeared to flow*
           With ⎱
227    *From*⎰ *its own pleasure and I breathed with joy*
228    *And from like feelings, humble though intense*
229    *To patriotic and domestic love*
230    *Analogous the moon to me was dear*
            ⎞For⎛
231    *[ ?And ]⎰ I would dream away my purposes*
232    *Standing to look upon her while she hung*
233    *Midway between the hills as if she knew*
234    *No other region but belong'd to thee*
235    *Yea, appertain'd by a peculiar right*
236    *To thee and thy grey huts my*

---

214    *no punct*
215    *no punct*
219    Not,] Not
222    cause,        had
223    His] The *altered to* His        hills,
224    mountains
225    an] a        hour,
227    With
229    analogous *erased at end of line*
231    And
233    Mid-way
235    Yea appertained
236    native vale *completes the line*

---

231    The penciled X preceded the revision.

290    Those incidental charms which first attach'd
My heart to rural objects day by day
Grew weaker and I hasten on to tell
How nature intervenient till this time
And secondary now at length was sought
For her own sake — But who shall parcel out
His intellect by geometric rules
Split like a province into round and square
Who knows the individual hour in which
His habits were first sown, even as a seed
Who that shall point as with a wand and say
This portion of the river of my mind
Came from yon fountain? Thou, my Friend art
                                    to the one
More deeply read in thy own thoughts, no share
Of that false secondary power by which
In weakness we create distinctions, then
                  deem that
these our puny boundaries are things
Which we perceive and not which we have made
To thee, unblinded by these outward shews
The unity of all has been reveal'd
And thou wilt doubt with me less aptly skill'd
Than many are to class the cabinet
Of their sensations and in voluble phrase
Run through the history and birth of each
As of a single independent thing.
Hard task to analyse a soul in which

| 237 | 200 | *Those incidental charms which first attach'd* |
| 238 | | *My heart to rural objects day by day* |
| 239 | | *Grew weaker, and I hasten on to tell* |
| 240 | | *How nature intervenient till this time* |
| 241 | | *And secondary now at length was sought* |
| 242 | | *For her own sake — But who shall parcel out* |
| 243 | | *His intellect by geometric rules* |
| 244 | | *Split like a province into round and square* |
| 245 | | *Who knows the individual hour in which* |
| 246 | | *His habits were first sown, even as a seed* |
| 247 | | *Who that shall point as with a wand and say* |
| 248 | | *This portion of the river of my mind* |
| 249 | | *Came from yon fountain? Thou, my Friend art* |

                                        one

                                   to thee

| 250 | *More deeply read in thy own thoughts, ~~no slave~~* |

    Science appears &c

| 251 | *Of that false secondary power by which* |
| 252 | *In weakness we create distinctions* ⎱ ~~and~~ *then* |

    Deem that

| 253 | ~~Believe~~ *our puny boundaries are things* |
| 254 | *Which we perceive and not which we have made* |
| 255 | *To thee, unblinded by these outward shews* |
| 256 | *The unity of all has been reveal'd* |
| 257 | *And thou wilt doubt with me less aptly skill'd*    220 |
| 258 | *Than many are to class the cabinet* |
| 259 | *Of their sensations and in voluble phrase* |
| 260 | *Run through the history and birth of each* |
| 261 | *As of a single independent thing.* |
| 262 | *Hard task to analyse a soul in which* |

237   attach'd *last three letters written over erasure*
241   secondary,
246   *no punct*
249   *no comma*
255   outward] owtward
256   has] hath
258   are,
259   sensasions
262   analiʃze

Not only general habits and desires
But each most obvious and particular thought,
Not in a mystical and idle sense,
But in the words of reason deeply weigh'd
Hath  no beginning.

                    Bless'd the infant babe
(For with my best conjectures I would trace
The progress of our being) blest the Babe
Nurs'd in his Mother's arms the Babe who sleeps
Upon his mother's breast who when his soul
Claims manifest kindred with an earthly soul
Doth gather passion from his mother's eye
Such feelings pass into his torpid life
Like an awakening breeze and hence his mind
Even in the first trial of its powers
Is prompt and watchful, eager to combine
In one appearance all the elements
And parts of the same object else detach'd
And loth to coalesce. Thus day by day
Subjected to the discipline of love
His organs and recipient faculties
Are quicken'd are more vigorous, his mind spreads
Tenacious of the forms which it receives.
In one beloved presence, nay and more
In that most apprehensive habitude
And those sensations which have been derived
From this beloved presence there exists

263     *Not only general habits and desires*

264     *But each most obvious and particular thought* ⟩

265     *Not in a mystical and idle sense,*

266     *But in the words of reason deeply weigh'd*

267     *Hath no beginning.*
                              *Bless'd the infant babe*

268     *(For with my best conjectures I would trace*

269     *The progress of our being) blest the Babe*

270     *Nurs'd in his Mother's arms the Babe who sleeps*

271     *Upon his mother's breast who when his soul*

272     *Claims manifest kindred with an earthly soul*

273     *Doth gather passion from his mother's eye*

                    *ass*⟩
274     *Such feelings p[ ? ]⟩ into his torpid life*

275     *Like an awakening breeze and hence his mind*

276     *Even in the first trial of its powers*

277  240  *Is prompt and watchful, eager to combine*

278     *In one appearance all the elements*

279     *And parts of the same object else detach'd*

280     *And loth to coalesce. Thus day by day*

281     *Subjected to the discipline of love*

282     *His organs and recipient faculties*

283     *Are quicken'd are more vigorous, his mind spreads*

284     *Tenacious of the forms which it receives.*

285     *In one beloved presence, nay and more*

286     *In that most apprehensive habitude*

287     *And those sensations which have been derive[   ]*

288     *From this beloved presence there exists*

---

265     sense,] sense
                              ⟨B
267     *no period*      ⟨babe
271     Mother's
273     Mother's
274     pass
281     dicipline
283     quicken'd,     are] and *altered to* are
284     *no punct*
287     derived

---

287     The last letter of "derived" is worn away.

A virtue which irradiates and exalts
All objects through all intercourse of sense
No outcast he, bewilder'd and depress'd
Along his infant veins are interfused
The gravitation and the filial bond
Of nature that connect him with the world
Emphatically such a being lives
An inmate of this active universe
From nature largely he receives nor so
Is satisfied but largely gives again
For feeling has to him imparted strength
And powerful in all sentiments of grief
Of exultation, fear and joy his mind
Even as an agent of the one great mind
Creates, creator and receiver both
Working but in alliance with the works
Which it beholds —          Such verily is the fir
Poetic spirit of our human life
By uniform controul of after years
In most abated and suppress'd, in some
Through every change of growth or of decay
Preeminent till death.
                            From early days    280
Beginning not long after that first time
In which, a Babe, by intercourse of touch
I held mute dialogues with my mother's heart
I have endeavour'd to display the means

289    *A virtue which irradiates and exalts*
290    *All objects through all intercourse of sense*
291    *No outcast he, bewilder'd and depress'd*
292    *Along his infant veins are interfused*

293    *The gravitation and the fil{ i {lal bond*
294    *Of nature that connect him with the world*
295    *Emphatically such a being lives*
296    *An inmate of this <u>active</u> universe*
297    *From nature largely he receives nor so*
298    *Is satisfied but largely gives again*
299    *For feeling has to him imparted strength*
300    *And powerful in all sentiments of grief*
301    *Of exultation, fear and joy his mind*
302    *Even as an agent of the one great mind*
303    *Creates, creator and receiver both*
304    *Working but in alliance with the works*

                              is the first
305    *Which it beholds— —Such verily*
306    Poetic spirit of our human life
307    *By uniform control of after years*
308    *In most abated and suppress'd, in some*
309    *Through every change of growth or of decay*
310    *Preeminent till death.*
                              *From early days*
311    *Beginning not long after that first time*
312    *In which, a Babe, by intercourse of touch*
313    *I held mute dialogues with my mother's heart*
314    *I have endeavour'd to display the means*

291    *no comma*
293    filial
296    *of*] in
305    *no period*    is the first
306    *no erasure*
307    controul
309    *second* of *inserted, possibly over erasure*
310    *no punct*
312    *no punct*
313    Mother's
314    endeavoured

305    Probably DW broke the line after "verily," necessitating erasure and correction where the penciled X was entered.

Whereby this infant sensibility,
Great birth-right of our being, was in me
Augmented and sustain'd. Yet is a path
More difficult before me & I fear
That in its broken windings we shall need
The Chamois' sinews & the eagle's wing
For now a trouble came into my mind
From          causes. I was left alone
Seeking this visible world, nor knowing why
The props of my affections were remov'd
And yet the building stood as if sustain'd
By its own spirit. All that I beheld
Was dear to me and from this cause it came
That now to Nature's finer influxes
My mind lay open to that more exact
And intimate communion which our hearts
Maintain with the minuter properties
Of objects which already are belov'd
And of those only. Many are the joys
Of youth but oh! what happiness to live
When every hour brings palpable access
Of knowledge, when all knowledge is delight
And sorrow is not there. The seasons came
And every season brought a countless store
Of modes and temporary qualities
Which but for this most watchful power of

315   *Whereby this infant sensibility,*
316   *Great birth-right of our being, was in me*
317   *Augmented and sustain'd. Yet is a path*
318   *More difficult before me, & I fear*
319   *That in its broken windings we shall need*
320   *The Chamois' sinews and the eagle's wing*
320   *For now a trouble came into my mind*
322   *From         causes. I was left alone*
323   *Seeking this visible world, nor knowing why*
324   *The props of my affections were remov'd*
325   *And yet the building stood as if sustain'd*
326   *By its own spirit. All that I beheld*

327   *Was dear to me and from this cause it c*[ ? ]$\}$ *me*
328   *That now to Nature's finer influxes*
329   *My mind lay open to that more exact*
330   *And intimate communion which our hearts*
331   *Maintain with the minuter properties*
332   *Of objects which already are beloved*
333   *And of those only. Many are the joys*
334   *Of youth but oh! what happiness to live*
335   *When every hour brings palpable access*
336   *Of knowledge, when all knowledge is delight*
337   *And sorrow is not there. The seasons came*
338   *And every season brought a countless store*
339   *Of modes and temporary qualities*
340   *Which, but for this most watchful power of love*

---

316   *no comma*
318   &] and
320   Eagle's
322   From obscure causes.
324   removed
327   came
333   *no punct; second half-line begins new para*     *of at end of line erased*
334   youth,
340   *no punct*

Had been neglected left a register
Of permanent relations, else unknown
Hence life and change, and beauty, solitude
More active even than "best society"
Society made sweet as solitude
By silent inobtrusive sympathies
And gentle agitations of the mind
From manifold distinctions, difference
Perceived in things where to the common eye
No difference is: and hence from the same source
Sublimer joy; for I would walk alone
In storm and tempest or in star light nights
Beneath the quiet heavens, and at that time
would feel
Whate'er there is of power in sound
To breathe an elevated mood by form
Or image unprofaned: and I would stand
Beneath some rock listening to sounds that are
The ghostly language of the ancient earth
Or make their dim abode in distant winds.
Thence did I drink the visionary power.
I deem not profitless these fleeting moods
Of shadowy exaltation not for this
That they are kindred to our purer mind
And intellectual life, but that the soul
Remembering how she felt, but what she felt
Remembering not, retains an obscure sense

341    *Had been neglected left a register*
342    *Of permanent relations, else unknown*
343    *Hence life, and change, and beauty, solitude*
344    *More active even than "best society"*
345    *Society made sweet as solitude*
346    *By silent inobtrusive sympathies*
347    *And gentle agitations of the mind*
                                ld ⎫
348    *From manifo[ ? ]⎬ distinctions, difference*
349    *Perceived in things where to the common eye*
                                            ⎧so ⎧rce
350    *No difference is: and hence from the same* ⎨cau⎨se
351    *Sublimer joy; for I would walk alone*
352    *In storm and tempest or in starlight nights*
353    *Beneath the quiet heavens, and at that time*
       *Would feel*
354    ₍ₐ₎*Whate'er there is of power in sound*
355    *To breath an elevated mood by form*
356    *Or image unprofaned: and I would stand*
357    *Beneath some rock listening to sounds that are*        320
358    *The ghostly language of the ancient earth*
359    *Or make their dim abode in distant winds.*
360    *Thence did I drink the visionary power.*
361    *I deem not profitless these fleeting moods*
362    *Of shadowy exaltation not for this*
363    *That they are kindred to our purer mind*
364    *And intellectual life, but* that the soul
                              '⎫
365    *Remembering how she felt* ⎬ *but what she felt*
                              '⎫
366    *Remembering not* ⎬ *retains an obscure sense*

---

341    neglected;
                     diff ⎫    ⎧nce
348    manifold      wh⎨ere⎨          *no punct*
349    Where to the common eye no difference *erased and overwritten with line as in V*
350    source
351    joy:
354    Would feel whate'er
358    ancient *omitted with no gap*
361    these]those
364    *no erasure*
365    felt, but
366    not,

---

348    The miswriting was first corrected in pencil with the letters "ol" above the line.
364    Again, the miswriting was first corrected in pencil, now erased.

Of possible sublimity to which
With growing faculties she doth aspire,
With faculties still growing, feeling still
That whatsoever point they gain they still
Have something to pursue.

And not alone
In grandeur and in tumult but no less
In tranquil scenes, that universal power
And fitness in the latent qualities
And essences of things by which the mind
Is moved with feelings of delight to me
Came strengthen'd with a superadded power
A virtue not its own. My morning walks
Were early oft before the hours of school
I travell'd round our little lake; five miles
Of pleasant wandering happy time more dear
For this, that one was by my side, a Friend
Then passionately loved; with heart how full
Will he peruse these lines this page, perhaps
A blank to other men, for many years
Have since flowed in between us, and our minds
Both silent to each other, at this time
We live as if those hours had never been.
Nor seldom did I lift our cottage latch
Far earlier, and before the vernal Thrush
Was audible, among the hills I sate

367    *Of possible sublimity to which*

368    *With growing faculties she doth aspire* ⸱⸴
369    *With faculties still growing, feeling still*
370    *That whatsoever point they gain they still*
371    *Have something to pursue.*
                                   *And not alone*
372    *In grandeur and in tumult but no less*
373    *In tranquil scenes, that universal power*
374    *And fitness in the latent qualities*
375    *And essences of things by which the mind*
376    *Is moved with feelings of delight to me*
                                        soul
377  340  *Came strengthen'd with a superadded pow*    ✕
378    *A virtue not its own. My morning walks*
379    *Were early oft before the hours of school*
380    *I travell'd round our little lake ; five miles*
381    *Of pleasant wandering happy time more dear*
382    *For this, that one was by my side, a Friend*
383    *Then passionately loved ; with heart how full*
384    *Will he peruse these lines this page, perhaps*

385    *A blank to other men* ⸴⸰ *for many years*
386    *Have since flowed in between us, and our minds*
387    *Both silent to each other, at this time*
388    *We live as if those hours had never been.*
389    *Nor seldom did I lift our cottage latch*
390    *Far earlier, and before the vernal thrush*
391    *Was audible, among the hills I sate*

---

368    aspire,
370    gain,
372    tumult,
377    strengthened      pow] soul
378    *no punct*; *second half-line begins new para*
379    early,
380    lake,
381    wandering,
383    loved :
384    *no punct*
385    men,

---

371    The upside-down "amens" show DW testing a pen.
377    The revision, over an incomplete word, is in pencil, as is the X.

Alone upon some jutting eminence
At the first hour of morning when the vale
Lay quiet in an utter solitude.
How shall I trace the history where seek
The origin of what I then have felt
Oft in those moments such a holy calm
Did overspread my soul that I forgot
The agency of sight, & what I saw
Appeared like something in myself—a dream
A prospect in my mind. 'Twere long to tell
What spring and autumn, what the winter snows
And what the summer shade, what day & night
The evening & the morning, what my dreams
And what my waking thoughts supplied to nurse
That spirit of religious love in which
I walked with nature. But let this at least
Be not forgotten, that I still retain'd
My first creative sensibility
That by the regular action of the world
My soul was unsubdued. A plastic power
Abode with me, a forming hand, at times
Rebellious, acting in a devious mood
A local spirit of its own, at war
With general tendency but for the most
Subservient strictly to the external things
    Which it communed. An auxiliar light

392 *Alone upon some jutting eminence*
393 *At the first hour of morning when the vale*
394 *Lay quiet in an utter solitude.*
395 *How shall I trace the history where seek*
396 *The origin of what I then have felt*
397 *Oft in those moments such a holy calm*    360
398 *Did overspread my soul that I forgot*
399 *The agency of sight, & what I saw*
400 *Appeared like something in myself—a dream*
401 *A prospect in my mind. Twere long to tell*
402 *What spring and autumn, what the winter-snows*
403 *And what the summer-shade, what day & night*
404 *The evening & the morning, what my dreams*
405 *And what my waking thoughts supplied to nurse*

406 *That spirit of religious lo[ ? ]} in which*
407 *I walked with nature. But let this at least*
408 *Be not forgotten, that I still retain'd*
409 *My first creative sensibility*
410 *That by the regular action of the world*
411 *My soul was unsubdued. A plastic power*
412 *Abode with me, a forming hand, at times*
413 *Rebellious, acting in a devious mood*
414 *A local spirit of its own, at war*
415 *With general tendency but for the most*
416 *Subservient strictly to the external things*
417 *With which it communed. An auxiliar light*    380

---

395 history,
399 &] and
403 &] and
404 The *written over erased word, probably* What    &] and
405 supplied,
406 love
408 *no comma*
411 unsubdu'd.
415 tendency,
416 Subservient *first two letters written over deletion*
417 commun'd.

---

401 A faintly penciled X probably marks a paragraph, as in 1805, II, 371.

Came from my mind which on the setting sun
Bestowed new splendour, the melodious birds
The gentle breezes, fountains that ran on
Murmuring so sweetly in themselves, obey'd
A like dominion, and the midnight storm
Grew darker in the presence of my eye.
Hence my obeisance, my devotion hence
And hence my transport.

        Nor should this perchance
Pass unrecorded that I still had loved
The exercise and produce of a toil
Than analytic industry to me
More pleasing and whose character, I deem
Is more poetic, as resembling more
Creative agency, I mean to speak
Of that interminable building rear'd
By observation of affinities
In objects where no brotherhood exists
To common minds. My seventeenth year was
— And whether from this habit rooted now
So deeply in my mind, or from excess
Of the great social principle of life
Coercing all things into sympathy
To unorganic natures I transferr'd
My own enjoyments, or, the power of truth
Coming in revelation, I conversed
With things that really are

418   *Came from my mind which on the setting sun*
419   *Bestowed new splendour, the melodious birds*
420   *The gentle breezes, fountains that ran on*
421   *Murmuring so sweetly in themselves, obey'd*
422   *A like dominion, and the midnight storm*
423   *Grew darker in the presence of my eye.*
424   *Hence my obeisance, my devotion hence*
425   *And <u>hence</u> my transport.*
                    *Nor should this perchance*

426   *Pa{s unrecorded that I still had loved*
427   *The exercise and produce of a toil*
428   *Than analytic industry to me*
429   *More pleasing and whose character, I deem*
430   *Is more poetic, as resembling more*
431   *Creative agency, I mean to speak*
432   *Of that interminable building rear'd*
433   *By observation of affinities*
434   *In objects where no brotherhood exists*
435   *To common minds. My seventeenth year was*
                                    *come*
436   *And whether from this habit rooted now*
437   *So deeply in my mind, or from excess*
438   *Of the great social principle of life*
439   *Coercing all things into sympathy*
440   *To unorganic natures I transferr'd*
441   *My own enjoyments, or, the power of truth*
442   *Coming in revelation, I conversed*
443   *With things that really are [          ]*

---

419   Bestow'{d
421   obeyd
424   *first* my *inserted with caret*
426   pass
428   an{yl[?]tic
443   are. I at this time

---

443   The end of the line is worn away.

saw blessings spread around me like a sea.
Thus did my days pass on, and now at length
From Nature and her overflowing soul
I had received so much that all my thoughts
Were steep'd in feeling, I was only then
Contented when with bliss ineffable
I felt the sentiment of being spread
O'er all that moves, and all that seemeth still
O'er all that, lost beyond the reach of thought
And human knowledge to the human eye
Invisible, yet liveth to the heart,
O'er all that leaps, and runs, and shouts and sings
Or beats the gladsome air, o'er all which glides
Beneath the wave, yea, in the wave itself
And mighty depth of waters: wonder not
If such my transports were, for in all things
I saw one life and felt that it was joy.
One song they sang and it was audible,
Most audible then when the fleshly ear,
O'ercome by grosser prelude of that strain,
Forgot its functions, and slept undisturb'd.

      If this be error, and another faith
Find easier access to the pious mind
Yet were I grossly destitute of all
Those human sentiments which make this earth
So dear if I should fail with grateful voice
To speak of you ye mountains! & ye lakes

444   *Saw blessings spread around me like a sea.*
445   *Thus did my days pass on, and now at length*
446   *From Nature and her overflowing soul*
447   *I had received so much that all my thoughts*
448   *Were steep'd in feeling, I was only then*
449   *Contented when with bliss ineffable*
450   *I felt the sentiment of being spread*
451   *O'er all that moves, and all that seemeth still*
452   *O'er all that, lost beyond the reach of thought*
453   *And human knowledge to the human eye*
454   *Invisible, yet liveth to the heart,*
455   *O'er all* that *leaps, and runs, and shouts and sings*
                          {*o'er*   *that*
456   *Or beats the gladsome air,* {*or all* ~~*which*~~ *glides*
457   *Beneath the wave, yea, in the wave itself*             420
458   *And mighty depth of waters: wonder not*
459   *If such my transports were, for in all things*
460   *I saw one life and felt that it was joy.*
461   *One song they sang, and it was audible,*
462   *Most audible then when the fleshly ear,*
463   *O'ercome by grosser prelude of that strain,*
464   *Forgot its functions, and slept undisturb'd.*
465         *If this be error, and another faith*
466   *Find easier access to the pious mind*
467   *Yet were I grossly destitute of all*
468   *Those human sentiments which make this earth*
469   [     ] *if I should fail with grateful voice*
470   [       ] *you, ye mountains! & ye lakes*

---

444/445  *extra space left between lines*
446  nature   *entire line inserted*
447  receiv'd   much,
         d}
448  steep't}   *no comma*
454  to] in *overwritten* to
455  that   *erased comma after* shouts
456  o'er   which] that
460  one *written over erasure*   *no punct*
461  sang,] sang
463  *no punct*
464  *no punct*
465  *no punct*
469  So dear; if   with *written over erasure, after gap*
470  To speak of you,   &] and

---

456  Deletion and revision are in pencil.
464/465  Sixteen lines of RV are here left out, and the line count excludes them.
469–470  The corner of the page is worn away.

sounding cataracts! ye mists and winds
That dwell among the hills where I was born.
If, in my youth, I have been pure in heart,
If, mingling with the world, I am content
With my own modest pleasures, & have lived
With God and Nature communing, remov'd
From little enmities, and low desires
The gift is yours: if in these times of fear,
This melancholy world of hopes o'erthrown
If 'mid indifference & apathy
And wicked exultation, when good men
On every side fall off we know not how
To selfishness disguised in gentle names
Of peace, and quiet, & domestic love
Yet mingled, not unwillingly with sneers
On visionary minds, if in this time
Of dereliction and dismay I yet
Despair not of our nature, but retain
A more than Roman confidence, a faith
That fails not, in all sorrow my support,
The blessing of my life, the gift is yours
Ye Mountains! thine O Nature! thou hast fed
Thy lofty speculations, and in thee
For this uneasy heart of ours I find
A never-failing principle of joy
And purest passion.

471     *And sounding cataracts! ye mists and winds*
472     *That dwell among the hills where I was born*

473     *If }in my youth, I have been pure in heart}*
474     *If, mingling with the world, I am content*
475     *With my own modest pleasures, & have lived*
476     *With God and Nature communing, remov'd*
477     *From little enmities, and low desires*                    440
478     *The gift is yours: if in these times of fear,*
                        waste
479     *This melancholy world of hopes o'erthrown*
480     *If, 'mid indifference & apathy*
481     *And wicked exultation, when good men*
482     *On every side fall off we know not how*
483     *To selfishness disguised in gentle names*
484     *Of peace, and quiet, & domestic love*
485     *Yet mingled, not unwillingly with sneers*
486     *On visionary minds, if in this time*
487     *Of dereliction and dismay I yet*
488     *Despair not of our nature, but retain*
489     *A more than Roman confidence, a faith*
490     *That fails not, in all sorrow my support,*
491     *The blessing of my life, the gift is yours*
                        O}
492     *Ye mountains! thine o}Nature! thou hast fed*
493     *My lofty speculations, and in thee*
494     *For this uneasy heart of ours I find*
495     *A never-failing principle of joy*
496     *And purest passion.*

---

472     born.
473     If,        heart,
475     &] and
477     *no punct*
479     world] waste
480     &] and        *no punct*
483     names] *miswritten* mames
484     quiet and
485     *no punct*
490     support,] support
492     Mountains!        O

---

479     Revision is in pencil.

Thou my Friend wast ——
In the great city 'mid far other scenes
But we, by different roads, at length have gain'd
The self-same bourne. And from this cause to thee
I speak unapprehensive of contempt
The insinuated scoff of coward tongues
And all that silent language which so oft
In conversation betwixt man and man
Blots from the human countenance all trace
Of beauty and of love. For thou hast sought
The truth in solitude, and thou art one,
The most intense of Nature's worshippers
In many things my brother, chiefly here
In this my deep devotion.

                    Fare thee well!
Health and the quiet of a healthful mind
Attend thee! seeking oft the haunts of men
But yet more often living with thyself
And for thyself, so haply shall thy days
Be many & a blessing to mankind.

        End of the Second Part

496                      *Thou, my Friend wast rear'd*
497    *In the great city 'mid far other scenes*
498    *But we, by different roads, at length have gain'd*
499    *The self-same bourne. And from this cause to thee*
500    *I speak unapprehensive of contempt*
501    *The* insinuated *scoff of coward tongues*
502    *And all that silent language which so oft*
503    *In conversation betwixt man and man*
504    *Blots from the human countenance all trace*
505    *Of beauty and of love. For thou hast sought*
506    *The truth in solitude, and thou art one,*
507    *The most intense of Nature's worshippers*
508    *In many things my brother, chiefly here*
509    *In this my deep devotion.*
                                  *Fare thee well!*
510    *Health and the quiet of a healthful mind*
511    *Attend thee! seeking oft the haunts of m{ᵉₐₙ*
512    *But yet more often living with thyself*
513    *And for thyself, so haply shall thy days*
514    *Be many & a blessing to mankind.——*


         *End of the second Part*

---

496    *no comma*
498    at length *inserted with caret*
500    speak,
501    *no erasure*
              ʃful
510    health{y
511    men
514    &] and       *no period*      End of the second Part *absent in U*

*The Prelude,* 1798–1799

Designed by R. E. Rosenbaum.
Composed by Syntax International Pte. Ltd.
in 8 and 10 point Monophoto Baskerville 169,
with display lines in Monophoto Baskerville.
Printed offset by Vail-Ballou Press, Inc.
on Warren's Olde Style Wove, 60 pound basis.
Bound by Vail-Ballou Press in
Joanna Arrestox B book cloth,
with stamping in All Purpose Gold foil.